Allah

Allah

A Christian Response

Miroslav Volf

HarperOne
An Imprint of HarperCollinsPublishers

HarperOne

FIRST HARPERCOLLINS PAPERBACK EDITION PUBLISHED IN 2012

Designed by Rosa Chae

Library of Congress Cataloging-in-Publication Data
Volf, Miroslav.
 Allah : a Christian response / by Miroslav Volf. —1st ed.
  p. cm.
ISBN 978–0–06–192708–9
1. God (Islam). 2. God (Christianity). 3. Islam—Relations—Christianity. 4. Christianity and other religions—Islam. I. Title.
BP166.2.V65 2011
261.2'7—dc22

2010040068

21 LSC (H) 10 9

To my father, a Pentecostal minister who admired Muslims and taught me as a boy that they worship the same God we do.

CONTENTS

The One God and the Great Chasm

A deep chasm of misunderstanding, dislike, and even hatred separates many Christians and Muslims today. Christian responses to Allah—understood here as the God of the Qur'an—will either widen that chasm or help bridge it. If for Christians Allah is a foreign and false god, all bridge building will suffer. Muslim responses to the God of the Bible matter as well, of course. But Muslim responses to the God of the Bible are a topic primarily for Muslims to explore. My interest here is the proper Christian stance toward the God of the Qur'an and what that stance means for Christians' and Muslims' ability to live together well in a single and endangered world.

The stakes are high. Muslims and Christians together comprise more than half of humanity.[1] Though charting the growth rates of world religions is a complex and disputed practice, most scholars agree that both Christianity and Islam will continue to grow numerically for the foreseeable future.[2] Equally significant, as the democratic ideal spreads and takes deeper root, Christianity and Islam are likely to assert themselves even more vigorously in public arenas worldwide than they have so far.[3] Consider also that we live in an increasingly interconnected and interdependent world with rapidly diminishing natural resources and explosive population growth.[4] Struggles between various groups are expected to increase, especially around water, the most vital of all resources.[5] Occasions for conflict between Muslims and Christians will multiply.

This book is about the extraordinary promise contained in the proper Christian response to the God of Muslims for easing animosities and overcoming conflicts. More, it is about opening up prospects for lasting peace. But let's stay for a while with conflicts and the role of religion in them, for good or ill.

History Matters

I was born and grew up in a country that no longer exists. It was called Yugoslavia, and it was destroyed by tensions turned into wars among some of its ethnic groups. Two of these wars were between Muslims and Christians (though Christians fought fiercely among themselves as well). As the weapons were thundering in the 1990s, outsiders would often ask me two questions: (1) How important is religion in the conflict? (2) Why do the centuries-old wrongdoings still stir such violent passions? After the terrorist attacks on the Twin Towers and the Pentagon, I was often asked those same two questions, now in regard to tensions between Christians and Muslims globally.

Let me start, briefly, with the second question, current passions about ancient grievances. The reason history matters is simple, though often difficult to fully grasp for citizens of fast-paced societies, who go through life vigorously leaning forward. The past is not simply past; it is alive in memory. But why, you may ask, do past wrongdoings and sufferings now brought alive in memory stir our aggressive energies? Because current events take us back to relive past ones. For example, when a person feels a stranger approaching from behind, it reminds her of an assault she had suffered. She feels in her gut: "This (the approaching stranger) is that (the past violent assault)." The present danger brings to memory the past injury, and the past injury is seen as likely to repeat itself in the present situation.

When Western powers colonized Muslim lands in the wake of the defeat of the Ottoman Empire at the beginning of the twentieth century, many Muslims thought, "This is that"—the Crusades of the Middle Ages are being reenacted and Christians are now emerging victorious. The same was true when coalition forces invaded Iraq. Similarly, when Muslim Albanians gradually became an overwhelming majority in Kosovo on account of their high birth rates, many Serbs thought, "This is that"—the victory of Ottoman Turks over the Serbian kingdom on Blackbird's Field in 1389 is happening once more in the very cradle of Serbian civilization. Or today, when some western Europeans see the percentage of the Muslim population steadily growing in their countries, they sense that the failed Ottoman siege of Vienna in 1529 is now being crowned with success. The present fears wake up dormant memories and project images of danger into the future: what happened (or was just about to happen) then is happening again. And so the passions are stirred. Their object is past events, but their reason is fears about the future.

In the course of this book, I revisit some events from the past whose memories disturb the peace of the present. How did the great Christian leaders of the past think of Islam and of Islam's God in the context of the deeply traumatic events of their lives and times—of the fall of Constantinople, the seat of Eastern Christianity for over one thousand years, into Muslim hands in 1453 (chapter 2) or of the successful march of Ottoman armies all the way to the gates of Vienna in 1529 (chapter 3)? The past responses of Christians to Muslims and their God can guide our responses today, maybe even help prevent our passions—our fears—from making us blind to the realities and possibilities of the present.

Religion Matters

Let's return to the first question I am frequently asked about conflicts between Muslims and Christians today. Why bother with God at all when dealing with conflicts between Christians and Muslims on the world stage? Even if the protagonists are religious people, are the conflicts themselves religious? Or are these, rather, conflicts about worldly goods, such as freedom or territory, economic resources (oil!) or political power, in which religion plays only a minor role?

Clearly, most conflicts between Muslims and Christians are not of a strictly religious nature. For example, even though in Nigeria religious issues matter in the conflict between Christians and Muslims—after the publication of the satirical cartoons of the Prophet Muhammad in Denmark (2006) more people died in clashes in Nigeria than anywhere else—the violence there is mainly about oil: the Muslim north resents the Christian south's hogging of Nigeria's oil money.[6] Similarly, as the term "ethnic cleansing" suggests, the war in Bosnia was, arguably, primarily about the exclusive possession of territory. And yet, even in such cases religion is obviously involved. It is people marked by distinct religions who fight one another, and in their minds and hearts religion plays a role (see chapter 10).

In other cases, tensions between Muslims and Christians directly concern *religious* issues, even if it is true that other matters, such as perceived economic injustices, disputed territories, or threatened language, are involved as well. Holy sites are often the source of tensions and wars; witness conflicts around Jerusalem from the time of its capture by Arabs in 638 CE through today. In recent years, the Christian practice of evangelism and the Muslim counterpart, *da'wa,* have caused serious conflicts (see chapter 11). As the case of the Danish cartoons makes plain, equally serious are tensions between Muslims and Christians around broadly conceived *moral* issues—about how to live in the contemporary world. For Muslims who believe that a woman should wear a burka, this is not merely an aesthetic or cultural issue, but a religious and moral one, a matter of following an explicit divine command. Similarly, the laws punishing apostasy, seen by most Christians as reprehensible, reflect injunctions in Muslim sacred texts (see chapter 12). Most pointedly, the prohibition against making drawings of the Prophet Muhammad concerns the very source of everything that is sacred. Religion *is* part of the conflict.

Sacred things need not be involved for people to fight and go to war. An insult, injury, or act of aggression or treachery may suffice. But when "holy" things are at stake, conflicts are exacerbated. Religious sentiments often give mundane goods a sacred aura, and the pursuit of private interests mutates into a transcendent and holy cause. It gets worse when it comes to tensions around specifically religious matters. If a single site is sacred to two religions, the fight seems almost preprogrammed. If what two groups consider to be divine commands are radically incompatible, they are likely to collide if they share the same space.

In recent years "God" has been the source of tension between Muslims and Christians. According to some Christians, Muslims worship a different God than Christians do, which leads to conflict. God, after all, is what ultimately matters for both. Let's meet some such Christians.

The Compassionate and Merciful One

For Barack Obama's inauguration as forty-fourth president of the United States on January 20, 2009, he asked Rick Warren to offer the inaugural prayer for the nation. Likely the most influential religious leader in the United States in the first decade of the twenty-first century and theologically conservative, Warren was a safe choice. Yet his prayer sparked a controversy. Here are its opening lines:

> Almighty God, our Father, everything we see and everything we can't see exists because of you alone. It all comes from you. It all belongs to you. It all exists for your glory! History is your story. The Scripture tells us, "Hear O Israel, the Lord is our God, the Lord is One!" And you are the compassionate and merciful one toward everyone you have made.[7]

The prayer seems innocuous enough. Warren is a Christian, and every orthodox Christian can affirm everything in his prayer without qualification. Look more carefully, though, and you will see Warren "nodding" in three directions. The claim that all comes from, belongs to, and exists for God echoes the words of the apostle Paul at the culmination of the great Letter to the Romans (11:33–36). Many Christians through the centuries have taken the three claims to refer to the activities of the Father, Son, and Holy Spirit, the Holy Three who are the Holy One. Then comes the affirmation of the unity of God through a quote from Deuteronomy, the classic expression of Jewish monotheism. Finally, Warren mentions the "compassionate and merciful one"—an expression almost identical to the one that appears at the beginning of all but one surah of the Qur'an and one that observant Muslims recite many times daily.

Not everyone was pleased. Joe Schimmel, a conservative Christian blogger from Good Fight Ministries, skewered Warren for praying a prayer that was "first and foremost an affront to the one true God."[8] Why an affront? By referring to God as the "compassionate and merciful one," Warren, blasphemously in Schimmel's opinion, identified the deities of Christianity and Islam as one and the same. As another blogger argued, "The one True God is known by his attributes," and since the attributes ascribed to God in the Qur'an are "diametrically opposed" to those found in the Bible, Allah cannot be God. "The meaning of the phrase, 'Allah is compassionate and merciful,' has a completely different meaning within the context of Islam and the Qur'an than the phrase, 'God is compassionate and merciful,' would have within the context of Christianity and the Bible."[9] Muslims and Christians worship different deities.

Notice that the bloggers did not object to the content of anything Warren actually said about God. How could they? All Christians believe that God is compassionate and merciful. Warren suggested—not stated!—that God's being "compassionate and merciful" means something similar in Christianity and Islam. And that was his transgression, a betrayal of the sacred cause during one of the most public political events. He was blurring the line between the God of Jesus Christ and the God of the Qur'an.

But why not rejoice over similarities, over the fact that Muslims invoke God as the compassionate and merciful one? Why insist that the attributes of God in Islam and Christianity are incompatible? What was at stake in what seemed like a debate about fine points of Christian and Muslim theologies?

"God Versus Allah"?

For monotheists, to worship God means, among other things, to espouse a set of values about what ultimately matters in human life. To worship a different god is to espouse a different set of such values. A clash of gods is a clash of ultimate values. That's why the question of whether a given community worships the same god as another community has always been a crucial cultural and political question and not just a theological one. Concern about ultimate values that underpin political life explains, for instance, why a document that claims that Muslims and Christians worship different gods would circulate through the Parliament of the United Kingdom.[10]

As the war in Iraq got under way and the tensions between Muslim communities and some Western governments escalated, U.S. Deputy Undersecretary of Defense Lt. Gen. William Boykin suggested that Allah is "not a real God" and that Muslims worship an idol.[11] Influential televangelist and former U.S. presidential candidate Pat Robertson stated the issue sharply. Contemporary world conflicts between Islam and the West, he said, concern the matter of whether "the moon God of Mecca known as Allah is supreme, or whether the Judeo-Christian Jehovah, the God of the Bible, is supreme."[12] The God of Muslims and the God of Christians are two radically different gods, he implied, and that conclusion ultimately explains and justifies the supposed clash between the two civilizations.

Robertson's claim that Allah is the "moon God of Mecca" is historically false[13] and turns differences between the God of the Qur'an and the God of the Bible into a bad and damaging caricature. Nevertheless, Robertson correctly expressed the political import of a radical difference between the gods that people variously worship. At the risk of oversimplification, one may generalize the issue at stake in this way. The stronger the tensions between adherents of different religions, the more likely that their gods will be held to be incompatibly different—if for no other reason than that, in their imagination, worshippers will draw their god into those conflicts too. Inversely, the more different the gods worshipped by various peoples, the more likely, all other things being equal, that their respective worshippers will come into conflict and the less likely that they will find peaceful resolution of conflict.

The point here is not that all conflicts between communities are reducible to religious differences, let alone to the more specific difference in the understandings of God. They are not. The point is rather that the differences between gods worshipped often spark, contribute to causing, and magnify conflicts between their respective worshippers. Since in monotheistic traditions convictions about God are repositories of ultimate values, if respective conceptions of God are radically different, then ultimate values are radically different. And if ultimate values are radically different, the people who espouse them will not be able to negotiate their differences successfully and will inescapably clash—especially so in a tightly interconnected and interdependent world. The claim that Muslims and Christians worship radically different deities is good for fighting, but not for living together peacefully.

One might be tempted to say that the only workable solution is for both Muslims and Christians to secularize some of their beliefs and practices and regulate their common life without reference to God. And yet, that won't work. For one thing, many contemporary secular thinkers believe that religion is important in the modern world, because it helps forge bonds of solidarity between people.[14] Moreover, Islam and Christianity continue to be vibrant and growing religions; even if one wanted to, one could not bypass God as the source of ultimate values (see chapter 13).

Muslims and Christians will be able to live in peace with one another only if (1) the identities of each religious group are respected and given room for free expression, and (2) there are significant overlaps in the ultimate values that orient the lives of people in these communities. These two conditions will be met only if the God of the Bible and the God of the Qur'an turn out to embody overlapping ultimate values, that is, if Muslims and Christians, both monotheists, turn out to have "a common God."

A common God does more to help bridge the chasm between Christians and Muslims than just provide a set of overlapping ultimate values. A common God "nudges" people to actually employ those common values to set aside their animosities. To see how, travel with me in time—away from tensions between Christians and Muslims and their understandings of God—to a time when the United States was forged into one nation in the crucible of the Civil War. Pay attention not so much to warring Christians, but to a great political leader who invoked God to call them to their better selves.

"Both Pray to the Same God"

On March 4, 1865, Abraham Lincoln delivered one of the greatest speeches in American history, his second inaugural address. By that time, the Civil War was almost as old as his presidency; it lasted nearly four long and brutal years. And his speech was a meditation on the proper moral stance toward two warring parties as well as on the role of God in the "mighty scourge of war."[15] Right in the middle of Lincoln's "sacred effort," as Frederick Douglass, the most prominent African American who heard the speech, called it,[16] we read the following lines:

> Both read the same Bible and pray to the same God, and each invokes His aid against the other. It may seem strange that any men should dare to ask the just God's assistance in wringing their bread from the sweat of other men's faces, but let us not judge, that we not be judged. The prayers of both could not be answered. That of neither has been answered fully. The Almighty has his own purposes.[17]

Should Lincoln have assumed that both Union and Confederate forces prayed to the *same* God? Both were Christians, readers of the same Bible, of course. It would seem obvious, then, that they prayed to the same God. And yet, can the God who helps people "wring their bread from the sweat of other men's faces" be the same God who says to each human being, "By the sweat of *your* face you shall eat bread" (Gen. 3:19, emphasis added)? Can the God of the pharaoh be the same God as the God of the Hebrew slaves? The one God must be either an oppressor or an indifferent spectator, and the other an engaged and just liberator. Two different Gods, then? Lincoln resists this conclusion. He warns against rushed judgment and advises humility. "Let us not judge, that we not be judged."[18] Both warring parties, he states, do pray to the same God even if they think of God, God's commands, and God's agency rather differently.

If the warring parties understand God somewhat differently, why does it matter, then, that both worship the same God? Why did Lincoln draw attention to the fact that "both read the same Bible and pray to the same God"? After noting in his "Meditation on the Divine Will" that both warring parties *may* be wrong, he writes: "One *must* be wrong. God cannot be *for* and *against* the same thing at the same time."[19] In the second inaugural, Lincoln makes the same point: "The prayers of both could not be answered" by one and the same God; the actions of both cannot be right in the eyes of the same God. *There is a tension between each party's claiming to give full allegiance to the same God and the discord between them.* The belief in the same God—the one true God of love and justice—puts pressure on those who maintain they believe to stop fighting and come to an agreement.

Lincoln was well aware that worshipping the same God will clearly not prevent strife and war. But it does serve as an obstacle to it, a hurdle the warring parties need to overcome, for there is an incongruity between appeals to the same God, the source of the same values, and profound differences in moral judgments that lead to strife. That incongruity gave rhetorical force to Lincoln's reference to the same God as he addressed a nation ravaged by the Civil War. That was the point of his twice saying "the same"—the same Bible, the same God.

Perspectives and Goals

In Lincoln's case, the people in the opposing trenches were mostly Christians. One could maybe assume that they did pray to the same God. But can it be said of Muslims and Christians, today caught in deep conflicts, that they too worship the same God? Yes, it can. That is exactly what I argue in this book. And it is only one of many controversial claims I make.

Sometimes when I observe contemporary U.S. culture, with its hard fronts and nasty culture wars, I have a strange sense that I've seen something like it before—in the Communist and semitotalitarian state in which I grew up. The issues and positions are very different, but the spirit is strangely familiar. In all public discussion, there was a party line that people had to toe; if you diverged, you were deemed disloyal and suspected of betraying the cause. I sense a similar spirit today among both progressives and conservatives in the United States when it comes to many hot-button issues, including Islam. Progressives and conservatives differ radically in their perspectives, but each group has a set of "politically correct" views about Muslims and Islam. In this book I am, roughly, an equal-opportunity offender when it comes to both of these "camps."

Here are some prefatory points about this book:

1. I write as a committed Christian who embraces classical expressions of the Christian faith, including the doctrines of the Trinity, the incarnation, justification by grace, and so forth. This I take to be part of the normative Christian tradition in which I happily stand. I offer here a Christian perspective, a Christian response to the God of the Qur'an.

2. I write both *as* a Christian and *for* Christians. I don't write

from some neutral perspective, from some vantage point suspended above Christianity and Islam; that would be disingenuous. And I don't write for Muslims, telling them what to believe and how to lead their lives; that would be condescending.

3. I write as a Christian, but I write in the presence of Muslims. They are more than welcome to look over my shoulder, and I am interested in hearing where they agree and disagree with me or where they feel understood or misunderstood. After all, this is a book about them, their God, their beliefs and practices, and their life in the imagination of Christians.

4. I write for Christians, but at the same time this book is an open invitation to Muslims to think along with me and, if so moved, reexamine their own stances toward the God of Jesus Christ in the light of what I have written.

5. There are many kinds of Muslims in the world today, just as there are many kinds of Christians. And just as I try to write from the perspective of what I believe to be the "normative mainstream" of Christianity, so I try to write about the "normative mainstream" of Islam. For me here the "paradigmatic" Muslim is the great and immensely influential thinker Abu Hamid al-Ghazali (1056–1111),[20] and not, for instance, Sayyid Qutb (1906–66), the most popular representative of radical Islam.[21]

6. As I write about Islam and Muslims, I seek to be both truthful and charitable. To love my neighbors as myself means to speak as well of them as I wish they would speak of me.

7. Except on the margins, I do not engage Judaism, the religious tradition through which the gift of the belief in one God came to the world. Jews and Christians have a different (though partly overlapping) set of issues when it comes to the identity of God and to living together in a single world than do Muslims and Christians. A different book is required to deal with those issues.

8. The goal of this book is to explore how Christian and Muslim

convictions about God bear on their ability to live together well in a single world. It is a book about God and *this* world, not a book about God and the world to come; it is primarily about socially relevant knowledge of God, not about saving knowledge of God. I leave the questions of salvation and eternal destiny aside. To use technical terms, the book is not an exercise in soteriology, but in political theology.

I was a child when I was first introduced to political theology, and the people who introduced me to it didn't even know that the term existed. I grew up in a small Christian community in an officially Communist and atheistic state. Our convictions about God organized a way of life for us, and it was distinct from the kind of social life mandated by the state. We were an alternative community giving ultimate allegiance to a Sovereign other than Marshal Tito; the state treated us as a threat to be contained. Both our allegiance to God and the state's denial of God were political stances. We found a way to coexist, sometimes clashing (I was jailed for obedience to God rather than to government officials), sometimes cooperating (I went to public school and got a decent education), sometimes going along while dissenting at the same time (I did compulsory military service with the understanding that I would not kill), and so on. As I reflected on how to live in light of my allegiance to God in a state that denied God and set itself up as the "earthly God" and the "absolute sovereign," I was doing political theology without knowing it.

When it comes to Muslims and Christians, the issue is not a conflict between allegiance to the Master of the Universe and to an earthly god. It is, rather, that the two religious communities give ultimate allegiance to two rival versions of the Master of the Universe. God matters to them in private as well as in public life, and this sometimes creates tensions. One of the defining challenges of our time is to find workable ways for Christians and Muslims to be true to their convictions about God and God's commands, while living peacefully and constructively together under the same political roof. The main purpose of this book is to help meet that challenge. In a broad sense of the term, the book is primarily about politics.

Hot and Spicy

Here is a small sampler of the hot and spicy dish I have prepared for you. Leaving the food metaphor aside, the theses below either make or break this book:

1. Christians and Muslims worship one and the same God, the only God. They understand God's character partly differently, but the object of their worship is the same. I reject the idea that Muslims worship a different God than do Jews and Christians.
2. What the Qur'an denies about God as the Holy Trinity has been denied by every great teacher of the church in the past and ought to be denied by every orthodox Christian today. I reject the idea that Muslim monotheism is incompatible with the Christian doctrine of the Trinity.
3. Both Muslims and Christians, in their normative traditions, describe God as loving and just, even if there are differences in how they understand God's love and justice. I reject the idea that the God of the Qur'an stands as a fierce and violent deity in opposition to the God of Jesus Christ, who is sheer love.
4. The God Muslims worship and the God Christians worship—the one and only God—commands that we love our neighbors, even though it is true that the meaning of love of neighbor differs partly in Christianity and Islam. I reject the idea that Islam is a religion of life-constricting laws, whereas Christianity is a religion of life-affirming love.
5. Because they worship the same and similarly understood God, Christians and Muslims have a sufficiently robust moral

framework to pursue the common good together. I reject the idea that Muslim and Christian "civilizations" are bound to clash.

6. Christians should see Muslims, who give ultimate allegiance to God as the supreme good, as allies in resisting the tendency in contemporary culture to see mere pleasure, rather than justice and love, as the hallmark of the good life. I reject the association of freedom to do what one pleases with Christianity and blind submission to the iron law of God with Islam.

7. What matters is not whether you are Christian or Muslim or anything else; instead, what matters is whether you love God with all your heart and whether you trust and obey Jesus Christ, the Word of God and Lamb of God. I reject making religious belonging and religious labels more significant than allegiance to the one true God.

8. Love and justice for all, rooted in the character of God, requires that all persons have the right to choose, change, and practice their religion publicly. I reject all attempts to control the decisions human beings make about what most profoundly matters in their lives.

9. All people have the right to witness about their faith; curtailing that right in any way is an assault on human dignity. At the same time, those who witness have an obligation to follow the Golden Rule. I reject *both* all suppression of freedom of expression *and* all uncharitable ways of exercising that freedom.

10. To give allegiance to the one God who enjoins humans to be loving and just to all, as Muslims and Christians do, means to embrace pluralism as a political project—the right of all religious people to articulate their views in public and the impartiality of the state with respect to all religions (and other overarching interpretations of life). I reject the idea that monotheism, properly understood, fosters violence and totalitarian rule.

The issues are hot and the claims are spicy, but this is how I see things.

Ever since I lived under the dead hand of a semitotalitarian regime, I have resisted toeing any party line. I know that the boundary separating truth and falsehood is not the same as the boundary between political parties or ideological combatants. I want the truth, not politically expedient or ideologically "correct" positions. And, as a follower of Christ, I want the truth seen with the eyes of inviting and reconciling love, not the truth born of cold indifference or simmering hatred. In this book, I apply lessons I learned living under Communist rule during the Cold War to relations between Christians and Muslims today. With regard to the central "ideological" question in relations between those two faiths—the identity and character of God—I resolutely try to expose encrusted positions and emotionally charged negative stereotypes and, instead, to speak truth in love. At the level of discourse, this is how wars are prevented and the road to peace is paved.

PART I

Disputes, Present and Past

CHAPTER ONE

The Pope and the Prince: God, the Great Chasm, and the Building of Bridges

In February 2006 the global crisis triggered by the Danish satirical caricatures of the Prophet Muhammad was at its peak. Leaders of many nations and transnational organizations, including the secretary-general of the United Nations, Kofi Annan, felt compelled to speak out. Peace and security were threatened in many parts of the world. Toward the end of that same month, the leader of over one billion Christians, Pope Benedict XVI, spoke up as well. Like most other international figures, he aligned himself squarely with those who insisted that freedom of expression does not include the right of desecration. "In the international context we are living in at present," he said, "the Catholic Church continues convinced that, to foster peace and understanding between peoples and men, it is necessary and urgent that religions and their symbols be respected." Such respect implies, the pope added, that "believers not be the object of provocations that wound their lives and religious sentiments."[1] Many Muslims felt that the most influential Christian in the world was on their side. But was he?

A mere seven months later, in September 2006, after the pope's now famous speech at the University of Regensburg, the fury of some Muslims fell on Pope Benedict XVI himself. As during the cartoon crisis, at issue again was Islam's denial of freedom and promotion of violence. Even earlier, in his statement against irreverent cartoonists and their mocking portrayals of the founder of Islam, the pope not only defended Muslims; indirectly and gently, he scolded the violent among them as well: "Intolerance and violence can never be justified as a response to offenses, as they are not compatible responses with the sacred principles of religion." He was referring to Muslim rioting, killing, and burning in response to the caricatures (even as he left unacknowledged peaceful protests, like the ones in Mauritania[2]). In the same breath, he raised another issue. Respect for religion and for religious symbols, he insisted, requires freedom of choice in religious matters, or, as he put it, the right to "the exercise of the religion freely chosen."[3]

In his brief statement about the caricatures, the pope demanded respect for religious symbols, condemned violence in response to desecration, and advocated freedom of religion. Many prominent Muslims agreed on all these matters. The pope and Muslims seemed aligned. So what broke the amity in the eyes of many? In his speech at Regensburg he picked up again, more extensively, the issues of religious freedom and violence and said something very different from his statement about the cartoons—or so many Muslims thought. An ally had turned adversary, and they felt betrayed and angry.

In the lecture, the pope seemed to argue that Islam is a violent religion and that the root cause of its violent nature lies in the character of the Muslim God. In scholarly prose, he made the same point Danish cartoonists made with satirical caricatures. As one Muslim commentator observed, he put "the caricatures into words."[4] That only two days before the lecture he once again urged respect for what is sacred to others rang hollow and self-serving in the ears of many Muslims, who saw the same disrespect in the pope's reasoned disagreement as they did in the cartoonists' satirical derision.[5]

The reaction of the "Muslim street" was swift and in many places extremely violent. As in the case of the Danish cartoons, a popular Muslim teacher, Yusuf al-Qaradawi, on the widely watched TV channel al-Jazeera, called for a "day of anger"—anger expressed, though, through demonstrations and sit-ins rather than violent attacks.[6] Many heeded his call to anger, but not to nonviolence. The pope's effigies were burned in Basra, Iraq; a Catholic nun was shot in Somalia; protests practically shut down the Kashmir Valley; and a branch of al-Qaeda vowed to conquer Rome, to "break the cross and spill the wine," and prayed to God to be able to "slit their throats and make their money and descendants the bounty of the mujahideen."[7]

Much more significant than the violent reaction of the extremists was a reasoned position taken by Islamic scholars ('ulama)—the voice of authoritative and moderate Islam. First came a direct response, an "Open Letter" that contained a point-by-point refutation of the pope's statements in the lecture about Islam from a group of the most renowned Islamic scholars of the day. Then, exactly a year later, came an alternative proposal, a highly authoritative and representative document titled "A Common Word Between Us and You." It is addressed to Christian leaders worldwide, but is directed above all to Pope Benedict XVI. On the surface it looks like another interfaith missive from one group of religious dignitaries to another—the kind of text that elicits a yawn from ordinary readers. But behind the document stood a young and brilliant Jordanian prince, and it contained one massive surprise: a new proposal about relations between Muslims and Christians. In it some of the most senior Muslim religious leaders from all around the world—grand muftis of many nations, popular preachers with large followings, and scholarly authorities from places like the famed al-Azhar University—argued that the commands of God unite Muslims and Christians much more than they divide them. Properly understood, God does not widen the chasm between Muslims and Christians as Benedict XVI suggested, but bridges it.

Before exploring the "Common Word" and some Christian reactions to it, we need to look more closely at the pope's offending speech. What did he say that caused such a stir—violence on some streets and a major alternative proposal about the relations between Islam and Christianity by leading Muslim scholars?

God and Democracy

Early on in the lecture, as a starting point for his reflection on faith and reason, the main topic of the speech, Benedict XVI reminded his audience of a fourteenth-century encounter between "the erudite Byzantine emperor Manuel II Paleologus and an educated Persian on the subject of Christianity and Islam, and the truth of both."[8] The emperor, ruler of a domain that by that time had shrunk to not much more than the city of Constantinople itself, had at one point issued a challenge to his interlocutor. It concerned the violent nature of Islam, especially as it relates to freedom of religion. He said: "Show me just what Muhammad brought that was new, and there you will find things only evil and inhuman, such as his command to spread by the sword the faith he preached."[9] These words, when the pope repeated them, triggered an explosion of Muslim anger.

The emperor may be excused for his "surprisingly brusque" words, as Benedict XVI has described them. Though the conversation had taken place in 1391, the emperor had recorded it during the eight-year Ottoman siege of Constantinople lasting from 1394 to 1402. By that time the Turks had conquered Thrace and Macedonia and had won, in 1389, the decisive victory against the Serbian Empire in the battle on Blackbird's Field. The minuscule empire of Manuel II had been a client state of the Turks since 1379 (and, by the end of the siege, the "empire" had paid the Turks the handsome sum of 345,000 ducats, roughly $47.5 million at the current value of gold!). During the siege, "hunger and desperation prevailed."[10] The sword of the Muslim Turks, deployed efficiently to conquer, subdue, and threaten, was in evidence everywhere. Who could object to a few brusque words by a powerless and besieged emperor about the evil and inhumanity of the mighty conquerors' religion?

To many hearers and readers of the pope's lecture, he seemed to make the emperor's words his own. Though he did not have Manuel's excuse—military, economic, and cultural power has shifted decidedly in favor of the West—rightly or wrongly the pope saw analogies between the situation of the Byzantine Empire in the late fourteenth century and that of the West today.[11] He distanced himself from some of the emperor's comments,[12] most likely those that associate *only* "evil and inhuman" things with Islam. In his earlier book on the relation between Christian faith and world religions, *Truth and Tolerance,* he distinguished between "destructive forms" of Islam and those forms in which "we can perceive a certain proximity to the mystery of Christ."[13] But the Regensburg address as a whole suggests that, whatever Islam's proximity to Christ, in its "inner nature" it also shows an undeniable connection to violence. Why? Not just because Islam is "a total organization of life . . . that embraces simply everything,"[14] but above all because of Islam's God.

In the dialogue between Manuel II and the learned Persian the most important words for Benedict XVI were not those that triggered the ire of many Muslims. Without any detriment to his main point, he could have easily left out the claim that Muhammad brought "things only evil and inhuman" into the world. His main concern was not even about Muslim violence, but about a deeper illness of which violence is a symptom—a profoundly mistaken idea about the nature of God, namely, that God is an unreasonable and capricious deity.

Benedict XVI zeroes in on the Christian emperor's claim that, in a Christian as distinct from a Muslim perspective, violence in advancing the truth is incompatible with God's nature. Drawing a contrast between Christianity and Islam, Manuel II said:

> God is not pleased by blood, and not acting reasonably is contrary to God's nature. Faith is born of the soul, not the body. Whoever would lead someone to faith needs the ability to speak well and to reason properly, without violence and threats. . . . To convince a reasonable soul, one does not need a strong arm, or weapons of any kind, or any other means of threatening a person with death.

Now, as it turns out, Muslim scholars almost unanimously *agree* with the Christian emperor in affirming that faith is born of the soul rather than of the body. Just because of that, they insist, in the words of the Qur'an, that there is "no compulsion in religion" (Al Baqarah, 2:256.[15] And even though both the ancient emperor and today's pope think differently about Islam's stance on freedom of religion, this too was not the pope's main point. In the lecture, his main concern was the *character of God*.

In Benedict XVI's view, Christianity is a marriage of biblical faith in God and Greek reason. The clearest demonstration of this marriage is the prologue of John's Gospel. Echoing the opening line of Genesis—"In the beginning God created"—John begins his Gospel with the words: "In the beginning was the *logos*." *Logos*, notes the pope, is both "word" and "reason"—"reason which is creative and capable of self-communication, precisely as reason." He continues:

> John thus spoke the final word on the biblical concept of God, and in this word all the often toilsome and tortuous threads of biblical faith find their culmination and synthesis. In the beginning was the logos, and the logos is God.

In Christianity, Reason is God and God is Reason. God does not just act reasonably; God is Reason itself.

In Islam, argues Benedict XVI, it is different. In Muslim teaching, "God is absolutely transcendent. His will is not bound up with any of our categories, even that of rationality."[16] So this, then, is the great contrast in the nature of the Ultimate Reality: the "God-as-reason" of Christianity stands over against the "God-as-pure-will" of Islam. The first encourages reasoning, deliberation, and persuasion; the second demands obedience and promotes violence. The "God-as-reason" of Christianity undergirds reasonable witness to one's faith and deliberative political procedures; the "God-as-pure-will" of Islam undergirds the spreading of faith by the sword and the totalitarian rule of the interpreters of God's will. In Benedict's view, the conception of "God-as-pure-will" is at the root of the challenge that Islam presents for democratic institutions and cultures. The Muslim God is a completely arbitrary deity, and therefore Islam is incompatible with deliberative democracy.[17]

For one of the most erudite and influential Christian leaders of today, a chasm yawns between Islam and Christianity. The organization of social life is "completely different" in the two, and at the heart of that social difference lie two distinct understandings of God.

An Open Letter

The first major reaction of the Muslim learned tradition to the Regensburg lecture came as an open letter to Benedict XVI. In contrast to the fury unleashed by some on the "Muslim street," the letter was a reasoned and measured response, point by point, to the pope's claims about Islam. The stated intention of the signatories was to be governed by the injunction in the Qur'an about debating with Jews and Christians: "Do not contend with people of the Book except in the fairest way" (Al 'Ankabut, 29:46).

First, the "Open Letter" takes up the claim that Muhammad commands faith to be spread by the sword. In his lecture, Benedict XVI mentioned the famous verse from the Qur'an that says, "There is no compulsion in religion" (Al Baqarah, 2:256). He dismissed it as coming from the early period of Muhammad's life, when he "was still powerless and under threat." This was superseded, the pope implied, by later instructions concerning holy war, which, he suggests, contain the injunction to spread faith by the sword. In response, the signatories of the "Open Letter" insist that the verse has permanent validity:

In fact this verse is acknowledged to belong to the period of Qur'anic revelation corresponding to the political and military ascendance of the young Muslim community. "There is no compulsion in religion" was not a command to Muslims to remain steadfast in the face of the desire of their oppressors to force them to renounce their faith, but was a reminder to Muslims themselves, once they had attained power, that they could not force another's heart to believe. "There is no compulsion in religion" addresses those in a position of strength, not weakness. The earliest commentaries on the Qur'an (such as that of al-Tabari) make it clear that some Muslims of Medina wanted to force their children to convert from Judaism or Christianity to Islam, and this verse was precisely an answer to them not to try to force their children to convert to Islam.[18]

The prohibition against compulsion in religion is binding in Islam, the "Open Letter" insists. All those who have acted against it and engaged in forced conversions in the course of history have "violated Islamic tenets."

But what about Islam's God—God's absolute transcendence, God's not being bound by "any of our categories, even that of rationality," indeed, God's not being bound "even by his own word"? That was the pope's main concern, the heart of the issue. The "Open Letter" responds:

> God has many Names in Islam, including the Merciful, the Just, the Seeing, the Hearing, the Knowing, the Loving, and the Gentle. Their utter conviction in God's Oneness and that "There is none like unto Him" (Al Ikhlas, 112:4) has not led Muslims to deny God's attribution of these qualities to Himself and to (some of) His creatures.

If justice, mercy, and knowledge are God's own attributes, then there is no room for divine capriciousness. At the least, there is the self-binding of God to mercy, justice, truth, and reason—which means that this is how God definitely *is* in relation to human beings even if God *could have been* different.[19]

Finally, the "Open Letter" reminds Benedict XVI that, at least since the Second Vatican Council (1962–65), the Catholic Church has affirmed that Christians and Muslims worship the same God. It quotes the words of the late pope John Paul II, "for whom many Muslims had great regard and esteem":

> We Christians joyfully recognize the religious values we have in common with Islam. Today I would like to repeat what I said to young Muslims some years ago in Casablanca: "We believe in the same God, the one God, the living God, the God who created the world and brings his creatures to their perfection."[20]

Even if it is true that Christians and Muslims differ in their understanding of God (Christians claim that the one God is the Holy Trinity, for instance, whereas Muslims deny this), they still worship the same God, the "Open Letter" argues. Even if it is true that Muslims and Christians may understand freedom of religion partly differently (Muslims, on the whole, insist on punishing conversion to another religion, whereas modern Christians do not[21]), Muslims and Christians both condemn compulsion in religion, the "Open Letter" suggests. Where the pope sees radical differences and incompatibilities, the signatories of the "Open Letter" see similarities amid the undeniable and ineffaceable differences. Muslims' and Christians' convictions about God, they believe, can serve as a bridge between the two communities, not simply as a source of division.

But who is right? Have the signatories of the "Open Letter" painted too rosy a picture? Have they contended "in a fair way"— in a way that is fair to sacred books as well as to the deeply held religious convictions of *both* Muslims and Christians?

Love of God, Love of Neighbor

Tucked in close to the end of the "Open Letter" is a truly revolutionary idea. It remained largely unnoticed by readers. The text winds down, as many such texts do, expressing hope that Muslims and Christians will "continue to build peaceful and friendly relationships based upon mutual respect, justice, and what is common in essence in our shared Abrahamic tradition." And then, just as one's hand starts moving to cover the yawn, one is startled by a pearl of surprising beauty and great value. The "common essence" of Christianity and Islam, states the "Open Letter" surprisingly, are the "two greatest commandments" as Jesus Christ formulated them in the Gospels: "The first is, 'Hear, O Israel: the Lord our God, the Lord is one; and you shall love the Lord your God with all your heart, and with all your soul, and with all your mind, and with all your strength.' The second is this, 'You shall love your neighbor as yourself'" (Mark 12:29–31).

Islam is at its heart a violent religion, say many of its fierce critics,[22] including Benedict XVI (at least in the Regensburg lecture). Islam is at its heart about obedience to God's law, the Shari'a, which is based on the Qur'an and authoritative oral tradition (*hadith*) and has been systematized over the centuries in the classical schools of law, say many of its devout advocates. Islam is at its heart about love of God and of neighbor, say the signatories of the "Open Letter."[23] In the minds of most people, Christianity is supposed to be about love of God and neighbor (even though it is true that at the heart of Christianity does not lie human love at all, but God's love for humanity[24]). But many—including many scholars of Islam—would need persuading that Islam is about love of God and neighbor.

As mentioned, exactly one year after the "Open Letter," on October 13, 2007, a longer text was published that expands upon this argument. Its title is "A Common Word Between Us and You," and it bears the stamp of authority of the most prominent and representative Muslim leaders in the world. Its birthplace was Amman, Jordan. The intellectual and organizational force behind it was Prince Ghazi bin Muhammad bin Talal.

Here is a bare-bones version of the argument. First, love of God. As recorded in the authoritative oral tradition (*hadith*), Muhammad said:

The best that I have said—myself, and the prophets that came before me—is: "There is no god but God, He Alone, He hath no associate, His is the sovereignty and His is the praise and He hath power over all things."[25]

"Love" for God does not appear in these words of Muhammad. Indeed, he says nothing about how humans should relate to God; rather, he describes God. And yet in every one of these descriptions of God, a human attitude toward God is implied. To the singleness and universal rule of God corresponds exclusive devotion to God on the part of humans. As the "Common Word" states, this text "reminds Muslims that their hearts, their individual souls and all the faculties and powers of their souls . . . must be totally devoted and attached to God."[26]

Second, love of neighbor. Again, according to the *hadith,* Muhammad said: "None of you has faith until you love for your neighbor what you love for yourself."[27] The "Common Word" explains: "Love of the neighbor is an essential and integral part of faith in God and of love of God, because in Islam without love of the neighbor there is no true faith in God and no righteousness."[28]

In Islam, as in Christianity, love of God and love of neighbor are central, argue the signatories of the "Common Word." Their point is not that Islam is no different from Christianity. They state explicitly that these two "are obviously different religions." Their point is, rather, that the two greatest commandments "are an area of common ground and a link between the Qur'an, the Torah and the New Testament."

The idea is ingenious and promising. But is it correct? Are love of God and love of neighbor at the heart of Islam? Many Christians are skeptical.[29] But Muslims themselves must answer this question. And they have given an initial answer through the representative character of the signatories of the "Common Word." Predominantly senior leaders and scholars, they come from all around the globe (from Chad to Uzbekistan, from Indonesia to Mauritania, from Canada to the Sudan), from all streams of Muslim thought

(Sunni, both Salafi and Sufi, Shiʻa, and ʻIbadi). How long this consensus will remain in place and how deeply it will penetrate Muslim communities remains to be seen.

Love and the Chasm

As a response to the pope's address at Regensburg, the "Common Word" has sidestepped the face-off between God-as-reason and God-as-pure-will. Prince Ghazi, who drafted it, felt that Muslim scholars dealt sufficiently with the issue in the "Open Letter." For relations between Muslims and Christians, as religious people as well as citizens, a common commitment to love is at least as important as a shared commitment to reason.

The occasion for issuing the "Common Word" was the Regensburg address, but its main concern was the deteriorated state of relations between Muslims and Christians. The document calls attention to the fact that these two religious communities make up more than half of the world population, and their number and influence continue to grow. "If Muslims and Christians are not at peace," we read in the "Common Word,"

> the world cannot be at peace. With the terrible weaponry of the modern world; with Muslims and Christians intertwined everywhere as never before, no side can unilaterally win a conflict between more than half of the world's inhabitants. Thus our common future is at stake.[30]

And yet today the two communities are deeply divided; suspicions, animosities, conflicts, and even wars mark their relations.

The critical question for the "Common Word" project is this. Is it possible to bring about a shift from what feels like a clash of civilizations to the peaceful coexistence of faith traditions by promoting what some may deem an esoteric feeling of human devotion to God and a soft and nebulous sentiment of neighborly love?

If religion has anything to do with conflicts between Christians and Muslims, religious passions stemming from single-minded devotion to God are the source of these conflicts, not a means to overcome them, many critics argue. Less religion is what we need, not more. Take God out of it all, critics conclude. Let people keep religious devotion locked in the privacy of their hearts. Instead, let's grapple with the harder and more secular realities of life—with poverty and economic development, freedom of expression, education, stewardship of the environment, political arrangements, the balance of power, and modes of countering violence with effective force.[31]

And yet today, as over the past millennia, faith profoundly matters to literally billions of people, the majority of whom are Muslims and Christians. And as democratic practices take root worldwide, religious people will continue to bring their faith into the public realm. This is where the significance of the "Common Word" comes in. First, the document points both Muslims and Christians to what is essential in each faith and common to both—love of God and love of neighbor. Second, it shows how what is essential in each faith and common to both has the power to bind them together, because it encourages—indeed, demands—that their adherents seek the good of others, not just their own good. If it is true that the dual command of love is the common ground of the two faiths, the consequences are momentous. We no longer have to say, "The deeper your faith, the more you will be at odds with others!" To the contrary, we must say, "The deeper your faith, the more you will live in harmony with others!" A deep faith no longer leads to clashes; it fosters peaceful coexistence.

What some deride as an impractical and soft commitment to love God and neighbor—but what is actually attachment to the Source of all reality and the practice of active care—can have real-life effects in defusing conflicts and fostering peace. It makes possible what would otherwise remain unattainable in a world of personally vibrant and socially assertive faiths. We can embrace deep faith while at the same time respecting the rights and promoting the well-being of those who do not share it. Deep faith expresses itself in love, and love, understood as active care, leads to respect for and struggle for others' rights. Put differently, and maybe surprisingly to some, *commitment to the properly understood love of God and neighbor makes deeply religious persons,* because they are deeply religious, *into dedicated social pluralists* (see chapter 12).

Obstacles

When Christians and Muslims commit themselves to practicing the dual command of love, they are not satisfying some private religious fancy; instead, they are actively fostering peaceful coexistence in an ineradicably pluralistic world plagued by deep divisions. They are making possible constructive collaboration between people of different faiths in the common public space and for the common good. That is the promise of the "Common Word"—to bridge the chasm between Muslim and Christian communities through a common commitment to love God and neighbor.

Promise, of course, is not yet fulfillment. First, it is one thing to agree that Muslims and Christians along with Jews share the two Great Commandments. It is another thing to act toward one another guided by these two commandments. Under the best of circumstances, loving one's neighbor as oneself does not come easy. And whole communities, which tend to be less moral than individuals, find it even more difficult to practice anything that comes close to love.[32] And yet, for moral action on behalf of others, love is crucial. Take, for example, respect for human dignity. Nobody respects the human dignity of another just for the sake of the abstract principle of respect for human dignity, just as nobody promotes justice for the love of the abstract principle of justice.[33] People do justice and respect dignity, because they care for others, because they want to be benevolent and beneficent toward them—in a word, because they love. You need love to have justice and human dignity—even if that love may be deficient and thoroughly mixed with self-interest.[34]

Second, Muslims and Christians may both commit themselves to love God and neighbor, but understand differently what it means to "love," who counts as "neighbor," and how to best describe "God." Is "love" unconditional or conditional? Is "neighbor" a fellow member of the same community (whether an ethnic, political, or religious community) or any human being anywhere in the world? What is the relation between God's justice and mercy? There is plenty of room for vigorous debate between Christians and Muslims on issues such as these (as there have been vigorous debates within each of these communities). All these issues and more would need to be sorted out patiently and responsibly.[35]

Finally, the most critical issue—an issue on which everything in the "Common Word" depends—is whether it can be said that Christians and Muslims believe in the same God. To be precise, the issue is not: Do Muslims and Christians have exactly the same beliefs about the one God they worship? Clearly, the answer is no. Nobody disputes this. Even among themselves Christians disagree—how would they then not disagree with Muslims? The same is true of Muslims as well. Muslim and Christian beliefs about God significantly diverge at points. The issue is, rather, this: Is the object of Christians' and Muslims' faith and love the same?

After we have visited Amman, Jordan, to hear what learned Muslims think about common ground between Christians and Muslims, we are back where we started: at the lecture hall in Regensburg, Bavaria, and the question of God.

Back to God

The "Common Word" does not state that Christians and Muslims believe in the same God. It did not need to do so; the Qur'an, to which the signatories owe obedience, says it for them. In the Qur'an it is written: "We believe what was revealed to us and what was revealed to you. Our God and your God is one, and to him we submit as Muslims" (Al 'Ankabut, 29:46). And again: "God is our

Lord and your Lord; we have our works and you have your works; there is no argument between us and you; God brings us together; and to him is the final destiny" (Al Shura, 42:15). The key signatories of the "Common Word" were also the authority behind the "Open Letter." To counter the opposition between the God of Christians ("God-as-reason") and the God of Muslims ("God-as-pure-will") set up by Pope Benedict XVI, the letter reminded him of the views of his predecessor, John Paul II, who clearly stated to the Muslim youth: "We believe in the same God."

Some Christians strenuously disagree not just with the Qur'an, but with John Paul II as well. One of the most passionate is John Piper, a learned and influential Pastor for Preaching and Vision at Bethlehem Baptist Church in Minneapolis, Minnesota. He was not responding directly to the "Common Word," but to what came to be known as the "Yale Response" to the "Common Word." The "Yale Response"—published originally in the *New York Times* in November 2007 under the title "Loving God and Neighbor Together: A Christian Response to 'A Common Word Between Us and You'"[36]—did not address directly the question of whether the God of the Bible and the God of the Qur'an are the same God. But the drafters—I was among them—worked with that assumption. Piper objected.

Piper's argument is simple. In the Gospel of John, a disciple of Jesus by the name of Philip says to Jesus: "Lord, show us the Father." The request is triggered by Jesus's famous claim: "No one comes to the Father except through me." Jesus's response to Philip is the cornerstone of Piper's argument: "Have I been with you all this time, Philip, and you still do not know me? Whoever has seen me has seen the Father. . . . Do you not believe that I am in the Father and the Father is in me?" (14:6–10). "The Bible is crystal clear," says Piper in a brief video on the issue, "that Jesus Christ is the litmus paper as to whether or not we are talking about the same God." To clarify the point, he gives an illustration:

I got help from a good friend of mine who said this: Suppose two people are arguing about their classmate from college thirty years ago, and they're starting to wonder if they are talking about the same person. . . . And somebody comes up and says, "Why don't you just open the yearbook?". . . They open it up and [one of them] says, "There she is!" And the other guy says, "Oh no, no, that's not who I was talking about!" And it's all clear now. [They] were not talking about the same person. And my friend said to me, "Jesus Christ, as he is revealed in the New Testament, is in the yearbook. You open the yearbook and you look at his picture and you say, 'Is that your God?' And the Muslims are going to say, 'No, that's not our God.' And you say, 'Well we're not talking about the same God then.'"[37]

Piper's assumption is that, for Muslims, God is very much unlike Jesus, that the differences are profound. It is "not honest" then, Piper argues, "to lead Muslims to think that we really have . . . a common vision of God."

This is not the place to respond to Piper's argument. The rest of the book is a response to arguments like his. I will propose, from a Christian perspective, a way to affirm that Christians and Muslims worship the same God even if their visions of God differ. Here, I am interested in the consequences of the claim that Christians and Muslims worship a different deity. What are they? Since both Christians and Muslims are monotheists, if they worship different gods, they will rightly accuse each other of worshipping a false god,[38] which is the worst of sins in both of these traditions. The love that Muslims and Christians have for the God they worship will pull them apart rather than bring them together. In the introduction I argued that the gaping chasm between Muslims and Christians will widen if it turns out that each community worships a profoundly different God. In this chapter we see that one of the most promising initiatives to bridge this chasm will fail if it happens that each community worships a completely different God. If Christians and Muslims love different and therefore competing deities, the whole "Common Word" project crumbles to the ground.

Now, if the followers of both faiths are committed to love of neighbor, that could come to the rescue. It is possible to be benevolent and beneficent toward those who worship a different God and with whom we therefore disagree on ultimate principles, but it's very difficult. In that situation love strains mightily. If, on the other hand, Muslims and Christians worship the same God, albeit partly differently understood, the love of each for God will help them live together and make neighborly love easier. That was the promise of the "Common Word."

It would be foolish, of course, to expect our wishes to determine the character of God. Neither Christians nor Muslims can design a God for themselves to suit the need for social harmony! Both religious communities definitely agree on one claim about God: God is God, the sovereign creator, not a malleable creature to be designed according to human need or fancy. So our task cannot be to *make* the two Gods the same. Instead, our task must be to *find out* whether the Gods that are worshipped are the same God. Christians cannot decide that question for Muslims; Muslims cannot answer that question for Christians. Each has to decide the question by examining what they believe to be the revelation of God. So for Christians the question is this: Is the God whose final self-expression is found in the life and teachings of Jesus Christ the same God as the God of the Qur'an? Much rides on the answer to this question.

The Pope in Amman

In Regensburg it seemed that Benedict XVI was suggesting that Muslims and Christians worship different deities, that Christians think of God as Reason and are therefore committed to freedom and deliberation, and that Muslims think of God as inscrutable and arbitrary Will and are therefore inclined to submission and prone to violence. And yet, even in the lecture, there were signals that the division between advocates of reason and advocates of will is not the same as division between Christians and Muslims. A similar division is to be found in Christianity itself, the pope conceded. Might the pontiff be open to seeing that an analogous division exists also within Islam, as some Muslim critics have suggested?

After the uproar in the aftermath of the Regensburg address, the Vatican went into high gear trying to control the damage. Less than two weeks after the address, on September 25, 2006, Benedict XVI invited the leaders of Muslim communities to the papal summer residence, Castel Gandolfo. Early on in his remarks to them, he quoted a passage from a historic document from the Second Vatican Council, *Nostra Aetate*. For the Catholic Church these words are, as he put it, "the Magna Carta of Muslim-Christian dialogue":

> The church looks upon Muslims with respect. They worship the one God living and subsistent, merciful and almighty, creator of heaven and earth, who has spoken to humanity and to whose decrees, even the hidden ones, they seek to submit themselves wholeheartedly, just as Abraham, to whom the Islamic faith readily relates itself, submitted to God.[39]

He underscored immediately that he places himself "firmly within this perspective."[40] The God whom Muslims worship and the God whom Christians worship are clearly not two different Gods. If Muslims worshipped a different God than Christians, they would be worshipping a false God, not "the one God living and subsistent, merciful and almighty, creator of heaven and earth." So the God is the same, notwithstanding many important differences.

How is the affirmation of the sameness of the Christian and Muslim Gods related to the contrast in the Regensburg address between "God-as-reason" and "God-as-will"? What implications does it have for the argument that the Muslim scholars and dignitaries, under the leadership of Prince Ghazi bin Muhammad bin Talal, offered in response to the pope—that what binds Christians and Muslims is commitment to love the one God and neighbor?

On May 9, 2009, during his visit to the Holy Land, Benedict XVI gave a speech in al-Hussein bin Talal mosque in Amman, Jordan. His host was Prince Ghazi bin Muhammad bin Talal. The pope took up both the issue of reason and the issue of love. He repeated the Christian description of God as reason as well as the correlative human capacity to participate in that divine reason. He dropped the reference to Islam's arbitrary God and Muslim violence. Instead, he said that, as believers in one God, Muslims and Christians "know that human reason is itself God's gift and that it soars to its highest plane when suffused with the light of God's truth." And he expressed his firm belief that Christians and Muslims can cultivate together "the vast potential of human reason."[41]

What about the "Common Word," with its suggestion that love of God and love of neighbor are common ground and an antidote to violence? The pope praised the document. The text, he declared, echoed "a theme consonant with my first encyclical: the unbreakable bond between love of God and love of neighbor and the fundamental contradiction of resorting to violence or exclusion in the name of God."[42]

Three years after the Regensburg address, reconciliation of sorts was achieved in Amman, in the persons of Benedict XVI and Prince Ghazi bin Muhammad bin Talal—a joint affirmation of a shared belief in one God and a common commitment to love God and neighbor.[43] Is this just a happy ending to a drama played out on the world stage between the current pope and an influential Muslim prince? Do Muslims and Christians in fact have a common God? How do we make an informed judgment about whether they do? If they worship the same God, what consequences follow for their relations with one another as faith groups and for their life together in a given state? I explore these issues in the reminder of the book.

The question of whether Christians and Muslims worship the same God is urgent for us today in an interconnected and interdependent world with scarce resources. But Muslims and Christians have faced the question before. A period of particularly intense Christian engagement with Islam is marked by two events, both of which involve the ascendant Ottoman Empire, the same power with which the Christian emperor Manuel II had to contend. The first event is the sack of Constantinople, and the second is the siege of Vienna. Two very different and very influential Christian thinkers, both Germans, wrestled with Islam and Islam's God in an environment marked by fear of Muslim conquests. One is a conciliatory Catholic cardinal, Nicholas of Cusa. The other is a fiery Protestant Reformer, Martin Luther. In my attempt to puzzle out whether Christians and Muslims have a common God, I turn to them for guidance in the next two chapters of the book.

CHAPTER TWO

A Catholic Cardinal and the One God of All

When Constantinople fell, all of Europe shuddered. On May 29, 1453, Ottoman armies led by the young and ambitious sultan Mehmed II entered the imperial city of Constantinople, which bore the name of the first Christian emperor and had stood at the center of Eastern Christendom for over a thousand years. The sack was brutal, but the thought of what was to come seemed even worse. Now that the walls of this "New Rome" had given way to enemy cannons and its streets had been overrun by enemy soldiers, the old Rome, the center of Western Christendom since the time of the apostles, was in danger as well. Indeed, many feared that the whole of Europe might face the fate of Constantinople. The immediate source of danger was the power of the Ottoman sword, but directing the sword and the hand that wielded it was the Muslim way of life, the Muslim religion. And at the heart of this religion was the Muslim vision of God.

At that time, Europeans had two distinct options in response to the fall of Constantinople and the rise of Ottoman power. One option had been tried several times before during the preceding centuries with varying degrees of success: organize a crusade. A second option was to engage in dialogue, a response that was new and untested. Aeneas Silvius Piccolomini (1405–64), later Pope Pius II, was the most vigorous and persistent advocate of crusades. The writings of Nicholas of Cusa (1401–64), who later earned a cardinal's hat, most ably represented the call for dialogue. Both men were committed churchmen, great Renaissance personalities, and, as it happens, also close collaborators.

Today tensions between the Muslim communities and the West are high and fears abound, but the situation is very different from that of the fifteenth century. It is not as if London has fallen to powerful Muslim armies and we have reason to fear for Washington. If anything, the situation is the reverse; Western armies are engaged in wars on the soil of majority Muslim countries. And yet today we face options similar to the ones exemplified by Pius II and Nicholas of Cusa—weapons or words (and a few other options as well, of course). It will pay to look carefully at why the great cardinal preferred dialogue and how he went about thinking through the thorny theological issues about God that spring up as soon as the dialogue begins.

Europe in Danger: "Now We Await the Fire"

Eyewitnesses paint a gruesome picture of the Turkish capture of Constantinople. Nicolo Barbaro, a surgeon and a member of one of the patrician families of Venice, witnessed the siege and sack:

> At sunrise the Turks entered the city near San Romano. . . . [They] went rushing about the city, and anyone they found they put to the scimitar, women and men, old and young, of any condition. This butchery lasted from sunrise, when the Turks entered the city, until midday, and anyone whom they found was put to the scimitar in their rage. . . . [They] were all running furiously like dogs into the city to seek out gold, jewels and other treasure, and to take merchants prisoner. They sought out the monasteries, and all the nuns were led to the fleet and ravished and abused by the Turks, and then sold at auction for slaves throughout Turkey, and all the young women also were ravished and then sold for whatever they

would fetch. . . . The Turks loaded all their ships with prisoners and with an enormous quantity of booty.[1]

Cardinal John Bessarion, a man prominent enough to have had a good chance of becoming pope, expressed the feelings of many when, in a letter to the Doge of Venice on July 13, 1453, he called the Turks "the most inhuman barbarians and the most savage enemies of faith."[2]

What troubled many Europeans, especially the Renaissance humanists, was not only the savagery of the sack of Constantinople—"rivers of gore" flowed through the city, as one of them noted. War was war, and they knew that European Christians could be as cruel as the Muslim Turks, especially when they fought for their "religion, freedom, and way of life," as Piccolomini noted in his letter to none other than Sultan Mehmed II.[3] Two other things worried them more. One was the irreparable destruction of classical culture, and the other was the potential disappearance of Christianity from Europe. In a letter to Nicholas written not long after the news of the fall of Constantinople had reached him, Piccolomini expressed both of these concerns with passion and eloquence.

First, he noted the threat to the legacy of classical culture. "The name for learning which Athens had when Rome was flourishing, Constantinople seems to have in our time," wrote Piccolomini. He continued:

> Whence was Plato restored to us; whence were the works of Aristotle, Demosthenes, Xenophon, Thucydides, Basil, Dionysius, Origen, and many others revealed to the Latins in our days? We hope many others also will be revealed to us in the future. But now, with the victorious Turks possessing all which Greek potency has achieved, I wonder what will be done about Greek letters. Never, in my opinion, was there a greater waste of the Greek name than has happened now.[4]

The lament rested on widespread and confirmed reports that

Turkish soldiers, simple and uneducated men, destroyed many books of poetry, philosophy, and theology. For Piccolomini this was "a second death for Homer, Pindar, Menander . . . the final destruction of the Greek philosophers."[5] After only three days of pillaging and wanton destruction of cultural artifacts by Turkish foot soldiers, the Turks became known in the West "as one of the worst threats to high culture and learning Europe has ever faced."[6] Barbarians, as Muslim Ottomans were then called, burst in through the gates, and the civilization itself was at risk.

Piccolomini was not just a Renaissance humanist; above all he was a churchman, the bishop of Siena, and the future Supreme Pontiff of the Catholic Church. The destruction of Greek letters and learning was a great loss, but he felt it was even worse to "see the Christian faith undermined and driven into a corner."[7] For some time, former Christian lands in Asia and Africa had been in Muslim hands; so also were parts of Europe. Worst of all, he said, "the blessed land . . . is subject to the rule of an impious nation. Already the hands and feet of the Saracens pollute with gore the city of the living God, the workshop of our redemption, and the principal sanctuary of the immaculate lamb."[8] After Constantinople had fallen, what "now lies between us and the Turks?" a despairing Piccolomini inquired rhetorically. "A little earth and a little water separate us," he replied in answer to his own question.

"These things seem to me . . . most wretched," he concluded in his lament over European civilization and religion. "We have a past which we bewail and a future which we fear. . . . We see the slaughter of the Greeks; next we expect the ruin of the Latins. The nearby house has been burned; now we await the fire."[9] How should Europe protect itself?

A New Crusade: Sword Against Scimitar

Piccolomini had a clear plan: a new crusade should be organized.[10] His letter to Nicholas does not end on a note of despair, but with a call to arms: "So it will be, believe me; the crusade will be launched with the common consent of all Christians"—if "the authority of the Roman pontiff has raised itself up again and if the faithful and eloquent voices of preachers . . . resound to the end of the earth."[11] He urged Nicholas to be such a voice and to exert his influence in Germany and especially in Rome, to help bring about a new crusade against the Ottomans.

Some five years after he wrote to Nicholas, on August 16, 1458, Piccolomini was himself elected pope. One of his first acts was to do himself what he urged Nicholas to press the prior pope to do: "Call kings and princes to some specific place . . . for a gathering."[12] The place was Mantua; the date was September 26, 1459. Piccolomini, now Pope Pius II, delivered an impassioned speech hoping to raise support for a crusade. But the ears of the gathered nobles were largely deaf. It was hard to get a crusade going when Europe was deeply divided and when the Germans suspected, in Pius's own words, that the pope was "false and greedy and wanted to rake in gold, not to make war."[13]

Although Pius II never gave up on the idea of a crusade, he also pursued a more peaceful alternative to deliver Christian Europe from the Ottoman threat. In 1461 he penned a surprising letter to Sultan Mehmed II in which he urged the sultan to convert to the Christian faith: "We do not seek you out in hatred nor do we threaten your person, although you are an enemy of our religion and press hard on Christian people with your weapons. We are hostile to your actions, not to you. As God commands, we love our enemies and we pray for our persecutors."[14] There may be some doubt about the authenticity of the crusading pope's love for the expansionist sultan. Be that as it may, it is clear from the letter that the pope wasn't concerned just for the eternal salvation of the sultan's soul, but above all for the future of Christianity in Europe.

In the letter the pope appealed more to the sultan's ambition than to his religious sensibilities. "A little bit of water by which you may be baptized and brought to Christian rites and to belief in the

Gospel," would make Mehmed II "the greatest, most powerful and illustrious man of all who live today";[15] it would make his rule over Christians legitimate and don him with the glory of being the one who restored peace to the world. "Only one man's will can pacify the entire world and it is yours, if it chooses to receive the grace of baptism. It is yours to put an end to cruel war and bestow an ineffable blessing on all men."[16] The example Mehmed II should follow is that of Constantine, the Roman emperor and a convert to Christianity, who eleven centuries earlier built the very city that Mehmed II had conquered.[17]

Pius II did not mince words. He argued for the truth and superiority of the Christian faith and against the falsehood of Islam. Islam, he wrote, is "not supported by arguments or reasons," but is instead "founded on pleasure and maintained by the sword."[18] This was a familiar complaint about Islam in the Middle Ages. It was thought that Muslims were commanded to spread their religion by the sword, and that the Qur'an allowed them to satisfy carnal desires by, for instance, practicing polygamy in this world and hoping for "plentiful women and concubines" in the next.[19] The core of Pius II's critique of Islam, however, was not its putative embrace of pleasure and violence, but its rejection of the true God.

Travel back with me in time for a moment. When the First Crusade was launched four centuries earlier, Pope Urban II delivered a famous sermon at Claremont in 1095, in which the question of God figured prominently. According to one account, Urban II said:

From the confines of Jerusalem and the city of Constantinople a horrible tale has gone forth and very frequently has been brought to our ears, namely, that a race from the kingdom of the Persians, an accursed race, a race utterly alienated from God, a generation forsooth which has not directed its heart and has not entrusted its spirit to God, has invaded the lands of those Christians and has depopulated them by the sword, pillage and fire; it has led away a part of the captives into its own country, and a part it has destroyed by cruel tortures; it has either entirely destroyed the churches of God or appropriated them for the rites of its own religion.[20]

The pope's tale of the woe caused by Muslim armies was similar to the one Piccolomini told after the fall of Constantinople. But Urban II also described the perpetrators of those crimes as "a race utterly alienated from God," a generation that had not "directed its heart and entrusted its spirit to God." Devout as Muslims are, they are worshipping a completely false God, Urban II seemed to imply, much as some Christians think today.

In his letter to Mehmed II, Pius II held the same opinion. He noted with approval that the sultan believed in "one God who created the earth and who cares for everything He fashioned in the world" as well as that this God "sees and judges all things."[21] Yet Pius II clearly rejected the idea that the sultan worshipped "the same God as [Christians],"[22] because Mehmed II, as a Muslim, did not believe in the triunity of the one God.[23] For Pius II, that seemed to settle the issue. Christians and Muslims worship different Gods; in this, as well as in other regards, the distance between their religions is "vast."[24]

We don't know the sultan's response to the invitation to convert; indeed, we don't know whether the letter was ever received or even sent. We do know, however, that the sultan neither converted nor brought to the world the kind of peace Pius II had hoped for. In calling the sultan to convert, Pius II likely saw himself as following in the footsteps of Francis of Assisi, who, during the Fifth Crusade, went to witness to Sultan al-Kamil of Egypt (1219). And just as Francis defended the crusade, so Pius II's letter to Mehmed II in no way meant that he was giving up on a crusade. His goal was the preservation of Christian Europe, and if the sultan would not let "the little bit of water" be applied to his head, Pius II was eager to have the sword applied to his neck!

Pius II continued to push for a crusade until the end of his life. He died in Ancona, where he went to lend support to what turned out to be a sorry band of would-be crusaders. Some of his last words were, "Bid my brethren continue this holy expedition, and help if at all you can; woe to you if you desert God's work."[25] The work did *not* continue. The aborted crusade was the last ever to be attempted.

Conference Versus Crusade

Nicholas did not quite do what Piccolomini had requested of him. Instead of pressing Pope Nicholas V to push for a crusade, as his friend had urged, Nicholas set his mind on writing a treatise titled *On the Harmonious Peace of Religions,* in Latin *De pace fidei.* In this short text, he advocated what is in effect a wholesale alternative to the Crusades.[26]

Nicholas was a friend of John of Segovia, a professor at the University of Salamanca, whom he met at the council in Basel in 1433. Unlike Piccolomini, John believed that "war could never solve the issue between Christendom and Islam" and that the mission to convert Muslims would have limited success. Instead, he advocated what he called a "conference" between Christians and Muslims. The goals of the "conference" were, perhaps surprisingly for that time, "political as well as a strictly religious."[27] Nicholas himself was by character a reconciler and deeply engaged with the cause of the unity of the church. Like John of Segovia, he much preferred "conference" to crusade.[28]

De pace fidei starts with a vision of a hearing "in the council of the loftiest beings and under the presiding direction of the Almighty."[29] It ends with the King of kings issuing a command for representatives of all nations to gather in Jerusalem, so that, in the name of their countrymen, they would "accept a single faith."[30] The existence of multiple faiths, Nicholas believed, fuels cruel interreligious violence, as was evident to all during the siege and fall of Constantinople. A single faith for all of humanity was needed. In Nicholas's view, a "conference," or a dialogue, as we would put it, was the best way to eliminate divisive differences, embrace a single faith, and achieve a "perpetual peace."[31]

Nicholas imagined a heavenly scene in which representatives of all nations were gathered and engaged in dialogue. But how would such a dialogue bring all nations to accept a single faith? Would ballots be cast and the decision of the majority prevail? Would participants hammer out some compromise faith, which all would oblige themselves to accept? Would they all agree that it does not really matter what people believe as long as they are sincere? None of these options would have been acceptable to Nicholas. Religions are about truth, not merely about sincere feelings; and one can neither determine what is true by vote nor forge the truth by a compromise. Instead, the conference—maybe designed in analogy to a church council[32]— is an instrument of a joint search for truth through argument, deliberation, and persuasion. The main body of the book *De pace fidei* is a portrayal of just such deliberation, conducted from a Christian standpoint.

Two Convictions and a Strategy

Two important and controversial basic convictions informed Nicholas's vision of the conference. First, Nicholas asserted, all people, whether they know it or not, worship the one and only true God "in everything they are seen to adore."[33] In the footsteps of many great Christian theologians from the past (such as Augustine and Bonaventure[34]) Nicholas here echoes Plato's belief that in all their immediate desiring, people ultimately desire the Good.[35] The purpose of the conference was for the representatives of all different religions to come to understand precisely how their specific religions were each a version of the worship of the one true God and how, from the very beginning, all people "have always presupposed God and worshipped Him in all their religious practices."[36] The rites may be many, but the religion is one. When people realize that, "the sword will cease, as will also the malice of hatred and all evils."[37]

For Nicholas, this did not mean that all religions are equal— equally true and equally efficacious as ways to the one God, whom all seek to worship. As a bishop and a cardinal—as a person left on one occasion in charge of the Vatican while the pope was traveling[38]—he was convinced both that the Christian faith is true and that it contains the final and most complete revelation of God, the criterion by which all other religions are to be judged. Correspondingly, he believed that all other religions—including Islam—are beset with error.[39] And yet, whatever religion people embrace, through it they worship the one true God.

The second conviction is as follows. Error rests ultimately on ignorance, not on the willful rejection of a manifest truth. This too he owed to Greek philosophy in its Platonic version.[40] No one departs from truth except out of ignorance, and thus no one abandons the true God "except because he is ignorant of" God.[41] When error about religion is overcome and people come to full understanding, they will believe what the Christian faith teaches. That is why Nicholas could hope for the conversion of Mehmed II no less than Pius II did. To that end, he himself addressed the sultan at the end of *A Sifting of the Qur'an* (*Cribratio Alkorani*)—a book he wrote after *De pace fidei* and roughly at the same time that Pius II wrote his letter to Mehmed II. *A Sifting of the Qur'an* ends with an extended prayer that God would grant "enlightenment" to the mighty ruler.[42] By "enlightenment" he clearly meant "conversion."

But how can Nicholas show that Muslims worship the same God as Christians (even if one grants his qualification that Muslims' understanding of that God is less adequate than the proper Christian understanding)? Muslims and Christians strenuously disagree on how they understand God's oneness, for instance. Christians affirm that the one God is the Holy Trinity. Muslims claim that this belief compromises God's unity. The issue is crucial, since the claim that "there is no god but God" (Muhammad, 47:19) is the central creed of Islam.[43] Here is Nicholas's strategy in a nutshell:

1. In response to the Muslim denial that there are three divine "Persons," Nicholas tries to show that Christians are *not*

affirming what Muslims are denying (namely, that there are
many gods).

2. In response to the uncompromising Muslim affirmation of
   God's unity, Nicholas tries to show that what Muslims say
   about the one God presupposes the kinds of beliefs Christians
   affirm about the Trinity.

From a Muslim perspective, Nicholas's dual strategy seems like
a distortion and an unwelcome appropriation of the Qur'an for
Christian purposes. From a Christian perspective, however, his
strategy can be seen as an exercise in charitable interpretation. In
what looks like an error, he finds that, if read carefully, truth is
hidden below the surface. Put differently, in another's flawed faith
he sees a distorted version of his own true faith. If you follow this
strategy, Nicholas believed, you will find "to be everywhere presupposed not a faith that is other but a faith that is one and the same."[44]
And that's how you get to "one religion in many rites," which is
necessary for peace.

Not all agree with Nicholas's approach to relations between
religions—all different religions being more or less adequate expressions of the one true faith, which Christ revealed.[45] It is useful,
however, to keep apart his overall project ("one religion in many
rites") and his general strategy ("all religions as versions of the final
and Christian religion") from his reflection on the relation between
God's oneness and God's triunity. It is possible to disagree with one
and still learn much from the other. So let's turn from the large
vista of relations between religions and zoom in on the central
question: Is it possible to affirm at one and the same time that God
is one and that God is the Holy Trinity?

Oneness and the Trinity

Nicholas discusses the relation between the claims that God is
one and that God is the Holy Trinity, and in the process he does

some very heavy intellectual lifting. Most of it happens in *A Sifting of the Qur'an,* which he ends with the aforementioned prayer for the enlightenment of the sultan. In his long letter addressed to Mehmed II, Pope Pius II also wrote about the Trinity. The pope's approach was simple, even simplistic. He stated that between Christians and Muslims "there is really no argument about unity" and then proceeded to state why Christians believe that the one God is properly described as the Holy Trinity.[46]

Nicholas, unlike Pius II, was a profound theologian and seminal philosopher who could not leave it at that. He had to explain *why* it is that there is no dispute between Christians and Muslims about God's unity. And to explain that, he needed to delve into the character of God's being, give an account of the kind of oneness that properly describes God, and show how the talk about "three Persons" does not subvert God's oneness. Finally, he had to show that Muslims *can* embrace this Christian account of God's unity *without denying* their basic beliefs about God. Only if he succeeded in all this could he reach his goal: to show that Christians and Muslims worship the same God.

Here is a brief sketch of Nicholas's complex argument, though each point he makes is worthy of hundreds of pages of explanation. First we will examine the nature of God. The three points he makes assume an important distinction: the way God is in God's own being is distinct from—but not contradictory to— how God manifests God's own being to humans and in human language.

1. God is infinite and boundless, not limited in any way.[47]
2. Since human beings cannot comprehend what is boundless, God is "incomprehensible and ineffable" to them; only God can comprehend and express properly who God is.[48]
3. As the infinite and incomprehensible one, God is "not said to be one or three or good or wise or Father or Son or Holy Spirit"; God "infinitely excels and precedes all such names."[49]

To many orthodox Christians, the last point will seem like a
bombshell. It is hard enough to absorb that the words "good" and
"wise" or "Father" and "Son" do not, strictly speaking, properly
describe God because God infinitely exceeds them. Nicholas also
believes that numbers, such as "one" and "three," do not strictly
apply to God either! Numbers are for creatures. God is not a creature. Therefore God is *beyond* number—beyond the number one
as much as beyond the number three. Nicholas writes: "When you
begin to count the Trinity you depart from the truth."[50] Of importance, Nicholas does not see this as some novel and revolutionary
idea he is introducing. On the contrary, he consciously leans on a
venerable Christian theological and philosophical tradition—that
of the greatest of the Western church fathers, Augustine (354–430),
and that of a profound Syrian philosopher-theologian, Dionysius
the Areopagite (likely sixth century, but information about his life
is uncertain).[51]

Now that we have established that, in the opinion of Nicholas,
God is beyond number, we can proceed with our summary. We
will zero in specifically on Nicholas's ideas about God's oneness
and God's triunity.

1. Oneness is prior to all plurality and is a source of all plurality.[52]
2. The "three" that comprise the Trinity are not three
   discrete entities; in Nicholas's words: "The Trinity in God
   is no composite or plural or numerical, but is most simple
   oneness."[53]
3. In God there is no opposition between "self" and "other"; in
   Nicholas's words: "'not-other' is not 'same'" and "'not-same' is
   not 'other.'"[54]
4. God is "one" in the sense of "absolute unity" rather than in
   the sense of a number; God is not first in a series or the only
   one in a set.[55]

These are some of the most basic convictions about God that
Nicholas brings to the question of whether Muslims and Chris-

tians worship the same God. They are Christian convictions held by the greatest and most influential teachers of the Christian tradition (like Augustine and Aquinas, to name just two), even if it is true that they may surprise many Christians today.[56]

How does Nicholas respond specifically to Muslim objections to the Christian claim that God is the Trinity? Here is a sample of statements from the Qur'an along with Nicholas's responses:

1. *The Qur'an:* "There is no god except One God" (Al Ma'idah, 5:73).

   Nicholas: To say that "there are several Gods implies a contradiction, since it follows therefrom that none of them are God, since each of them lacks supreme glory, which befits only God."[57]

2. *The Qur'an:* "They do blaspheme who say: Allah is one of the three in the Trinity" (Al Ma'idah, 5:73).

   NICHOLAS: God is most definitely *not* one of the three in the Trinity; God is the "most simple oneness"; the three divine "Persons" are "three in oneness, not in number."[58]

3. *The Qur'an:* (stating that Christians claim that Jesus said): "Worship me and my mother as gods in derogation of [or beside] Allah" (Al Ma'idah, 5:116).

   Nicholas: Christ never taught people to worship him or his mother "in place of God."[59]

4. *The Qur'an:* "No son did Allah beget" (Al Mu'minun, 23:91).

   Nicholas: (a) Together with Muslims, Christians insist that "it is impossible for God to have a son who is another God."[60] (b) God is not corporeal and cannot beget a son in a literal sense; sonship in God an "intellectual sonship,"[61] so that "Word" and "Son" are interchangeable. (c) God is eternal and so the generation of the "Son" is eternal, never resulting in a self-standing entity next to God.[62]

5. *Muhammad* (summarizing "the best" that he and the prophets that came before him said): "There is no god but God, He Alone, He hath no associate."[63]

Nicholas: "To confess the Trinity is to deny a plurality, and association, of gods."[64]

In sum, Nicholas argued that the Qur'an is not denying the authentic Christian doctrine of the Trinity, but is rightly rejecting a bastardized version of this doctrine. He stated tersely and categorically: "In the manner in which Arabs and Jews deny the Trinity, assuredly it ought to be denied by all."[65]

Supreme Bliss and Fecundity

Everything Muslims reject in regard to God as the Holy Trinity Christians reject as well. That is Nicholas's first and main point. His second, and maybe more controversial, point is that everything Christians affirm about the Trinity Muslims ought to affirm as well. Nicholas believed that all human beings ought to believe that God is the Holy Trinity; that is simply what the truth about the one God is as revealed in Jesus Christ. But Muslims, he thought, have their own reasons to embrace a trinitarian understanding of God. The Trinity, he believed, is "presupposed" in the Qur'an. To show that this is so, he engaged in a "devout interpretation" of the Qur'an[66]—an attempt to show that if you dig below the surface of some of its claims, you will find the Trinity.

Here are two of Nicholas's arguments. The first builds on God's creative activity; the second, on God's presence in Jesus. They both rest on one peculiar feature of God as distinct from creatures, designated in theological terms as "divine simplicity." Put concisely, divine simplicity means that God is what God has; God does not have attributes, God is God's attributes.

1. *The Qur'an:* "To Him is due the primal origin of the heavens and the earth: When He decreeth a matter, He saith to it: 'Be,' and it is" (Al Baqarah, 2:117).
   Nicholas: (a) If God creates through word, then God's Word is "eternal and uncreated," an "inward, intellectual word," a "conception begotten of the intellect."[67] (b) "If it is true that God has a Word, then it is true that the Word is God. For *having* does not properly befit God, because He *is* all things [that He has], so that in Him having is being."[68] (c) Therefore God is the Word with which God creates.

2. *The Qur'an:* "Christ Jesus the son of Mary was a Messenger of Allah, and His Word, which he bestowed on Mary, and a Spirit proceeding from Him" (Al Nisa', 4:171).
   Nicholas: If Christ was God's Word, then he was God, not a second God, but the one true God.

Nicholas also offers a slightly different version of this argument for the Trinity. This time around, he builds not so much on how God's creativity and God's presence in Christ are portrayed in the Qur'an, but on the belief in God's perfection, which Muslims and Christians share. First, he takes up what he calls God's "fecundity" or fruitfulness: "Unless the Trinity were present in the oneness, the Omnipotent Beginning would not exist in order to create the universe."[69] This tersely stated argument is complicated, but it boils down to this. To create, you need a mental image of what you will create—an "intellectual word." For God to be fecund in the sense of giving rise to something other than God, God must create; to create, God must have an internal word; and if God has an internal word, God is the Word and the Word is God. Divine creative activity presupposes internal distinctions in God, and that implies the Trinity.

Second, there is the matter of divine "supreme happiness." Love is the supreme divine perfection. But who is it that God would love if there were not three divine Persons to love? Not the world, because then God's supreme happiness would depend on the existence of the world. Hence Nicholas writes that if God were not triune, God would lack "the sweetness of paternal love and joy, of filial love and joy, and of love and joy common to the Father and the Son."[70] Put simply, the twofold argument is this. It is part of God's perfection that God is loving in God's own being apart from the world, and it is part of God's perfection that God is able to create the world. Neither would be possible if God were not the Holy Trinity.

This, then, was Nicholas's approach to the central question regarding relations between Muslims and Christians—the question of God's unity, the core message of Muhammad. First, he contested that Christians believe those things that Muslims reject with regard to the Trinity. Second, he argued that, based on the Qu'ran, Muslims should accept what Christians in fact do believe about the Trinity. In this way he hoped to show that Christians and Muslims name "in different names" and worship in "different ways" the one true God,[71] while at the same time insisting that the Christian faith offers the most reliable and complete revelation of that one God.

The Trinity and Revelation

Some may object to Nicholas's claim that the Christian revelation is ultimate; most Muslims certainly would, since they consider Muhammad to be the Seal of the Prophets (Al Ahzab, 33:40). Nicholas's stated reason for the finality of the Christian revelation takes us back once more to the doctrine of the Trinity.

Recall that God, according to Nicholas, is utterly unknowable, beyond all human concepts—not just invisible to the human eye, but also unreachable for every created mind. Can we therefore know nothing about God? We can know, but our knowledge is dependent on God's self-revelation. Addressing God in prayer, Nicholas says: "But You are able to manifest Yourself as visible to whom You will."[72] Now, many have claimed to be vehicles of God's self-manifestation, offering knowledge of God and describing the way to God. But how do we know which one of these ways is true? Since mere human beings cannot conceive of God, how can they "disclose" God to others, and how can we trust that what they have disclosed is true? And even if we grant that revelation has been "infused into them," how can they, mere human beings, "explain" to others words they themselves don't understand?

Since only God knows God, only the one who is utterly one with God—the Word incarnate—can reveal God. And so we have arrived back to the distinction within God—to the trinitarian nature of God—as the presupposition of the self-revelation of God, who is utterly unknowable. To be love in God's own being and to create the world, God must be the Holy Trinity, argued Nicholas earlier. Now he argues that to reliably reveal God's very self to human beings, God must be the Holy Trinity.

Must be? *Must* God be anything? A more accurate way of stating Nicholas's arguments is this. *If* we say that God is love, *then* we must also say that God is the Holy Trinity; *if* we say that God created the world, *then* we must say that God's nature is trinitarian; and *if* we claim that God reliably revealed God's very self to human beings, *then* we must also say that God is the one who is also in a mysterious way "three"—three beyond number as God is one beyond number.

Conversation Versus Crusade

There is no need here to go into a full-scale assessment of Nicholas's positions. I pick up some of his central claims in chapter 7, where I discuss God's unity and trinity. For now, let me highlight only a few significant aspects of his approach.

First, faced with a powerful enemy, Nicholas offers an alternative to war. It consists in argumentative engagement with Muslims. War, he believes, can never resolve issues between Christians and

Muslims. The battle to be won is the battle of ideas, not the battle of swords. Hence he recommends a "conversation," a "council," a "dialogue."

Second, for Nicholas, conversation is not about hammering out some mutually acceptable compromise. The issue is not simply clashing interests, but competing truth claims. And we deal with competing truth claims not by "striking deals," but by arguing respectfully.

Third, in the battle of ideas, we are interested in truth being embraced by all, not in portraying our opponents as being in the wrong and ourselves as being in the right. That's why it is not only possible but also wise to give "charitable interpretations" of others' views—as a way of teasing out the truth contained in their positions.

Fourth, when it comes to truth about God, we have to affirm that God is beyond the comprehension of any human being. Even our true statements about God—for instance, that God is good or that God is one—manifest as much ignorance as they do knowledge.

Fifth, we do not need to agree on everything we say about God to agree that we worship the same God. Our knowledge of God may be more or less adequate, and our worship may be more or less appropriate, and yet the "object" of our worship can still be the same.

Martin Luther, to whom I turn in the next chapter, was less interested in "charitable interpretation" than Nicholas was. He knew Nicholas's texts, in particular his more polemical *Sifting of the Qur'an*. But Nicholas was by nature a mediator, and much of his professional life was devoted to forging unity between estranged groups within the church, above all between the Christian West and the Christian East, between Rome and Constantinople. Luther, on the other hand, was a Reformer, fierce and unbending in defending what he believed to be true. And one of those things was, perhaps ironically, the utter gratuity of God's infinite

love. Islam falls short in this regard, he argued forcefully, though
not much shorter than Catholicism and Judaism. Significantly, for
Luther that falling short of Catholics, Jews, and Muslims never
cast doubt on the conviction that Christians and Muslims have a
common God. In many ways, the "drama" of Luther's encounter
with Islam consists in the tension created by affirming two things
at once: (1) that Muslims worship the same God as Christians, and
(2) that they miss what is the most important characteristic of God,
God's absolutely unconditional love. Luther sets the stage for my
own later reflection on sameness and difference in Christian and
Muslim understandings of God's love.

CHAPTER THREE

A Protestant Reformer and the God of the Turks

Within the confines of Europe [the Turks] have usurped no mean dominion with the effusion of much Christian blood. They could easily transport themselves to the gates of Rome in the space of one night."[1] With these urgent words, the archbishop of Spalato (today's Split in Croatia, which was not far from the advancing Ottoman armies) addressed representatives from across the Western church at the opening session of the Fifth Lateran Council (1512–17). In the midst of this overwhelming sense of threat, the Protestant Reformer Martin Luther grappled with the question of whether Christians and Muslims have a common God. As in the controversies with Catholic theologians, the central issue for him, a dividing line between true and false faith, was an understanding of God's love and its utter gratuity. Can we say that Muslims and Christians have a common God if they differ about God's love? The question is particularly important today, as many Westerners think of the God of the Qur'an as a fierce deity, issuing unbending rules and brutally enforcing them.

Ottoman troops never reached the literal "gates of Rome," as the archbishop feared. Yet the "Turkish threat" loomed heavily in the consciousness of sixteenth-century Europeans across the continent. The situation was deemed so critical that a system of *Türkenglocken* (literally, "Turk bells") was set up in central Europe to warn local troops of a Turkish attack and to remind Christians to pray for deliverance.[2] In German Saxony, where Luther lived and worked, the *Türkenglocke*'s call to prayer rang every day at noon.[3]

The "Turkish threat" was no mere phantom of the European imagination. By the first few decades of the sixteenth century, kingdoms in Asia, Africa, and Europe had already fallen under Ottoman control, positioning the empire as "one of the greatest existing political and military powers" of its time.[4] As I noted in the previous chapter, in 1453, thirty years before Luther's birth, Ottoman forces conquered Constantinople, spelling the end of the great Byzantine Empire of the Christian East. Less than a year before Luther nailed his *95 Theses* to the door of the Wittenberg Castle Church, Sultan Selim I defeated the powerful Mamluk dynasty in Egypt, further enriching the empire. Before long, Ottoman sultan Suleiman the Magnificent's armies were making major inroads into western territories, capturing large portions of eastern, central, and southern Europe. As Luther wrote in 1530, with very little exaggeration, "We now have the Turk and his religion at our very doorstep."[5] Europeans' fears that after the sack of Constantinople the Turks would overrun Europe were not completely without basis.

Despite the urgent focus of European fears, Arab and Islamic cultures were known for far more than the military prowess of Ottoman armies. Medieval Arab and Islamic civilizations had long outstripped much of Europe in sophistication; Piccolomini's fears of the onslaught of barbarianism after the fall of Constantinople were proven unfounded (see chapter 2). As one historian writes, while al-Rashid and al-Mamun, caliphs of the Baghdad-based 'Abbasid dynasty, "were delving into Greek and Persian philosophy, their contemporaries in the West, Charlemagne and his lords, were reportedly dabbling in the art of writing their names."[6] Creative achievements in Islamic architecture, music, and literature were apparent to Christian Europeans in religiously pluralistic regions such as Spain and Sicily.[7] Throughout Europe, medieval Arab and Islamic treatises on algebra, medicine, and chemistry influenced scientific endeavors for centuries.[8] Considering both the military might and cultural advancement of Islamic civilizations, it is not surprising that historian Marshall G. S. Hodgson asserts that "in the sixteenth century . . . a visitor from Mars might well have supposed that the human world was on the verge of becoming Muslim."[9]

Yes and No

A thousand miles away, Suleiman the Magnificent was preparing to lead troops—numbering at least a hundred thousand—on the march to secure Hungary and lay siege to Vienna. In Wittenberg, Germany, Luther was laying out the basic contours of his position in texts like the *Large Catechism* (1529), a teaching tool to help Lutheran clergy understand the heart of the Christian faith as he proclaimed it. In the *Large Catechism,* after expounding the articles of the Apostles' Creed, Luther underscores that those very articles "divide and distinguish us Christians from all other people on earth." He then goes on to note an important difference between his view of God and the view of many monotheists, including Muslims:

> All who are outside this Christian people, whether heathens, Turks, Jews, or false Christians and hypocrites—even though they believe in and worship only the one, true God—nevertheless they do not know what his attitude is toward them. They cannot be confident of his love and blessing, and therefore they remain in eternal wrath and condemnation.[10]

Leaving aside for the moment the questions of whether indeed non-Christians and wayward Christians "cannot expect any love and blessing" from God and abide "in eternal wrath," let us consider Luther's opinion about whether they believe in the same God as do "true" Christians. We might expect a categorically negative answer. After all, Luther was known for seeing the world in sharp contrasts, dividing people into two camps, those with him on the side of God and the gospel and those gathered against him under the banner of Satan. The latter camp included above all the "Anti-Christ" pope[11] as well as "blind, venomous Jews"[12] and Muslims, whom he claimed were "all . . . possessed by the Devil."[13] And yet Luther's answer was neither a simple yes nor a simple no. Instead, he believed that monotheistic non-Christians and wayward Christians *do* believe in the one true God, but know that God mistakenly and therefore do not worship the "right God."

The idea of believing in the true God whom one knows mistakenly may seem puzzling. It contains a peculiar blend of knowing and not knowing, a mixture of being right and profoundly wrong at the same time. At a later point, I explore this idea on its own, but here I want to understand what Luther meant by it. For that, it is helpful to look at one of his last sermons, which he preached less than three weeks before his death. Sick and exhausted from years of carrying on his shoulders the burden of the Protestant Reformation, he traveled to Eisleben, his hometown, to undertake the troublesome task of mediating in a quarrel between two powerful brothers, the Counts of Mansfeld.[14]

There, on January 31, 1546, Luther preached a sermon on Matthew 8:19–27, a text about Jesus's calming a storm. In his sermon, the boat carrying Jesus and his disciples represents the church, Luther's struggling band of Christians. The sea, in which Jesus's boat threatens to sink, is the world. And the perilous wind and waves are the assaults of the Devil, above all in the form of expansionistic Turks.[15] In a sense, Luther was preparing the congregation for his own departure as well as for the great tribulation preceding the seemingly imminent Last Judgment. His message? Just as Christ calmed the storm on the Sea of Galilee, so Christ will bring today's church safely through the rough seas.

And rough seas they were! By the time of Luther's sermon, Suleiman the Magnificent had completed his fifth campaign in Hungary, capturing the Hapsburgs' forts and annexing nearly all their Hungarian territory. Two and a half months before the sermon, on November 10, 1545, the mighty sultan, with a realm extending all the way from Persia in the east to Croatia and Hungary in the west, agreed to a truce with the Hapsburgs. But Luther, along with everyone in Europe, must have wondered: Is this merely a lull before the final burst of the Devil's fury? How long will the truce last? Will the Ottomans attack, sink the boat of the Christian church, and with it all of Christian civilization in central Europe?

Eternal Creator, Wise Lawgiver

With these concerns undoubtedly simmering in the background of his sermon, Luther devoted much attention to identifying non-Christians' erroneous beliefs about God and contrasting them with proper Christian convictions. His aim was to highlight the identity of the one around whom "true" Christians are gathered—the one who is the ultimate object of the Devil's fury, the cause of the Devil's demise, and the agent of the church's liberation. That one is Christ, both a human being who sleeps while the storm rages and God who calms the elements by the word of his mouth. Affirmation of Christ's storm-conquering divinity led Luther to discuss similarities and differences between Christian and other monotheistic notions of God.

The thrust of Luther's comments in this sermon is the same as in the section of the *Large Catechism* I quoted earlier: to show that Muslims—along with other monotheists—do not know the true character of the one true God they worship, but informed Christians do. And yet he also recognized—maybe a bit against his will—that Muslims are not completely mistaken about God. That may be small comfort to Muslims, especially since Luther puts them, devout confessors that there is "no god but God," in the same company as the enlightened heathen (mainly Greek philosophers who wrote about the one God). When Luther speaks of other faiths, he remains a radical reformer, not an irenic ecumenist. Nonetheless, in the reformed convictions of Christians as he envisages them, an important bridge to Muslims remains intact: the belief that they worship the one true God.

Scattered throughout the sermon are descriptions of the God Muslims, along with Jews and some heathens, worship: the one eternal God, the wise and just creator of heaven and earth to whom all human beings owe obedience. Luther echoed with a twist the apostle Paul's claim about Gentiles—non-Jews and non-Christians—at the beginning of the Letter to the Romans: "For what can be known about God is plain to them, because God has shown it to them. Ever since the creation of the world his eternal power and divine nature, invisible though they are, have been understood and seen through the things he has made" (1:19–20). All people—even polytheistic heathens, let alone radical monotheists like Muslims—have some share in the proper knowledge of God. Following the apostle, this is what Christian theologians have believed for centuries, especially when it comes to Muslims. Luther was no exception, notwithstanding the mighty Turkish armies looming on the horizon.

For Luther, just as for other classical theologians, the *sensus divinitatis*—the sense of God that all people possess—is not a matter merely of knowing the existence and power of God as the one creator. For his views, he leans on the Letter to the Romans, where the apostle writes that Gentiles, and not just the recipients of God's revealed law, also know the moral demands of the one true God and often follow them. True, all human beings are "under the power of sin" and "'no human being will be justified in his [God's] sight' by deeds prescribed by the law" (3:9, 20). And yet, even without knowing God's revealed law, the Gentiles often act in accordance with moral law. How does the apostle explain this? "When Gentiles, who do not possess the law, do instinctively what the law requires, these, though not having the law, are a law to themselves. They show that what the law requires is written on their hearts, to which their own conscience also bears witness" (2:14–15). Summarizing the apostle, Luther put the idea very succinctly and pointedly in his *Large Catechism:* the Ten Commandments—the basic content of God's law—are "written in the hearts of all people."[16] That means Muslims too.

Luther was impressed by the moral achievements of the Ottoman Muslims. True, there is ambivalence in his descriptions of them, similar to the ambivalence we just noted in the apostle's description of the Gentiles. After the Turks captured Belgrade (1520) and at the Battle of Mohács (1526) killed King Louis II of Hungary and defeated his troops, Luther wrote "On the War Against the Turk" (1529). In it, he warned that Islam undermines the foundations of the Christian civilization. Muslims destroy true religion by "denying Christ as God's Son and his sacrifice." In addition, he wrote, they trample underfoot the true form of government by engaging in the forceful expansion of Islamic lands. Finally, they violate the estate of marriage by freely divorcing women and holding them "immeasurably cheap" and "despised." For Luther, this three-pronged attack on spiritual life (religion), temporal government (politics), and home life (economics) threatened all spheres of life. If the Turks succeeded in conquering Europe, he asked rhetorically, what would be left in the society but "flesh, world, and devil?"[17]

And yet, perhaps surprisingly, Luther thought that Muslims followed the precepts of God's law more closely than most Christians of his time did. In the preface to a 1530 pamphlet on the customs of the Turks, written only months after the Turkish siege of Vienna, as well as in many of his sermons, he did not hesitate to point out that Ottoman Muslims were superior to Christians in many ways, including moral ones: "The modesty and simplicity of their food, clothing, dwellings, and everything else, as well as the feasts, prayers, and common gatherings of the people" that prevail under Ottoman rule "are nowhere to be seen among us." More significant, as far as "good customs and good works" are concerned, "the Turks are far superior to our Christians."[18] In the same text, Luther even added, not without some hyperbole: "I sincerely believe that no papist, monk, cleric, or their equal in faith would be able to remain in their faith if they should spend three days among the Turks. Here I mean those who seriously desire the faith of the pope and who are the best among them."[19] If you want religion centered on morality, as Luther thought Catholics mistakenly did, Islam is more attractive. In a sermon delivered in 1544, Luther commended the Turks for exceeding Christians in doing works of mercy, adding that they "regard it the greatest unfaithfulness and most shameful vice not to share bread with a neighbor in times of hunger."[20]

In Luther's view, Muslims worship the one true God, the wise and just creator of heaven and earth, and they often display enviable moral qualities. His claim that Muslims undermine religion, government, and economy notwithstanding, he was aware that these qualities provided religious and moral underpinnings to a highly successful Muslim civilization. His primary concern, however, was not with "civilization," but with the salvation of the human soul. And for that, Muslim convictions about God and their spirituality were, in his opinion, utterly inadequate. They were good for this life, but not for the life of the world to come.

The Abyss of God's Heart

It is "not enough," Luther believed, to know that God is the eternal and just creator to whom we owe obedience. To worship and obey God as such is "not yet to worship the right God."[21] Indeed, in his judgment, to know only this about God is to miss by far the most important thing, namely, "the most profound depths of his [God's] fatherly heart and his pure, unutterable love."[22] This is what the Apostles' Creed, which differentiates Christians from all other religious people, describes. And at the heart of the creed are two claims about God: first, that God is the Holy Trinity—Father, Son, and Holy Spirit—and second, that Jesus Christ died for the sin of the world. Put simply, the Holy Trinity tells you who God is; Jesus's death on the cross tells you what God thinks and does.[23] Along with all other non-Christians, Muslims miss these two essential things about God. And they miss them for the same reason that all non-Christians do: human beings cannot come to these convictions on their own, using only reason and disregarding God's self-revelation.

Take, first, the Holy Trinity. Luther knew that for Muslims, no less than for Jews, the idea that there may be more than one "Person" in God is the "greatest folly," "abomination," and "frightful blasphemy."[24] In the minds of Muslims, this would be to divide the one indivisible God. From their perspective, to hold that God is triune is, as the Qur'an puts it, to add an associate to God and therefore to overturn the most important pillar of Islam: the radically monotheistic claim that there is no god but God.

Like Nicholas of Cusa and many others (see chapter 2), in response Luther insisted that Christians never believed that God has an associate or that there is more than one God: "Christians in the whole world say that God is one and undivided, and that nothing can be more united than God or the divine essence."[25] But even though—or maybe just because—God is so much one that "nothing could be more singular" than God,[26] God exists as Trinity. For reasons similar to Nicholas's, Luther insisted that the unique singularity of God is not compromised if we say that God is the Father, Son, and Holy Spirit. He knew, of course, that the affirmation of the Trinity further complicates matters that are already complicated. Why do Christians affirm that God is triune? This is how God is revealed in the holy scriptures, and this is who God is, Luther insisted. When it comes to God, God's self-revelation is ultimate. Since there is only one God, there is no other God than this. The consequence? Any god different from this God is "no God at all."[27] And yet, as we shall see, he believed that even when they deny the Trinity, Muslims believe in the one true God; they just understand God mistakenly (see also chapter 7).

Closely tied to the conviction that the one God is the Holy Trinity is the belief that God manifests unutterable love toward humanity in Jesus Christ. This claim is at the center of Luther's theology. In Luther's view, the belief that God was in Christ for the salvation of the world is both the heart of the Christian faith and what differentiates the Christian faith from all other faiths. Everything in

Christianity depends on the cluster of convictions that tell the story of God's coming to redeem sinful humanity in love, namely, the convictions "that Christ is the son of God, that he died for our sins, that he was raised for our life, that justified by faith in him our sins are forgiven and we are saved, etc."[28] God's unconditional love for humanity, displayed in Christ's bearing of the sin of the world, is the most telling expression of God's very being. This is where we see most clearly who God is and how God relates to humanity. As Luther explained in the *Heidelberg Disputation,* one of his early writings, God loves human beings not because they are or strive to be godly, but in spite of the fact that they are ungodly; and God loves them so as to create godliness in them, transforming them into beings who reflect God's love in the world.[29]

A Dream of a God?

When it comes to faith and reason, Muslims have it easier, according to Luther. Reason halts before the central and defining claims of the Christian faith—that the indivisibly one God exists as three "Persons"; that Christ, true God and true man, died for human sin; and that God's love is utterly unconditional. The wisdom of these convictions, Luther wrote, "surpasses and exceeds the wisdom, mind, and reason of all men" and is perceived by most people as foolishness. Along with the greatest Christian minds through the centuries (like the great Thomas Aquinas, for example), Luther was undeterred by this seeming irrationality of the Christian faith. For him more than for many other Christian theologians, this is part and parcel of the incomprehensibility of God, who on account of being God must be utterly beyond human reason. Without God's self-revelation, no one can know God properly. Without the incarnate Word, "it is impossible to know or say anything for certain of his [God's] divine essence or will."[30]

The inaccessibility of God to reason alone has consequences for knowledge of God in non-Christian religions. It is not that God remains utterly unknown to those who seek to know God apart from revelation in Christ—"heathens," Jews, Muslims. Rather, they always already distort the God they know. They correctly believe in the one God, but they fail to see that the very being of that God is triune love. In Luther's view, they therefore have in God "nothing more than a mere name" and "a mere dream."[31] There is a bit of the rhetorical bluster of a radical reformer and a passionate preacher in these statements—"nothing more" and "mere" go too far. But his main point is that without God's self-revelation in Christ, one cannot know God's essence and God's will; everything else one knows about God gets twisted, and one cannot know of and experience the most important thing: God's unconditional love.

As Luther the preacher developed his position before the congregation in Eisleben, he invoked the words of Jesus to the Samaritan woman, recorded in John's Gospel. In the course of the conversation about proper worship, this shrewd woman asks Jesus where one should worship God, on Mount Gerizim in Samaria or at the temple in Jerusalem. On the surface, the issue seems to be the place of worship. Deeper down, the issue is identifying whether the God of the Samaritans or the God of the Jews is the true God. "You [Samaritans] worship what you do not know," Jesus responds. He then adds, "We [Jews] worship what we know, for salvation is from the Jews" (4:22).[32] In Luther's account, true Christians are like the Jews in Jesus's statement: they worship the true God whom they know. All others—heathens, Jews, Muslims, even "false" Christians—are like Samaritans: they worship that same true God whom they do not know.

Where does this leave us with regard to whether Christians and Muslims worship the same God? It may look as though Luther has taken away with one hand what he has given with the other. First he affirmed that Muslims worship the one true God, creator of heaven and earth and moral lawgiver. Then, because they believe in neither the Holy Trinity nor the death of God's Son on the cross, Luther claimed that in Muslims' hearts and mouths this true God morphs into no God at all. What they think of God is so far from who God in fact is, that they worship the God whom they do not know.

Is it possible to worship the true God without adequately knowing God? Imagine, Luther urges the congregation in Eisleben, that you say that you know the Count of Mansfeld. But when you are asked to describe him, it turns out you don't know that he is, by nature, a being with feet, arms, and head! So it is with Muslims and their claim to know God. By saying that there is no divine Son in the one and indivisible being of God, they are taking away from God, metaphorically speaking, "hands and feet, which is to say his perfect divinity."[33] They direct worship to the correct object—the one true God—but they distort that object almost beyond recognition. The "being" is right; the "character" is mostly wrong.

Extreme Polarities

What do we make of Luther's complex, almost paradoxical position on whether Muslims and Christians worship the same God? Let's look first at what seems to me the shady side of his position, paying attention to both the tenor and the content of it. My evaluation will be based on how well Luther's position reflects what he insists lies at the heart of the Christian understanding of God—namely, that God is infinite and unconditional love.

First, Luther's tone, evident in his liberal use of vicious name-calling and negative stereotyping, is troubling. In his view, the Turks are not just the "enemies of God"; the struggle against them is a struggle against "the Devil himself."[34] True, as a person of fierce and volatile temperament, Luther was in this regard an equal-opportunity name-caller, hurling insulting epithets with similar vehemence against the pope, Jews, and sectarians. But there is something deeply ironic about a person's defending God's unconditional love by using the same kind of brutal rhetoric violent extremists use.

Second, Luther's uncharitable tone makes him draw unfavorable caricatures of the Muslim understanding of God. Since he considers the Turks to be Satan's instruments, Luther is interested in highlighting how their religious beliefs differ from Christian beliefs. Take, for instance, how Luther employs the analogy of knowing the Count of Mansfeld to illustrate the extent to which Muslims can be said to know God. With massive exaggeration, Luther states that not knowing that God sent the Son into the world to die for human sin is analogous to not knowing that the count has "hands and feet." A more fitting use of this analogy might go something like this. A person who knows that the one God is the eternal creator, but not that God sent the Son as the Savior of the world, is like a person who knows and honors the Count of Mansfeld simply as a majestically aloof but wise and just ruler, but is unaware that the count's heart is good, that he visits his impoverished subjects, and that he is beneficent to a fault. Certainly, the count's good heart would affect the character of his rule, so that one could not understand him fully as a majestic ruler if one did not know of his good heart. But would it be true to say that a person does not know the count's character *at all,* if she or he does not know that his heart is good?

Is it not a significant part of God's character to be "almighty Lord of all, who has created all men and given them the law according to which they are to live"?[35] Luther affirms that Muslims believe this, and yet he seems to consider this belief of little significance. He also says that Turks, along with Jews and "false" Christians, "boast that God is merciful" and that they know "something of the grace of God."[36] Yet again, this seems to be of little significance for Luther. For him, everything depends on one thing: if human beings must acquire God's mercy by "their works, rigid life, and their own holiness,"[37] they do not know God, for God's mercy is a completely gratuitous gift and in no way a reward. To want to earn God's mercy in even a smallest way is to dishonor God, to malign God's character. But even if one agrees with Luther, the Master of the Universe, understood as one whose mercy is conditional, is not the same as Satan appearing as the angel of light. That God, as Luther also states, is still the one true God, even though the description does not express God's character adequately. Despite this, Luther chooses to reject instead of correct, exclude instead of recast, and proclaim to be "no God" what is merely God mistakenly understood.

Third, seemingly without a second thought, Luther declares that Muslims—along with Jews, Catholics, and Anabaptists—are objects of God's wrath. They do not know what God's "mind toward them is," he explains, and they abide "in eternal wrath and damnation."[38] By trying to gain God's favor with their good works, they "only make the wrath and displeasure of God the more grievous."[39] Luther is willing to admit that one can have all the right convictions about God—which the devils have as well—and be damned. But he does not seem ready to grant that one can have partly wrong convictions about God and still be saved. But why not? After all, Luther believes that God is the God of unconditional love and that faith in God is itself a gift of that utterly generous God. It is not our convictions about God that save us; God saves us.

All three of these issues—negative stereotyping, refusal to assign positive significance to clear overlaps in understandings of God, and seeing Muslims as objects of God's wrath—seem incongruous with the main emphasis of Luther's theology: God's unconditional love. His explosive personality and the widespread fears that Europe would be overrun by a powerful enemy may help explain Luther's attitudes and stances, but cannot justify them. At least one contemporary thinker with whom Luther debated vigorously and, ironically, whom he accused of slighting God's unconditional love, did better than Luther in this regard. Erasmus of Rotterdam (1469–1536), a humanist and Catholic theologian, complained against those who "forget first that [the Turks] are human beings, and second that they are half-Christian."[40] But those whom Erasmus considered "human beings" and "half-Christians" were no more than "servants of the devil" for Luther.

Common Ground?

So far, the main lesson from our engagement with Luther has been a negative one. In theological encounter with Muslims, especially in situations of intense conflict, avoid inconsistency. The way you think about others and act toward them should not clash with the beliefs about God you espouse and seek to commend to them. If you say that God is unconditional Love, you should show unconditional love toward Muslims. Luther did the one, but failed miserably at the other. But are there any positive lessons we can learn from Luther's engagement with the question of whether the God of the Qur'an and the God of the Bible are the same God? Two lessons are particularly significant.

First, in an important sense, Luther refuses to answer the question as I have posed it. His predilection for extreme polarities notwithstanding, he does not simply contrast the God of Muslims and the God of Christians. In his view, Christians too have deeply inadequate convictions about God; indeed, the great majority of them do. And their convictions are inadequate for basically the same reason that Muslims' convictions are: they too miss the fact that God's love is utterly unconditional and God's favor is a pure gift, which cannot be earned in any way. With this image of God in view, Luther insists that there are Christian "infidels" as well as Muslim, Jewish, and heathen infidels. For Luther, the polarity of "us" versus "them" is not a polarity of "Christians" versus "Muslims" and other non-Christians. Rather, it is a polarity of those who rightly know how God relates to them and how they ought to relate to God (some Christians) and those who do not (the majority of Christians and all non-Christians). Muslim "distortions" of who God is are not categorically different from the "distortions" of fellow Christians. An important consequence follows. The "clash of gods" is not a "clash of religious communities," let alone a "clash of civilizations," pitting Christian communities, cultures, and nations against Islamic ones. Since Luther's God is above such culturally and politically defined clashes, the importance of religious, moral, or cultural achievements is relativized, and the importance of unconditional care for others—God's care as well as human care—is elevated.

Second, Luther maintains consistently that there is a great deal of commonality between Muslim and Christian views of God—even Christian views of God as defined by Luther himself. But because his primary concern is with human standing before God, he considers these major overlaps to be ultimately unimportant. I disagree, as will be clear from subsequent chapters, where I argue that the overlaps in views about God in Islam and Christianity matter for the flourishing of the individuals and communities involved. What is plain is that Luther never denies significant overlap, despite the pressures of his explosive and polarizing temperament, the exclusivity of his apocalyptic theological framework, and the presence of mighty Ottoman armies at his "very doorstep." Significant differences in the views of God notwithstanding, his belief that Muslims and Christians have a common God was sufficiently robust to withstand even such a powerful cluster of forces.

Luther is a resource for us today, both in what he got right and what he missed or got wrong. So is Nicholas of Cusa, whose stance toward the God of the Qur'an I examined in the previous chapter. They shed light on our path, but they cannot walk the path for us. Today, we need to pick up the relationship between the God of the Bible and the God of the Qur'an afresh. Three sets of questions about this relationship are especially important today.

First, how do we decide whether the two, though partly different in character, are the same God? Neither Nicholas nor Luther gives us a comprehensive answer. I take up this question in part II of this book.

Second, what do we do with different understandings of God's nature—with the Christian affirmations that God is the Holy Trinity and that God is love and the Muslim denial of or hesitation about these claims? Nicholas and Luther dealt with these issues, but a lot has changed in the ensuing five hundred years. They demand the fresh look that I give them in part III.

Finally, what difference does the claim that Muslims and Christians have a common God make in their daily encounters with one another? Nicholas and Luther, I believe, were right to make this theological claim, but neither of them lived in a society that included both Christians and Muslims or faced the particular daunting challenges of today's interconnected, interdependent, and rapidly changing world. I explore the practical ramifications of the claim that Christians and Muslims have a common God in part IV.

PART II

Two Gods or One?

CHAPTER FOUR

How Do We Decide?

For Muslims, the question of whether Christians worship the same God they do is in one respect settled. The Qur'an, considered to be God's very Word, clearly states that they do:

> And we dispute not with the People of the Book, except with
> means better (than mere disputation), unless it be with those
> of them who inflict wrong (and injury); But say, "We believe
> in the Revelation which has come down to us and in that
> which came down to you; Our God and your God is One:
> and to Him we bow (in Islam)." (Al 'Ankabut, 29:46)[1]

However, if you dig deeper than just one or two verses, things get more complicated. The Qur'an suggests that Christians "join gods" to God by considering Jesus Christ and the Holy Spirit to be divine (see Al Baqarah, 2:135). Muslims seem to reject some central Christian convictions about God, notably the belief that God is the Holy Trinity. As we have seen in chapter 2, Cardinal Nicholas of Cusa believed that the Muslim rejection of the Trinity rests on a misunderstanding; in affirming God's triunity, Christians do not compromise God's oneness. I'll reinforce that argument in a later chapter. But most Muslims, including scholars, either have never heard these arguments or are not persuaded. So Muslims make two affirmations that don't sit easily next to each other: (1) that Islam's God and Christianity's God are one and the same, and (2) that central Christian beliefs seriously compromise the most important characteristic of God, God's oneness. The challenge for Muslims in relation to Christian views about God is to deal with this tension, a tension that is similar to the one we found in Luther's assessment of Muslim views about God (see chapter 3).

The Christian holy book, the Bible, does not say that Christians have a common God with Muslims. The reason is obvious. The Bible was completed by about 100 CE, some five centuries before the birth of Islam. So Christians have no explicit guidance in this matter from their sacred text. As a consequence, opinions range widely. Some, like the controversial and influential televangelist and erstwhile U.S. presidential candidate Pat Robertson, believe that Muslims worship a completely different deity (see the introduction). Others, like the erudite and ecumenically minded Pope John Paul II, unambiguously affirm that Muslims and Christians worship the same God (see chapter 1).

Who is right? And how should Christians decide? In the next two chapters, I mount an argument that, not surprisingly, John Paul II was right and Pat Robertson was wrong. But before I delve into that argument, it is important to be clear about how to mount such an argument. This is what the present chapter is about. I start with the controversy about "Allah" as the term for God.

Designation

Under the influence of Malay militants, in 2007 the Malaysian Home Ministry decided to enforce the 1986 law prohibiting use of the word "Allah" in non-Muslim publications. The Malay-language edition of the Catholic weekly *Herald* was forbidden to use "Allah" to denote the God Christians worship. In a parallel move, in 2009 the government also ordered customs officials to seize some fifteen thousand Bibles, because they used "Allah" as a translation for "God." The *Herald* filed a suit, and at the beginning of 2010 Judge Lau Bee Lan of Malaysia's high court overturned the government ban. She ruled that "Allah" is not exclusive to Muslims. In response, angry mobs attacked churches, often with firebombs.

The government itself was displeased by Judge Lan's decision, and it appealed the ruling. "Allah" is the God of Muslims, the government lawyers insisted, and "Allah" is different from the God of Christians, because Christians recognize a "trinity of gods" while Islam is "totally monotheistic." If Christians were to use "Allah" to designate their own God, Muslims would be "confused."[2] From these arguments, it almost seemed as if "Allah" was a name for a tribal deity, not a designation for the Creator of the Universe.

Surprisingly, Malay Islamic militants can find soul mates among some Christian theologians. R. Albert Mohler Jr., president of the Southern Baptist Theological Seminary, strenuously disagrees with the idea that it is appropriate for Christians to pray to Allah (as they do in some Malaysian churches). The key condition for Christians' calling God "Allah" is that "Allah" must refer to the same God as is revealed in the Bible. But that is not the case, according to Mohler. He writes:

> From its very starting point Islam denies what Christianity takes as its central truth claim—the fact that Jesus Christ is the only begotten Son of the Father. If Allah has no Son by definition, Allah is not the God who revealed himself in the Son. How then can the use of Allah by Christians lead to anything but confusion . . . and worse?[3]

Rather than examining what Christians *mean* when they speak of "God's Son" and what Muslims *mean* when they contest the claim that "God has a son," as, for instance, Nicholas of Cusa did (see chapter 2), Mohler takes Christian and Muslim claims in their surface sense and concludes that Muslims and Christians worship two different Gods. If so, then it would be confusing to designate them with the same name.

Should Christians reject "Allah" as a term for God? Should they insist that "Allah" is the Muslim God, whereas Christians worship the "Father of Jesus Christ" or the "Lord God"?[4] They should not. "Allah" is simply Arabic for "God" (with the definite article) just as

Theos is Greek for "God" and *Bog* is Croatian for "God." A slightly different way to make the same point is that "Allah," like "God," is not a proper name, but a descriptive term. "Barack Obama" is a proper name; "president" is a descriptive term. "Zeus" and "Hera" are proper names; *theos* is a descriptive term. For the most part, we don't translate proper names; Obama is "Obama" (transliterated) in all languages. We translate descriptive terms; "president" is *predsjednik* in Croatian. "God" is "Allah" in Arabic, and "Allah" is "the God" in English.[5]

Even more important than the meaning and the character of the word "Allah" is the millennia-long practice of Christians. "Arab Christians and Arabic-speaking Jews since long before the time of Muhammad have used the name 'Allah' to refer to God. . . . Thus all Arabic Christian Bible translations of John 3:16 say, 'For Allah so loved the world . . .'"[6] Today, all Arabic-speaking Christians use "Allah" for God. The Copts, one of the oldest Christian communities in the world, going back to the first century, are a good example. Living as they do in Egypt and speaking Arabic, they use "Allah" for God. Witness, for instance, what happens in a Coptic ceremony after a cross has been tattooed onto the wrist of an infant as a sign of religious and ethnic identification in a predominantly Muslim and Arab society.[7] The whole assembled congregation shouts "Allah!"[8] Are they, a presently beleaguered Christian minority in a predominantly Muslim country, betraying Christian faith and invoking a foreign god by that shout? No, they are unmistakably affirming the Christian faith, and they are doing so by exclaiming the same word for God their Muslim compatriots use.

The whole heated discussion about the proper designation for God is a bit futile. Those who insist that Christians and Muslims must use different designations for God generally think that the two groups worship different deities. But a different *word* for God, obviously, does not mean that *God* is different. You can use different words to refer to the same thing. That happens all the time, of course, when you translate from one language into another. But it happens even within a single language and even when two words for the same thing are not synonyms. To use an example famous in philosophy, the "evening star" and the "morning star" refer to the same heavenly body, the planet Venus.[9] Even if Muslims and Christians are using different designations for God, they could be worshipping the same God. The question is, do they?

Inversely, the mere fact that Muslims and Christians use the same word for God does not mean that their Gods are the same. Take the case of the same name. If in the company of my friends you start talking about Miroslav playing soccer, for a while they may think you are talking about me. I am Miroslav, and I play soccer. But if you say, "Miroslav is set to terrorize defenses at the 2010 World Cup in South Africa," anybody who knows anything about me and about soccer will immediately realize that you are talking about another Miroslav, the famous striker from Bayern München. The name is the same—Miroslav. The referent is different—in one case a Croatian-born theologian and in the other a Polish-born soccer superstar.

With the distinction between the "designation" (or term) and the "referent" (or object) in mind, the crucial question is not whether Christians and Muslims should or should not use the same word for God. Rather, it is whether Christians and Muslims refer to the same "object" when they speak of "God" or "Allah." Whatever the designation, is the *referent* the same?

A Bit of Ground Clearing

Let me make three brief preliminary and somewhat technical observations about the phrase "the same referent." First, a comment about the word "same." An annoyed woman at a party might whisper to her companion about another woman, "She is wearing the same dress I am!" "Same" in this example means that the two dresses are almost identical, not that somehow both women have squeezed into one and the same dress. Consider a different situation. Surprised, a woman might say to her companion, "Two years

ago, in Cairo, I was at a dinner party with that same woman."
Now "same" designates a single thing—one and the same woman;
it is used in the sense of "numerical identity." Christians and Muslims are monotheists; for them there are not two gods, which could
be either the same or different. There is only one single God. So
the question of whether Christians and Muslims worship the same
God is about whether they refer, with the word "God" or "Allah,"
to the same, numerically identical "object."

Second, one way Greek philosophers entertained themselves
while puzzling over the problem of "sameness" was by trying to
figure out whether the famous ship of Theseus, whose decayed
planks were gradually replaced by new ones, had remained the
same ship through the process.[10] The question they were pondering was, roughly, this: How many properties does an object need to
retain in order to remain the same?

The question we are pondering is different. God is one, eternal,
and unchanging. It does not make any sense to inquire about how
many properties the Muslim God and the Christian God have to
have in common for us to consider them the same. Keith DeRose,
a philosopher at Yale, puts the question we are pondering this way:
the issue is "whether the thoughts and utterances of Muslims that
are expressed in terms of being about 'God' (if they are speaking
English) have the God that Christians worship as their object."[11]

Finally, before I argue that Christian and Muslim descriptions of
God are sufficiently similar and that they refer to the same object,
consider the alternative. What happens if we deny that Muslims
and Christians are worshipping the same God? From a Christian
standpoint there are three options. In their thoughts and utterances
about God, Muslims are referring to (1) another God, (2) no real
object, or (3) an idol. The first option is closed. As monotheists,
Christians believe that there is and there can be only one God.

So we are left with the second option ("no real object") or the
third option ("an idol"). But in the end, these two options are the
same. Recall the statement of the apostle Paul: "We know that 'no
idol in the world really exists,' and that 'there is no God but one'"
(1 Cor. 8:4). For the apostle Paul, as well as for the prophet Isaiah

before him (see Isa. 44:9–20), idols are not active supernatural powers; they are human creations.[12] So from a Christian perspective we are left with two options: when Muslims talk about God, they are referring either to a mere collective projection or to the God Christians worship.

Of course, some people believe that *both* Christians and Muslims—indeed, that all religious people—worship nothing more than human projections. The German philosopher Ludwig Feuerbach is well known for his "projection theory" of religion.[13] He argued, as atheists do, that God does not exist, except in human imagination. But then he added that God lives in human imagination, because human beings as groups project what they find valuable onto a heavenly screen. In religious worship and daily efforts to imitate God, human beings extol and try to appropriate for themselves those very qualities they have projected there as their ultimate values!

To a religious person, Feuerbach is all wrong in claiming that God does not exist and that human ultimate values make up God. It is the other way around: God, the creator of all there is, is the source of values that humans ought to consider ultimate. For my present purposes, I will simply assume that religious people are right and Feuerbach is mistaken in the main thrust of his argument. Christians worship the one God, creator of all that is seen and unseen. I believe that Muslims have that same object in mind when they worship God. But how can we show that? There are three plausible ways to approach the issue.

General Knowledge of God?

The first approach is based on an analogy to the way in which early Christians dealt with the worship of Samaritans, non-Jews who were not pagans. John's Gospel reports an encounter between Jesus and a Samaritan woman. In the course of the conversation, Jesus tells her: "You worship what you do not know; we worship what we know, for salvation is from the Jews" (4:22). Jesus assumed that the Samaritans and the Jews worshipped the same God, the Samaritans on Mount Gerizim and the Jews in Jerusalem. But the Samaritans' worship was not pure. According to 2 Kings 17:41, it had an admixture of foreign worship in it, because Samaritans "served their carved images" as well (or served the Lord by means of worshipping those carved images[14]). So they worshipped God, but without true knowledge of God.

Now apply this model to Muslim worship. On the one hand, Muslims are unlike Samaritans because they adamantly reject "carved images" and affirm as the central pillar of their faith that "there is no god but God." On the other hand, according to this analogy, they are like Samaritans, because they worship the one true God, but they don't truly and adequately *know* the God they are worshipping. This is, roughly, how Martin Luther thought about the issue, as we have seen in the previous chapter.

Let's say we go along with this suggestion and maintain that Muslims don't adequately know the one true God, whom they are in fact worshipping. But how do we *know* they are indeed worshipping the one true God? Nicholas of Cusa provides us with one possible answer. Building on Plato's views about the relation between human desire and the ultimate Good,[15] he argues that *all* people adore the one true God in everything they adore (see chapter 2). Like all people, Muslims desire what they think is good, and in doing so they are stretching themselves out to the one who is the Ultimate Good.

First, many people today find this argument unpersuasive. But even if it were persuasive, it would put Muslims in the same company with idolaters and atheists. Given Muslims' robust beliefs about God, that seems implausible. Second, it may well be that the desire for the one true God is driving all human desires. Does it follow that the thoughts and utterances of these same people about God have as their object the God Christians worship? It does not, for we are comparing explicit beliefs and practices, not hidden desires. In order to decide whether Christians and Muslims have the same object in view when they talk about God, we need to look for something that would tell us about actual descriptions of God that Christians and Muslims share, some common elements in their descriptions of God.

Building on what the apostle Paul wrote in Romans 1:20 about Gentiles ("Ever since the creation of the world God's eternal power and divine nature, invisible though they are, have been understood and seen through the things he God has made"), Luther thought that all people have some knowledge of the one true God. This suggestion gives Christians scriptural reason to affirm some significant common elements in Christian and Muslim descriptions of God. But it again treats Muslims as if they were generic non-Christians and proceeds as if it did not matter at all what the Qur'an actually says about God.

Common Scripture?

The second approach takes the Muslim holy book, the Qur'an, into account. The approach is modeled on the way in which early Christians related to Jews and their worship. Early Christians had a common scripture with Jews; indeed, the earliest Christians were Jews who considered Jewish scripture to be their scripture. The question of whether they worshipped the same God as the Jews never even arose for them. Why? Not so much because their "statements" about God were obviously similar, but because their God was the one who said and did what the Hebrew Bible describes God as having said and done. That settled the issue as far as early Christians were concerned. (That did not settle the issue for the Jews who remained non-Christians, but that is a different matter.)

One might argue that Christians and Muslims also share scripture, even if not quite in the same way as Christians and Jews do. For starters, there are parallels and overlaps in sections of the Bible and the Qur'an. More important, the Qur'an requires Muslims to say, "We believe in God, and the revelation given to us, and to Abraham, Ishmael, Isaac, Jacob, and the descendants (children of

Jacob) and that given to Moses and Jesus and that given to (all) Prophets from their Lord: We make no difference between one and another of them" (Al Baqarah, 2:136; cf. Al Nisa', 4:136). In the Muslim view, Muslims and Christians share God's revelation. Therefore they worship the same God. The statement in the Qur'an that "our God and your God is One" is preceded and justified by the claim: "We believe in the Revelation which has come down to us and in that which came down to you" (Al 'Ankabut, 29:46). If one were to ask Muslims, "To whom do you refer in your thoughts and utterances about God?" they could respond, "To the God revealed to Abraham, Moses, the Prophets, and Jesus."

Would this settle the question for Christians? It would—under one condition. That Muslims agree with Christians that the Bible contains the authentic *content* of God's self-revelation to Abraham, Moses, the Prophets, and Jesus. Some Muslims do agree; they believe that the Torah, the Psalms, and the Gospel[16] are authentic revelations from God. If so, Christians and Muslims, then, have a significantly overlapping and therefore common scripture.[17] To the question, "Who is the God you worship?" Christians and Muslims could both respond, "The God who said and did what our common scripture says that God said and did." And then a debate—a vigorous and protracted debate, I am sure—could begin about the proper understanding of the God in whom both believe.

But suppose Muslims were to say, "We believe in God's revelation to Abraham, Moses, the Prophets, and Jesus, but not as it is recorded in the Bible." Then Christians and Muslims would no longer have a common scripture. Muslims would derive from the Qur'an the content of God's self-revelation to Abraham, Moses, the Prophets, and Jesus (and agree with what the Bible says about God to the extent that the Bible agrees with the Qur'an). Christians, on the other hand, would derive God's self-revelation to Abraham, Moses, the Prophets, and Jesus from the Bible (and agree with what the Qur'an says about God to the extent that the Qur'an agrees with the Bible). Now Christians and Muslims could no longer say,

"When we talk about God, we both refer to the God whose words and deeds are recorded in these jointly recognized sacred texts." Instead, we would have to *compare the content* of what is said in the Bible and the Qur'an about God and determine whether Muslims, when they speak about the God they worship, refer to the same object Christians do.

Sufficient Similarity

As it turns out, the majority of Muslims do not believe that they have a common scripture with Christians—at least not a common scripture in the sense in which I have defined it. The Qur'an, the measure of revelation for Muslims, explicitly states that many Christians have gone astray from the original revelation given to Moses and Jesus (Al Ma'idah, 5:14, 66, 68). Drawing from classical commentators,[18] contemporary Qur'anic translator and scholar Muhammad Asad takes this to mean that, over the millennia, fabrications and alterations have distorted the message of the Bible.[19] Moreover, the Bible contains legislation that is different from that contained in the Qur'an. Muslims therefore do not believe that the Bible, as it exists today, is a true revelation. In the minds of most Muslims, Muslims and Christians today do not have a common scripture; the common scripture would have been the original revelation, which has since been lost or altered.

Hence we need a third approach. It consists in comparing the content of what Christians and Muslims say about God and determining whether the descriptions of God are sufficiently similar for us to claim that they speak of the same object when they refer to God. In the subsequent chapters I argue that this indeed is the case. The crucial term in this third approach is "sufficient similarity."

If Muslims' and Christians' "thoughts and utterances" about God were the same, the problem would more or less disappear. We could rightly conclude that they refer to the same object. But the descriptions of God in the Bible—for Christians both the Hebrew scriptures and the New Testament—and in the Qur'an are not identical; what Muslims and Christians say about God does not always match. And these discrepancies give rise to our problem.

It is clear that we cannot have *radically* different descriptions of God and still say that they refer to the same object. If I say that God is the result of premarital relations between Zeus with Letho and that he has a chaste sister called Artemis, and you say that God is the Spirit who created the world out of nothing, we would clearly *not* be talking about the same God. In this case I would be mistaken, because I would be describing the Greek god Apollo, not the God of Jesus Christ. Consequently, my description would fail to refer to the true God at all.[20]

But we don't need to subscribe to *identical* descriptions of God to be referring to the same object. When my sons were young, before meals we would sometimes pray a simple prayer: "God is great and God is good, and we thank God for our food." I am a theologian who has spent much of my life pondering God's nature; they were young and boisterous boys who thought about it only when I nudged them to do so. Our understandings of God—of God's greatness and goodness and of what it means to thank God—were *very* different. Yet it would be absurd, I think, to say that, sitting around our dining-room table, we were not praying to the same God.

Or take a dispute between theologians as an example. If you say that God predestined some people to eternal salvation and others to eternal damnation, and I insist that it would be unworthy of God to predestine anyone to eternal damnation, we can still be talking about the same God. Indeed, it never occurred to Calvinists and Arminians,[21] who thought the issue was sufficiently important to debate it vigorously for centuries, that they were not debating about the nature and purposes of the same God.

Two simple preliminary conclusions about descriptions of God and their referring to the same object follow:

1. To refer to the same object, descriptions of God need not be identical.

2. To refer to the same object, descriptions of God may not be radically different.

Now apply these conclusions to the question of whether Muslims and Christians worship the same God. Muslim and Christian descriptions of God are clearly not "completely identical." Therefore, our question is this: Are they so radically different that they cannot be referring to the same object, or are they sufficiently similar so that they are referring to the same object? And to what extent and in what regards must they be similar to be referring to the same object? I take up these questions in chapter 5.

The Common Versus the Distinctive

For two things to be similar, they must have both commonalities and differences. What significance does each of these categories have in our decision about whether Muslims worship the same God as Christians?

My rules in approaching similarities in Muslim and Christian understandings of God are:

1. Concentrate on what is common.
2. Keep an eye out for what is decisively different.

Not all people agree with these rules. Instead, they concentrate on differences in the description of God and consider commonalities largely irrelevant. Let Australian scholar and vicar Mark Durie represent this group. He agrees that God as described in the Bible and God as described in the Qur'an share certain similarities. In both, God is said to be "the creator, all-powerful, merciful, and the judge of humanity."[22] Yet for Durie this does not suffice to say that Christians and Muslims worship the same God. He maintains that if you don't have a *complete* match between descriptions of God in Islam and Christianity, you don't have identity. To find out whether the God of the Qur'an is a genuine or false God, the procedure should be the same as when trying to figure out whether a banknote is genuine or counterfeit. If there are *any* differences from the banknote you know is genuine, then it's counterfeit.

The two approaches—the "commonalities" approach and the "differences" approach—yield very different results. If differences are decisive and similarities don't count, then to Christians the God of the Qur'an will appear as an alien deity, a false god. If similarities are important and differences matter when they signal major incompatibilities, then we will possibly conclude that Muslims have a common God with Christians. But which approach is correct? In answering the question, we need to keep in mind two considerations: biblical example and moral stance.

First, *biblical example.* A famous text from John's Gospel seems to offer biblical support for Durie's counterfeit test. During a conversation with Philip, Jesus says:

> "If you know me, you will know my Father also. From now on you do know him and have seen him." Philip said to him, "Lord, show us the Father, and we will be satisfied." Jesus said to him, "Have I been with you all this time, Philip, and you still do not know me? Whoever has seen me has seen the Father." (14:7–9)

It would seem that Jesus encourages here the position Durie advocates: "Look at Jesus, and if your picture of God matches what you see, you have the right God; if not, you have the wrong God."[23] And yet, this is not the case.

Certainly, John's Gospel affirms that Jesus is the self-revelation of God. If you know Jesus as the incarnate Word, you know God, and you know God truly (though not exhaustively!). And yet, according to that same Gospel, if you *reject* Jesus, you can still be worshipping the God whom Jesus truthfully revealed. According to John's Gospel, Jewish leaders did not even recognize Jesus as a prophet, let alone as the self-revelation of God. Instead, they rejected him as a blasphemer. But when Jesus engaged in debates with them about the nature of God, including the question of whether Jesus blasphemed by making himself equal to God (see 5:18; 8:39–58), the assumption was that opponents were disagreeing about the same God, the God of the Hebrew Bible. The contested issue was whether it was appropriate for Jesus to call God his "Father" (5:18) and whether honoring God requires honoring Jesus (see 5:23). The issue was not whether Jews worshipped the God revealed by Jesus. John's Gospel assumes they did. When it came to the question of God, in John's Gospel Jesus's approach was that the commonalities were more important than the differences.

The "differences" approach excludes Jews, the people to whom belong "the covenants, the giving of the law, the worship, and the promises" (Rom. 9:4), from worshipping the same God as Christians. Against the opinion of a great majority of Christian theologians from the apostles to just about all contemporaries, the proposed counterfeit test would mean that devout Jews worship a different God than do Christians. And since there is only one God, it follows that the God whom Jews worship is either an idol or a projection, and in any case *nothing*. Clearly, notwithstanding the shared scripture, there are major differences between Jewish and Christian understandings of God—so much so that there is a powerful tradition within Judaism of considering Christians to be idolaters.[24] And yet Christians have always maintained that the God is the same.

Second, *moral stance*. In the book *Idolatry* Moshe Halbertal and Avishai Margalit note that the two opposing approaches I have just sketched are partly "a product of the religious ideology itself."[25] An exclusivist religion, a religion committed to showing its adherents "that there is something unique in their belief," will tend to highlight differences. An inclusivist religion, a religion operating on a great-believers-think-alike principle, will zero in on commonalities.

Now, I don't find the contrast between "inclusivist" and "exclusivist" religions entirely compelling. Most religions are exclusive in some regards and inclusive in other regards. Still, Halbertal and

Margalit make an important point: religious outlook itself—the way persons of faith see themselves in relation to others—shapes how they approach the question of commonalities and differences between religions. So what is a Christian way to see oneself in relation to others? It is very simple. Commanded, as Christians are, to love their neighbor as themselves, their stance should be that of discerning generosity toward others—toward them as persons as well as toward their beliefs and practices.

In the famous love chapter in 1 Corinthians, the apostle Paul writes that love "does not rejoice in wrongdoing, but rejoices in the truth" (13:6). Those who take the "differences" approach are a bit like those who rejoice in wrongdoing. Those who take the "commonalities" approach are a bit like those who rejoice in the truth. The first are like a nagging partner, who seems not to see any good in the other and always complains about anything that's wrong. The second are like a generous and wise lover, who celebrates the good while not being blind to what might be wrong. Christians are called to rejoice in whatever truth there may be in the Muslim understanding of God. It follows that they should adopt the "commonalities" approach to the question of whether Muslims and Christians worship the same God. Concentrating on what is common and keeping an alert eye to critical differences are but two aspects of "rejoicing in truth."

This chapter was about procedures to follow and a stance to adopt as we seek to decide whether Muslims and Christians have a common God. I have concluded that convictions about God must be sufficiently similar if we are to claim that Muslims and Christians have a common God. But are the beliefs of Muslims about God sufficiently similar to the beliefs of Christians? And are they similar in relevant ways? I turn to these questions in the next two chapters.

CHAPTER FIVE

A Common God and the
Matter of Beliefs

The closest thing Christians have to an authoritative statement about whether Muslims worship the same God they do comes from the Second Vatican Council (1962–65), an assembly of Catholic bishops from the whole world called by Pope John XXIII. A short and, for that time, bold document on non-Christian religions, *Nostra Aetate* (1965), contains a brief section on Islam. Its first lines address Muslims' worship of God: "They adore the one God, living and subsisting in Himself; merciful and all-powerful, the Creator of heaven and earth, who has spoken to men."[1] The text doesn't state explicitly that Muslims and Christians worship *the same* God, only that Muslims worship "the one God." But the description of God, highlighting as it does beliefs shared by Muslims and Christians, and the use of the definite article ("*the* one God") suggest that the one God each group worships is the same God, even if there are differences in their understanding and worship of that God.

To support its assertion about the God of Muslims and Christians, *Nostra Aetate* appeals to a medieval pope, Gregory VII. In 1076, some twenty years before the First Crusade, he wrote a letter to al-Nasir, the Muslim king of Mauretania. Although relations between the pope and the king had not been smooth, they saw eye to eye on the consecration of a certain Servandus as bishop, and the pope wrote a friendly letter to the king. Keep in mind that Gregory VII had also made a failed attempt at a crusade and insisted, as every pope would, that Christianity is the only saving faith.[2] But the situation was different now. The letter was friendly, and it highlighted commonalities, especially with regard to faith in the one God:

> Almighty God, who desires all men to be saved (1 Tim. 2:4) and none to perish is well pleased to approve in us most of all that besides loving God men love other men, and do not do to others anything they do not want to be done unto themselves (cf. Matt. 7:12). We and you must show in a special way to the other nations an example of this charity, for we believe and confess one God, although in different ways, and praise and worship Him daily as the creator of all ages and the ruler of this world. As the apostle says, "He is our peace who has made us both one" (Eph. 2:14).[3]

In the mind of the pope, he and the Muslim king belong to the same company of those who worship the one God. It is clearly the same God, even if Christians and Muslims worship that same God "in different ways."

But how do Popes Gregory VII and Paul VI (who issued *Nostra Aetate*) *know* that Muslims and Christians worship the same God? They appeal to a brief description of God with which Muslims and Christians agree. Sufficiently similar descriptions of the object of worship imply that the object of worship is the same. In other words, they decide the matter the way I argued in favor of in the previous chapter.

Both Gregory VII and *Nostra Aetate* imply that Muslims' description of God is sufficiently similar to the Christian description of God. But is it? It depends, in part, on which Muslims and which Christians you have in mind. There are Muslims and Christians who disagree so radically about God's character that they, in fact, do worship very different Gods. But then it would be easy to find Christians who disagree among themselves so radically that we may be tempted to conclude that they too worship different Gods. The same is true of Muslims and Jews,[4] I suspect. In this book I have in mind Muslims and Christians who embrace what I will call here normative versions of their religions, those with robust ties to the Bible and the Qur'an who also have some appreciation for the tradition of interpretation and debate about these sacred texts. These believers are, arguably, the mainstream majority in both faith traditions; they take their faith seriously while at the same time realizing that many great teachers have disagreed on and argued about many major issues, including important questions about the character of God.

Now that I have identified which Muslims and Christians we are talking about (those who embrace the normative traditions of their respective religions) and what we are looking for (sufficient similarity in beliefs about God), the examination can start. First, I address *similarity in descriptions of God* to establish the claim that Muslims and Christians worship the same God. Then I discuss *similarity in God's commands* in the two faiths to reinforce that claim. Remember, this all is written from a distinctly Christian perspective; Muslims might or might not agree, and they will have their own ways of approaching the issue.

One God and Creator

Consider the following three beliefs together, all central to Muslims and Christians alike:

1. There is only one God, the one and only divine being.
   Bible: "Hear, O Israel: the Lord our God, the Lord is one." (Mark 12:29)
   Qur'an: "Know, therefore, that there is no god but God." (Muhammad, 47:19)
2. God created everything that is not God.
   Bible: "In the beginning . . . God created the heavens and the earth." (Gen. 1:1)
   Qur'an: "(He is) the Creator of the heavens and the earth." (Al Shura, 42:11)

3. God is different from everything that is not God.[5]

   Bible: God "dwells in unapproachable light, whom no one has ever seen or can see." (1 Tim. 6:16)

   Qur'an: "No vision can grasp Him. But His grasp is over all vision: He is above all comprehension, yet He is acquainted with all things." (Al An'am, 6:103)

Since both Christians and Muslims embrace these three affirmations, it follows that *if they could point to God, both would point to the same thing.* Why? Because in addition to everything that is not God, there would be nothing else to point to![6]

"*If* they could point to God," I wrote above. But, of course, God is not the kind of thing one can point to. God is not an object in the world, a thing of space and time. God is in principle inaccessible to our senses and incomprehensible to our minds—an important point to which I return in the discussion of the Trinity in chapter 7. When it comes to knowing God, we are always thrown back on God's self-revelation—on how God has manifested God's own character and will to humans, whether that manifestation takes place in the "book of nature," the "book of scripture," or the life and teachings of Jesus Christ.

The terse argument I have offered is based on the claims about God contained in the Bible and the Qur'an, which Christians and Muslims, respectively, believe to contain God's final revelation. It is not an argument from a general sense of what all people mean by "God"—the one who brought the world into existence, its ultimate Cause. Instead, it's an argument from specific but overlapping convictions about God found in the holy books of Christians and Muslims.

Is this simple argument persuasive? I think it is, as far as it goes. With it, we have shown that Muslims and Christians refer to the same object when they speak about worshipping God. The three features of God they jointly affirm allow Christians and Muslims to "pick out" the one they both designate as "God" among all the possible candidates.

These three things—that God is one, creator of all, and incomparably and incommensurably different from the world—are not all that Muslims and Christians will want to say about God. These statements may not even be the most important things Christians would want to say about God. Yet they are sufficient for identifying, at least initially, the one both groups refer to when they talk about the God whom they worship. They are both worshipping "that one"—a single creator of everything different from God—rather than a member of some pantheon (like Zeus) or a deity indistinguishable from the world (like Spinoza's God).

And yet, if everything else Christians and Muslims said about God were radically different, Christians would have to insist that Muslims' God is *not* the God they worship! True, if they could point, they both would be pointing to the same object. From a strictly linguistic standpoint, this would suffice to establish the identity of the referent. But from a religious standpoint, the object of worship of one group would not be worthy of being called "God."

Beneficent God

Imagine a person who believes that the one and only God of infinite power created the world out of nothing. She believes about God what I said earlier that Muslims and Christians believe, namely, that God is one, creator, and different from the world. Imagine that she also has a child suffering in terrible pain caused by an incurable disease. The experience of coping with her child's illness has affected her theological judgment. She has come to believe that God is evil and had a perverse plan in creating the world. God wanted to make creatures suffer as much pain as possible and yet maintain the belief that God is absolute love; according to this plan, this sadistic God could inflict maximum pain as well as laugh at the idiocy of humans for considering their malefactor to be utterly good. When such a believer talks about God, is she referring to the one whom Christians worship? Is she just wrong about the moral character of God? Or is she referring to the wrong God?

When it comes to human beings, we can have radically divergent views of another's moral character and still be talking about the same person. Take the case of Slobodan Milošević. During the early years of the wars in the former Yugoslavia (1990–95), many Serbs thought of him as their savior, the one who would restore their nation to its proper glory and at the same time protect Europe from being overrun by Muslims; in their eyes, he was a person with lofty ideals, ably fighting for most noble causes. Muslims of Kosovo and Bosnia, on the other hand, thought of him as the "butcher of Belgrade," an incarnation of evil. The two groups assessed the moral character of one and the same man in radically discordant ways; they were both referring to the same person, yet assessing his character *very* differently.

Would the circumstances be the same if two groups assessed the moral character of God in radically discordant ways? They would not. Whether Milošević was evil or good, he was still a human being. By definition, human beings can either be good or evil, because they are morally ambivalent beings. But this is not true of God. "A radically evil creator of the world" is not a partially false description of God; it is simply not a description of God at all. Those who would have such a monster in view when talking about God would be gesturing toward the same "object" as Christians do when they speak about God, but they would be distorting God beyond recognition. Take away God's goodness, and you've taken away God's divinity. Now, once we affirm God's goodness, we have to figure out how God's goodness is compatible with evil in the world. But that reinforces my point: the problem of evil looms so large just because we cannot give up on God's goodness.

After the ravages of World War II and the terrible misuse of power by the Nazi regime in Germany, the great Protestant theologian Karl Barth strenuously urged against using the term "the Almighty" for God. He did not disagree that God is almighty, but he insisted that if you worship "the Almighty" pure and simple, you are worshipping "Chaos, Evil, the Devil."[7] Christians don't just add the attribute of love to the creative power, which they recognize as divine. Such power is divine only if it is the power of love. Love *is* the divinity of God, and that's why only the absolute power of love deserves to be called divine.

For Muslims and Christians to refer to the same God in their worship, they need to affirm not just that God is the creator of all that is not God, but that God is good in God's own being and beneficent toward creatures. As it turns out, Christians and Muslims agree on this, as can be seen from the following comparison of verses from the Bible and the Qur'an. Thus we add a fourth element of "sufficient similarity":

4. God is good.
   Bible: "God is love." (1 John 4:16)
   Qur'an: "And He is Oft-Forgiving, full of loving-kindness." (Al Buruj, 85:14)

So now we have four important convictions about God on which there is agreement. These beliefs sufficiently establish that Christians and Muslims have a common God. Whoever agrees on these four convictions about God refers to the same "object" when talking about God.

I write of "agreement" on the four convictions. However, if you peek just below the surface, you will see spirited debates and even outright intellectual wars within each religious group and between these two groups about how to best understand these convictions. Both Christians and Muslims believe that the other holds some erroneous views about these convictions. But these errors do not necessarily indicate that they are talking about a different "thing"; they are disagreeing about the God they both worship, not talking about two different Gods. Just as different Christian groups do, Muslims and Christians disagree about the God they both worship.

Worship

The argument I have offered, that Christians and Muslims worship the same God, is tight and persuasive. But it can be strengthened. To show how, I need to explain what Christians mean by "worshipping" God.

Many think of "worship" as something people do either together with others in houses of worship (when they participate in religious rituals, such as the Eucharist) or in the privacy of their homes (when they pray or read the Bible alone). But this is a narrow and one-sided description of worship, mistakenly reduced to specifically "religious" activities. Properly understood, worship of God is much broader and is summed up in the two Great Commandments: "'You shall love the Lord your God with all your heart, and with all your soul, and with all your mind.' This is the first and greatest commandment. And the second is like it: 'You shall love your neighbor as yourself'" (Matt. 22:37–39). When we strive to obey these two commandments, we worship God (Mic. 6:8; Isa. 58:3–7).

Note the three important features of worship. First, worship of God consists in love. Worshipping God is much richer than merely describing God adequately. When we worship, we relate to God with our whole being. Yes, we relate to God with our cognition, or our "mind," as the first commandment says; but we also relate to God with our emotions and desires, energies and activities, and more. To worship God means to have one's whole being oriented toward God (and precisely in that to find one's true freedom, of course).

Second, as worship of God, love has two objects—God and neighbor. When we love God, we worship God directly by attending to the many ways God commands that we relate to God. When we love our neighbor, we worship God indirectly by attending to the many ways God commands us to relate to neighbors (above all, by doing for them what we want done to us and not doing to them what we don't want done to us). The first commandment about loving God is the "greatest," as Jesus said, because it is the source of the second. The second commandment about loving our neighbor is "like" the first, because we cannot fulfill the first without fulfilling the second. The two components of worship are intertwined; since neighbor love is what God commands, neighbor love is a form of love of God.

Third, our whole life before God is—or should be—worship of God. Love of God and neighbor are not only the greatest commandments; they also sum up all other commandments of God. "On these two commandments hang all the law and the prophets," Jesus said (Matt. 22:40). They sketch in the broadest strokes the kind of life human beings need to lead in relation to God, to others, and to themselves. This life itself is the proper worship God requires.[8]

Does the worship that God requires tell you something about who God is, so that if two people's worship is similar, their views about God are likely to be similar as well? It does. Who God is shapes what God requires. That's why you can know something about who God is from what God requires. It is more likely that people are relating to the same God if their claims about the commands of God are highly similar; the more similar the commands are, the more likely that the One issuing them is the same. If what God is said to command in the Bible were similar to what God is said to command in the Qur'an, then this would suggest that the character of God is similar and that Muslims and Christians have a common God. If what God is said to command in the Bible were incompatible with what God is said to command in the Qur'an, this would suggest that the character of God is very different and that Muslims and Christians do not have a common God.

But how similar is the worship God requires in Islam and Christianity? Is there significant agreement between the two faiths on the summary of true worship as Christians understand it, namely, on the two Great Commandments? As I explained in chapter 1, the famous document "A Common Word," behind which stands the authority of many of the most prominent Muslim leaders, argues persuasively that there is agreement. This argument is echoed in the responses of many of the most influential Christians to that document.[9] Let's look briefly at the bearing that this agreement has on the question of whether Muslims and Christians have a common God.

Keep in mind that agreement on commandments will not by itself establish that Christians and Muslims worship the same God. Indeed, this agreement has significant content only *if* they do worship the same God (see chapter 1). But if we have established independently that Christians and Muslims do worship the same God—as I believe we have done—then agreement on God's commandments reinforces the claim that Muslims and Christians have a common God.

The Two Great Commandments

We can quickly deal here with the first and greatest commandment—the commandment to love God with our total being. Jews, Christians, and Muslims agree on this:

1. God commands us to love God with our whole being.
   Bible: "You shall love the Lord your God with all your heart, and with all your soul, and with all your mind." (Matt. 22:37, citing Deut. 6:5)
   Qur'an: "God, One and Only." (Al Zimar, 39:45)[10]

The one true God is the absolute Good and, as the creator and sustainer, the source of all finite goods. Therefore God ought to be loved with our total being. The command to love God above all things is embedded in the definition of "God," so to speak.[11] Once you embrace the belief in the one true God and know what you are talking about when you say "God," you've bought into the commitment to love God with your whole being. Muslims' and Christians' agreement on this reinforces the claim that they have a common God.

The same is true of the second Great Commandment, which is "like" the first in importance (Matt. 22:39). It too tells us something about the character of God and reinforces the claim that Muslims and Christians have a common God:

2. God commands that we love our neighbors as ourselves.
   Bible: "In everything do to others as you would have them do to you." (Matt. 7:12)
   Hadith: (authentic sayings of Muhammad): "None of you has faith until you love for your neighbor what you love for yourself."[12]

My purpose here in this brief comparison between the commands of God in Christianity and Islam is to indicate that similar commands suggest similarity in understandings of God. To reinforce this point, consider the relation between the command to love your neighbor and the character of God in a classic Christian text about loving our neighbors, 1 John 4:7–8, 16:

Beloved, let us love one another, because love is from God; everyone who loves is born of God and knows God. Whoever does not love does not know God, for God is love. . . . God is love, and those who abide in love abide in God, and God abides in them.

"Love one another!" is not an arbitrary command of a whimsical God, who, if God had wanted, could have commanded the exact opposite. The command to "love one another" is also not motivated merely by the kind of creature God has created—human beings who need the mutual help of loving relationships. More fundamentally, the command to love one another is an expression of God's character. Why should humans love one another? Ultimately, because God *is* love. As Christians see things, God commands humans to love so that they can align their character with God's character. God's commands speak of God's character.

There is a large overlap in what God is said to command in the Bible and the Qur'an. In addition to the two central commandments given by Christ mentioned above, for every one of the Ten Commandments—except the Sabbath commandment, which most Christians do not hold to be obligatory—there is a corresponding commandment in the Qur'an.[13] Here is the comparison, commandment by commandment:

1. *Bible:* "You shall have no other gods before me." (Exod. 20:3)
   Qur'an: "Thy Lord has decreed That ye worship none but Him." (Al Isra', 17:23)

2. *Bible:* "You shall not make for yourself an idol." (Exod. 20:4)
   Qur'an: "Lo! Abraham said to his father Azar: 'Takest thou idols for gods? For I see thee and thy people in manifest error.'" (Al An'am, 6:74)

3. *Bible:* "You shall not make wrongful use of the name of the Lord your God." (Exod. 20:7)
   Qur'an: "And make not God's (name) an excuse in your oaths against doing good, or acting rightly, or making peace between persons; for God is one who heareth and knoweth all things." (Al Baqarah, 2:224)

4. *Bible:* "Remember the sabbath day, and keep it holy." (Exod. 20:8)
   Qur'an: "We commanded them: 'Transgress not in the matter of the Sabbath.'" (Al Nisa', 4:154) (This is not a commandment to Muslims, but a report of the commandment given to the Jews.)

5. *Bible:* "Honor your father and your mother." (Exod. 20:12)
   Qur'an: "Thy Lord had decreed that ye . . . be kind to parents. Whether one or both of them attain old age in thy life, say

not to them a word of contempt, nor repel them, but address them in terms of honor." (Al Isra', 17:23)

6. *Bible:* "You shall not murder." (Exod. 20:13)
   Qur'an: "Take not life, which God hath made sacred, except by way of justice and law." (Al An'am, 6:151)

7. *Bible:* "You shall not commit adultery." (Exod. 20:14)
   Qur'an: "Nor come neigh to unlawful sex for it is a shameful (deed) and an evil, opening the road (to other evils)." (Al Isra', 17:32)

8. *Bible:* "You shall not steal." (Exod. 20: 15)
   Qur'an: "As to the thief, male or female, cut off his or her hands: a punishment by way of example, from God." (Al Ma'idah, 5:38)

9. *Bible:* "You shall not bear false witness against your neighbor." (Exod. 20:16)
   Qur'an: "And the servants of (God) Most Gracious are those . . . who witness no falsehood." (Al Furqan, 25:72)

10. *Bible:* "You shall not covet." (Exod. 20:17)
    Qur'an: "And in nowise covet those things in which God hath bestowed His gifts more freely on some of you than on others." (Al Nisa', 4:32)

Similarities in commands go even deeper. In regard to neighbors, for instance, the Qur'an contains more than just the prohibitions found in the Ten Commandments—against murder, adultery, stealing, bearing false witness, and coveting. It commands that we care for others, especially the underprivileged. That is a central message of the Hebrew prophets (see Isa. 58), and it is reaffirmed in the New Testament (see Matt. 25). Consider the following verse from the Qur'an:

It is not righteousness
That ye turn your faces
Towards East or West;
But it is righteousness—
To believe in God
And the Last Day,
And the Angels,
And the Book,
And the Messengers;
To spend of your substance,
Out of love for Him,
For your kin,
For orphans,
For the needy,
For the wayfarer,
For those who ask,
And for the ransom of slaves;
To be steadfast in prayer,
And practice regular charity. (Al Baqarah, 2:177)[14]

In the Bible and the Qur'an, the things that God commands are sufficiently similar for us to say that, to the extent that God's commands express God's character, Muslims and Christians have a common God.

Clearly, there are also differences between God's commands in the Bible and in the Qur'an. In a subsequent chapter (chapter 9) I explore whether and to what extent the New Testament command to love not just neighbors, but also "enemies" (Matt. 5:43–48) presents an important difference between Christianity and Islam. An explicit command to do so is not found in Muslim sacred texts. Though Christians have not always obeyed this command, to say the least, the command to love enemies is nonetheless central to the Christian faith—as central to the way Christians should live in the world as is the message of God's unconditional grace to their standing before God. It is a clear consequence of the Christian conviction that God is love.

Differences go even deeper. Sometimes commands are the same, but punishments for breaking them are different. Because of certain harsh temporal punishments of transgressors in the Qur'an, some Christians have argued that the God of the Qur'an is radically different from the God of the New Testament.[15] For stealing, the Qur'an's God demands that the thief's hands be cut off: "As to the thief, male or female, cut off his or her hands: a punishment by way of example, from God" (Al Ma'idah, 5:38). The New Testament, on the other hand, imposes no temporal punishments for stealing. Similarly, for adultery the Qur'an prescribes flogging ("Flog each of them with a hundred stripes: Let not compassion move you in their case" [Al Nur, 24:2]), and there are instances in the *hadith* in which Muhammad prescribed stoning[16] (though there are also instances in which he concealed cases of adultery for the sake of mercy[17]). Christ, on the other hand, showed mercy and forgave the woman caught in adultery and brought to him to be stoned according to the law of Moses. He said to her, "Neither do I condemn you. Go your way, and from now on do not sin again" (John 8:11).

What do we make of such differences in commands and punishments? In regard to beliefs, I argued that convictions about God need not be identical for Muslims and Christians to have a common God. The same holds true in regard to commands; they need not be identical, only sufficiently similar, to suggest that Muslims and Christians have a common God. Here the analogy to the way Christians relate to the God of the Jews is again helpful. In the Hebrew Bible there is no command to love the enemy, and severe temporal punishments are imposed on those who transgress the law, including the death penalty for adultery (see Lev. 20:10). Does this difference suggest that Christians and Jews do not have a common God? It does not.

Sufficient Similarities

In sum, Muslims and Christians agree on the following six claims about God:

1. There is only one God, the one and only divine being.
2. God created everything that is not God.
3. God is radically different from everything that is not God.
4. God is good.
5. God commands that we love God with our whole being.
6. God commands that we love our neighbors as ourselves.

For Christians, from the agreement on these six claims, it follows that Muslims' and Christians' object of worship is the same. The first four, which describe God, establish the claim that in their worship of God, Muslims and Christians refer to the same object. The next two, which sum up the principal commands of God, reinforce this claim.

I propose that this argument holds true for *normative* Christianity and Islam, for the two religions as they are expressed in their respective sacred books and interpreted by their great teachers. Of course, Islam and Christianity are complex religions, and individual Muslims and Christians have widely differing opinions, some of them contrary to normative Islam and Christianity. So I need to make my claim more precise: *When* Christians and Muslims agree on the above six claims about God, *then* in their worship of God they refer to the same object. Arguably, the majority of Muslims and Christians in the world would agree on these claims. Therefore, the majority of Muslims and Christians refer to the same God in their worship.

Muslims and Christians *refer* to the same God in their worship. Does it follow that they *in fact worship* the same God? Not yet. To answer that question, we need to examine not just what Muslims and Christians say about God, but how they live, for worship of God is more about living than about thinking and speaking.

CHAPTER SIX

A Common God and the Matter of Practices

The question of whether Muslims and Christians worship the same God has led a kind of subterranean existence in the West over the past century. Scholars specializing in relations between Islam and Christianity were aware of its immense importance and of formidable challenges in answering it well, but they did not bother to try.[1] For the general population it was a nonissue. When speaking about their work to church audiences, Christians who lived and worked in majority Muslim countries were almost never asked whether Muslims and Christians worship the same God. It's not that the answer was assumed; rather, it's that the question didn't matter.

In 2001, this lack of attention changed after the attacks on the Twin Towers and the Pentagon. Now, when relations between Muslims and Christians are discussed, the "same God" question almost *always* comes up. The terrorists who flew the planes on their suicidal mission were carefully instructed in their manual: "Remember, this is a battle for the sake of God."[2] In the name of God and with expectations of glory in this world and rewards in the next, they killed themselves and thousands of innocent civilians. To many Christians it seemed obvious that the God who demands the blood of the innocent and rewards suicidal missions with paradisiacal pleasures isn't the God they worship. And since the terrorists were Muslims, then the God Christians and Muslims worship must not be the same.

There is something peculiar about the way in which a "terrorist God" has been associated with Islam. First, only a minuscule fraction of 1.6 billion Muslims are suicide terrorists and only a small minority of Muslims approve of their acts; and not all suicide terrorists are Muslims (as the case of the secular Sri Lanka Black Tigers, the only professional cadre of men trained for suicide missions in the world, shows[3]). Second, normative Islam condemns suicide as well as the killing of the innocent.[4] It therefore also condemns suicide terrorism,[5] and doubly so when it is directed against civilians.[6] We need not try to explain here the quick and unwarranted mental leap from seeing a terrorist attack perpetrated by a group of Muslims in the name of God to declaring the God of Islam to be radically different from the God of Christianity (and Judaism). I mention this mental leap, because it illustrates well what actually triggered concern in the West about the God Muslims worship. It was not primarily the teaching of the Qur'an or even the beliefs of Muslim majorities. It was the appalling practice of a small but dangerous minority, justified by appealing to God.

But what do the practices of Muslims and Christians, the noble practices no less than abominable ones, tell us about whether they worship the same God?

God Identified, God Worshipped

In the previous chapter I made the following argument. Christians and Muslims describe God's character and God's commands in similar ways. They agree, roughly, on six central claims about God—that (1) God is one, (2) God is the creator, (3) God is different from the world, (4) God is good, (5) God commands love of God, and (6) God commands love of neighbor. From this agreement it follows that they refer to the same object in their thoughts and utterances about God. This is an argument about *normative* Islam and *normative* Christianity—about what Muslims and Christians *are taught* to believe about God in their holy books and by their great teachers. It is not an argument about what *all* Muslims and *all* Christians, in fact, believe, though I

would venture to say that many Muslims and Christians do agree
with these six propositions.

There are two basic and intertwined ways in which human
beings properly relate to God, not one. The first concerns thinking.
It concerns believing the right things about God, about who God
is and what God commands. Put differently, this way of relating
to God concerns *rightly identifying* God. If we have misidentified
God—say by subscribing to a seriously erroneous description of
God—we are talking about the wrong God (which for all monotheists means that we are not talking about *God* at all). The second
way of properly relating to God concerns doing what God requires,
or *rightly worshipping* God. If we fail to do what God requires—for
Christians, if we aren't obeying the two Great Commandments to
love God and neighbor—we are neither fulfilling our most central
duty before God nor fully flourishing as human beings.

It is clear, then, that to believe the right things about God isn't
yet to worship God rightly. Worship is above all a matter of practice—of actively loving God and neighbor. Muslims and Christians
may well refer to the same object in their thoughts and utterances
about God and still *not worship* the same God. To know whom
people worship, we cannot just look at what they say about God;
rather, we need to pay attention above all to how they live.

Talking about false prophets who come in "sheep's clothing but
inwardly are ravenous wolves," Jesus says:

> You will know them by their fruits. Are grapes gathered
> from thorns, or figs from thistles? In the same way, every
> good tree bears good fruit, but the bad tree bears bad fruit. A
> good tree cannot bear bad fruit, nor can a bad tree bear good
> fruit. (Matt. 7:15–18)

The deeds people do indicate the kind of people they are. Those
same deeds also help identify the kind of God they worship. As
Alon Goshen-Gottstein, of the Elijah Interfaith Institute, argues
in his discussion of whether Jews and Christians worship the

same God, "God can be known through the fruits of contact with Him."[7]

There is a distinction to be made here, however, and the matter is not as straightforward as it may seem. Imagine a group of religious people who affirm what their holy book says about God: that God, the one creator of the world, is both just and loving to all human beings and requires human beings to love God and neighbor. They describe God and God's commands correctly. Imagine that they also consistently perpetrate injustice and are indifferent to injustice done to others. You can draw one of two conclusions. You can say either that (1) notwithstanding what these people say about God's love and justice, their God is an oppressive deity, or that (2) this is a group of mean and devious hypocrites whose behavior is at odds with their convictions about God.

The great nineteenth-century critic of Christianity Karl Marx drew the first conclusion: the Christian God is an oppressive deity. But his reason was not simply that Christians went about oppressing others, but that some of their other convictions about God neutralized what they said about God's justice and love. In Marx's reading of Christianity, God created human beings dependent and unfree;[8] God reserved effective implementation of justice and love for the afterlife; and God designed the present world as a valley of tears to craft human beings into better people. When it comes to life in the here and now, such a God is oppressive, he believed.

But what if we believed, as I think Christians should, that dependence on God sets you free to act responsibly in the world; that God desires justice to "roll down like waters" in the here and now (Amos 5:24); and that we are crafted into better people in the valleys of tears in part by striving to make life better for all? Would we not then be pushed to the second conclusion, not that God is an oppressive deity, but that it is inconsistent for people who believe this about God to oppress and tolerate oppression?

Most religious people—and not just religious people—are painfully aware of a gap between what they believe and how they actually live. As the apostle Paul put it, you can "boast of your relation to

God and know his will and determine what is best because you are instructed in the law," and still live in such a way that, because of you, "the name of God is blasphemed" among nonbelievers (Rom. 2:17–18, 24). We fail often, and fail miserably, not because of our convictions, but despite them. We believe rightly, but act wrongly. Practices of Christians and Muslims are ambiguous when it comes to identifying the God to whom Muslims and Christians *refer* in their worship. And that brings me to the important distinction mentioned earlier, between the God we *actually* worship and the God we *say* we worship, between the God of our everyday practices and the God of our holy books and great teachers.

Practices disclose the God (or the gods!) individual Christians or Muslims *actually worship* better than anything they or their holy book says about God's character or God's commands! So, let's step away from words about God to consider the deeds.

Believing Rightly, Acting Wrongly

In the second half of the twentieth century, a debate about atheism was going on between the West and the world behind the "Iron Curtain." Both Christian theologians and Marxists participated in it. In this debate, the term "practical atheism," introduced by the French Catholic philosopher Jacques Maritain, played a role, partly to make "theoretical atheism" seem less threatening. "Theoretical atheists" are those who find the belief in God intellectually implausible and socially harmful; they deny the existence of God. "Practical atheists," according to Maritain, are those "who believe that they believe in God, but who in actual fact deny His existence by their deeds and the testimony of their behavior."[9] They intellectually affirm the existence of God, but live as if there were no God, often contrary to God's commandments. They *profess* the right God with their words, yet they deny God with their lives.

The term "practical atheism" may be relatively recent. The phenomenon itself, however, is as old as the belief in God itself. Recall the famous passage in Isaiah in which the prophet castigates those who participate in religious rituals, but fail to do God's will. In response to people's complaint that, although they fast and pray, God does not respond, Isaiah berates them, speaking on behalf of God:

> Look, you serve your own interests on your fast day,
> and oppress all your workers.
> Look, you fast only to quarrel and to fight
> and to strike with a wicked fist.
> Such fasting as you do today
> will not make your voice heard on high. . . .
> Is not this the fast that I choose:
> to loose the bonds of injustice,
> to undo the thongs of the yoke,
> to let the oppressed go free,
> and to break every yoke?
> Is it not to share your bread with the hungry,
> and bring the homeless poor into your house;
> when you see the naked, to cover them? (58:3–7)

When people disregard God's commands—especially the commands that concern justice for the powerless—and serve their own interests at the expense of others, they are not worshipping God. They can pray to the right God, they can fast as instructed, they can participate in prescribed religious rituals—and still not worship God. Doing justice is the "fast" God chooses, and without it any other form of fasting is simply not reaching God. The Qur'an has similar warnings: worship is not to turn piously "faces towards East or West," but to "believe in God" and to "spend out of your substance, out of love for Him, for your kin, for orphans, for the needy, for the wayfarer" (Al Baqarah, 2:177).

The New Testament echoes the prophets in this regard. "Those who say, 'I love God,' and hate their brothers or sisters, are liars," we read in 1 John (4:20). Whoever does not love their neighbor does not worship God. The reason is simple. As we have seen in the previous chapter, worship of God has two components: love of God and love of neighbor. The love of neighbor, whom we see, is the test of our love of God, whom we do not see (see 1 John 4:20). Not to love the neighbor means not to know God and not to love God and therefore not to worship God. The fifth-century church father Augustine, one of the most influential Christian theologians ever, put it well: "Whosoever therefore violates charity, let him say what he will with his tongue"—let him have all proper beliefs about Christ and God—he still denies Christ and "acts against God."[10]

A pattern of disobedience to God's commands tells you that a person is *not* worshipping the one true God. And it tells you more.

Believing the Right God, Serving the Wrong God

Jesus added a twist to Isaiah. It is not merely that religious people committing injustice aren't worshipping rightly and therefore aren't really worshipping God. They are, in fact, worshipping *a false god*. Jesus contrasted serving God and serving wealth, implying that, when people serve wealth, it becomes a god for them: "No one can serve two masters; for a slave will either hate the one and love the other, or be devoted to the one and despise the other. You cannot serve God and wealth" (Matt. 6:24). In the Letter to the Ephesians, the greedy person of the type described by the prophet Isaiah is explicitly called "an idolater"—a worshipper of a false god (5:5; see also Col. 3:5).

Martin Luther pushed the thought to its conclusion: wealth is just one of many things that can become a god. Explaining the first commandment, which says, "You shall have no other gods before me," Luther writes in his *Large Catechism*:

What does "to have a god" mean, or what is a god? Answer: A "god" is the term for that to which we are to look for all good and in which we are to find refuge in all need. Therefore, to have a god is nothing else than to trust and believe in that one with your whole heart.[11]

Seen from Luther's perspective, the term "practical atheism" is misleading, for it suggests that when people reject the true God, they live without any god. Most often, this is not the case. Something else, like money or power, becomes a god—a source of "all good" and "a refuge in all distress"—through the trust people place in it. For Luther, our god is not who we *say* our god is, but what we *make* to be our god by trusting it and loving it. That's why the pattern of our deeds doesn't just disclose what we aren't worshipping; it also indicates what we are worshipping.

Consider the Crusaders' capture of Jerusalem in June 1099, "on noonday hour on Friday, the day of the week when Christ redeemed the whole world on the cross," as Fulcher of Chartres, who accompanied the Crusaders to the Holy Land, writes. The purported servants of the Redeemer of the world had proven themselves to be merciless murderers on the very day of the week on which redemption was accomplished! "Nowhere was there a place where Saracens could escape the swordsmen," reports Fulcher, not even in Solomon's Temple. He continues:

> On the top of Solomon's Temple, to which they had climbed in fleeing, many were shot to death with arrows and cast down headlong from the roof. Within this Temple, about ten thousand were beheaded. If you had been there your feet would have been stained up to the ankles with the blood of the slain. What more shall I tell? Not one of them was allowed to live. They did not spare the women and children.[12]

What butchery! The Crusaders could have had all the right beliefs about God, and yet they in fact worshipped a very different god than the God who in Christ "was reconciling the world to himself" (2 Cor. 5:19)!

Now, next to this scene of cruel Crusaders from the Middle

Ages imagine a contemporary scene—a Muslim terrorist blowing himself up to kill and maim the innocent and spread uncertainty and fear. Are the Crusaders and the terrorist worshipping the same God? A Crusader shouts *Christus dominus* ("Christ is the Lord") while cleaving the head of an infidel. A terrorist shouts *Allahu Akhbar* ("God is the greatest") as he pulls the fuse of the bomb strapped around his waist. They are naming God very differently, and yet they are, alas, worshipping the same god—a bloodthirsty god of power, not the God of justice and mercy of the normative Christian and Muslim religious traditions. When it comes to practices, the fundamental issue is not whether Muslims and Christians worship the *same* God. It is whether they both worship the *true* God.

Deeds reveal which god we worship—the true God or a false god—better than words; and it matters little which god we profess to be worshipping. True convictions about the one true God can serve as sheep's clothing donned to hide a rapacious wolf god. Our god is known by our fruits.

Believing Wrongly, Worshipping Rightly

Is the opposite possible? Is it possible to worship the one true God with deeds while erroneously identifying God with words? A radical version of this possibility was seriously entertained during the Cold War in the debates about atheism to which I referred earlier. Some atheists, it was suggested, seem to lead more godly lives than many believers in the one true God; they worship God with their deeds, whereas ungodly theists—or "practical atheists"—deny God with their deeds. Whatever we decide about atheists as possible worshippers of the one true God, does this view make sense when applied to those who may be described as "deficient theists"—who believe in the one God, but do so in a flawed way? From a Christian standpoint, might it be that some Muslims (and some Christians!) who have a deficient view of God's nature and

God's commandments nonetheless worship the one true God by means of their godly lives? I think so.

In the previous chapter I argued that love of neighbor is worship of the one true God for the simple reason that it is the second of the two Great Commandments, which together sum up all of God's requirements for humanity. In this chapter I argued that deeds more accurately disclose the god people actually worship than do their words. Put the two together, and it follows that those who love their neighbors worship the one true God (though not knowing that God adequately, they may be doing so deficiently). This is not a statement about people's "eternal destiny" or "salvation," but about everyday acts that honor God, whether that honoring is done intentionally or not.

Consider a crucial passage about God and love from 1 John. Earlier, I examined the passage for what it says about the relation between God's nature and God's command to love neighbors (see chapter 5). Notice now what it says about the *origin* of love of neighbor:

> Beloved, let us love one another, because love is from God; everyone who loves is born of God and knows God. Whoever does not love does not know God, for God is love. . . . God is love, and those who abide in love abide in God, and God abides in them. (4:7–8, 16)

The passage is about love among Christians—the "beloved" who need to learn to love one another. But if "love is from God," then *all* genuine love is from God. Those who love love through God—in that they are born from God, in that God abides in them, in that God works through them. With God's help they do God's will. They may or may not be aware that they are doing God's will, or they may be able to articulate only very inadequately who God is and what God's will is. Yet if they love, they "know" God even without adequately acknowledging God; they worship God, without believing properly.

Does it then matter at all what people believe about God? It does. The same letter, which says that love of neighbor is a sign of true knowledge of God, also stresses the importance of correct belief. "Every spirit that does not confess Jesus is not from God," we read in 1 John 4:3. It is simple: error about God and Christ cannot be from God. And the error has consequences. Let's say that a person believes in the one true God, but thinks that all God's favors must be earned by strict obedience to the commands of a stern God. She may live in terror of God, whom she could never satisfy; and she may both have inordinate expectations of others and suffer under the compulsion to impress them. Correct beliefs matter, for those who believe and for their neighbors. Still, those who love do obey the second Great Commandment, and they worship the one true God, even if that worship may be deficient in many ways.

Saladin Versus the Crusaders

Return for a moment to the struggle of Christians and Muslims for rule over Jerusalem in the Middle Ages. We pick up the thread of the story almost a century after the Crusaders have sacked Jerusalem and killed all its Muslim inhabitants. In the year 1187, the Muslim ruler Salah ad-Din, or Saladin, recaptured Jerusalem. Unlike the Crusaders a century earlier, he spared its inhabitants' lives. He offered safe passage with all their possessions to those who could pay ransom—ten dinars for males, five for females, one for children. Those who could not pay the ransom were less fortunate; they became booty, to be sold or killed.

Commenting on Saladin's offer, a Christian eyewitness wrote, "This agreement pleased the lord Patriarch and the others who had money." What about those who did not have money? "Crowds throughout the city wailed in sorrowful tones: 'Woe, woe to us miserable people! We have no gold! What are we to do?'" Significantly, the anger of the poor was not directed against Saladin, but against the wealthy fellow Christians who would not help their poor coreligionists. The same eyewitness commented, "Alas, by the hands of wicked Christians Jerusalem was turned over to the wicked."[13] The "wicked Christians" looked even worse after Saladin, their enemy and conqueror, released one thousand of the poor residents without ransom.[14] Given this report, did Saladin not come nearer to worshipping the one true God than did the Crusaders who took Jerusalem a century earlier?

Notwithstanding Saladin's widely admired nobility, in initial Christian reports he, the enemy, was portrayed as a wicked villain. However, gradually over the centuries, he was transformed in the Western imagination into an adoptive hero.[15] The case in point is Gotthold Lessing's play *Nathan the Wise* (1779). Ensconced as the ruler of Jerusalem, Lessing's Saladin is the very incarnation of magnanimity and generosity. Poverty made people into beggars, and Saladin so strongly hates the humiliations beggars have to endure that, as his treasurer bitterly complains, he helps them to the point of having "to become a beggar himself."[16] For the sake of argument—we are not talking history now—let's assume that Lessing's portrayal is correct. Imagine, moreover, that in other ways as well Saladin led a life of righteousness; he practiced the kind of love that "does no wrong to a neighbor" and is therefore, as the apostle Paul says, "the fulfilling of the law" (Rom. 13:10). Would we not have to say that in loving his neighbors Saladin was, in fact, worshipping the one true God? After all, such love is the second requirement of the proper worship of the one true God.

As a Muslim, it is likely that Saladin would have explicitly denied that God is the Holy Trinity and that Jesus Christ died on the cross for the sin of the world. Why would his inadequate convictions about God transform his love of neighbor from worship of the one true God into something ignoble? How could his convictions have that effect, when the only possible source of that love is the same God who commanded it? To the extent that people love their neighbors, they worship the one true God, even if their understanding of God is inadequate and their worship is seriously lacking in other regards.

What do people's practices tell us about their worship of God?

1. A pattern of wrong practices overshadows correct beliefs about God and exposes those who engage in them as worshippers of false gods.
2. Wrong beliefs about God do not invalidate right practices as worship required by God.

As indicators of the god people actually worship, both good and evil deeds tower over beliefs. With their deeds, people can worship both the false gods of this world and the one true God.

Same God?

Let me sum up my argument so far. My original question was, "Do Christians and Muslims worship the same God?" In trying to answer the question, I distinguished between "referring to the same object with a similar character" (discussed in chapters 4 and 5) and "actually worshipping" (discussed in the present chapter). The summary of my findings, reached from a Christian perspective, therefore has two parts:

1. *To the extent that* Christians and Muslims embrace the normative teachings of Christianity and Islam about God, they believe in a common God.
2. *To the extent that* Christians and Muslims strive to love God and neighbor, they *worship* that same true God.

No simple yes or no is possible in answering the question of whether Muslims and Christians worship the same God. Some do and some don't. If we were to leave it at that, the result of our long study would admittedly be rather meager. But there is a robust and very important yes to be said as well. All Christians have solid reasons to affirm two things:

1. The God of whom their holy book and their great religious teachers speak is the same God of whom the holy book and the great religious teachers of Muslims speak.

2. That God requires Muslims and Christians to obey strikingly similar commands as an expression of their worship.

Are there then no important differences between the God of the Qur'an and the God of the Bible, the God of the normative tradition of Islam and that of Christianity? Yes there are. Two of these differences concern the very core of the Christian faith—the Christian claims that God is the Holy Trinity and that God is love. I discuss these differences as well as similarities the next three chapters (chapters 7–9).

Assume for a moment that there are no deal-breaking disagreements over God as the Holy Trinity and God as love, at least as far as Christians are concerned. Under this assumption, the normative Islamic and the normative Christian traditions urge the adherents of these two faiths to believe in and worship the same God. Of course, we will still find differences in Christian and Muslim understandings of God. The differences that exist *between* Muslim and Christian understandings of God are then loosely analogous to the corresponding differences that exist *within* the Christian and Muslims faiths. Now the question arises, if the God Muslims and Christians worship is the same, does that mean that the way of Muhammad is the same as the way of Christ? Or are Islam and Christianity simply two different but equally good paths to the same God? Or is one of them the only true faith? I explore this issue in chapter 10.

But even now, before discussing God as the Trinity and God as love and before deciding on whether the way of Christ and the way of Muhammad are two versions of the same religion, we can affirm one important thing with confidence. The conclusion that we have already reached provides a solid foundation for Christians and Muslims to engage with one another in fruitful public debate about human flourishing and the common good and to practice the solidarity necessary for living peacefully in a common world. More on this in chapters 12 and 13.

PART III

Critical Themes: The Trinity and Love

CHAPTER SEVEN

The One God and the Holy Trinity

In the fall of 2008, I spent an afternoon at the home of one of the Muslim world's most prominent clerics, Sheikh Habib Ali al-Jifri. Joined by David Ford, professor of theology at Cambridge University, we discussed a number of topics, but foremost among them was the problem of violence in the Qur'an and the Bible. Like most Muslims, Sheikh al-Jifri was concerned that many non-Muslims, especially in the West, consider Islam an irredeemably violent religion. The gist of his argument in response to critics of Islam was that violence in the Qur'an is always tied to a just cause. It is never indiscriminate and never directed against noncombatants, women, and children.

In highlighting the connection between violence and justice, Sheikh al-Jifri offered guidelines for interpreting passages in the Qur'an that deal with violence—say, for instance, the famous "Verse of the Sword" (Al Tawbah, 9:5) about slaying pagans wherever one finds them.[1] But there was a polemical sting to his comments as well. He intended to favorably contrast the Qur'an with the Bible, in which God commands whole peoples to be wiped out, such as the Amalekites (see Deut. 25:17–19) or the peoples exterminated in the course of the conquest of Canaan (Josh. 8:23–25).[2] We went back and forth on the issue, and Professor Ford and I explained that all Christians consider Christ's command to love our enemies (Matt. 5:43–44) to abrogate the injunctions to obliterate entire nations.

The discussion on violence was involved and illuminating, but I didn't get to explore with Sheikh al-Jifri the question of greatest interest to me. As we left his home and began driving to meet with the minister of higher culture, I decided to raise my question, even if only briefly.

"Do you think that Muslims and Christians worship the same God?"

Sheik al-Jifri answered without hesitation: "Yes, they do. In the Qur'an it is written: 'Our God and your God is One.'"

"But Christians believe that God is the Holy Trinity, and Muslims disagree. How do you then still affirm that the two worship the same God?" I pressed him.

He smiled enigmatically and said, "What the archbishop of Canterbury wrote about the Trinity in his response to the 'Common Word' was very helpful."

Only a few months previously, in July of that year, Dr. Rowan Williams, the archbishop of Canterbury, had published a response to the Muslim "A Common Word." A highly prominent church leader and one of the great theologians of today, he titled the letter "A Common Word for the Common Good." "God exists in a threefold pattern of interdependent action," he wrote there, referring to the Father, the Son, and the Holy Spirit. But Christians, he insisted, uncompromisingly affirm that "there is only one divine nature and reality."[3]

"The archbishop is a great and creative theologian," I responded to Sheikh al-Jifri, "but he said nothing new in his comments on God as the Holy Trinity."

"Yes?" he inquired. There was a note of mild surprise and curiosity in his voice. In his lecture at Yale University some six months earlier, Sheikh al-Jifri had stressed that Muslims "do not believe that God, mighty and majestic is He, can be divided."[4] He seemed to imply, of course, that Christians do. I wanted to reassure him that Christians and Muslims agree on this point.

"After the early centuries of intense debates, Christians have come to affirm what some theologians have described as 'the numerical identity of the divine substance,'" I continued, knowing full well that the phrase is inexact, but wishing to underscore an important and valid point. "For us, the divine 'three' are one single and undivided divine essence, not three divine essences next to each other comprising some kind of a divine troika."

I could not read his expression, but I sensed gravity in his manner as he slowly turned to face me. "Miroslav," he asked, "do you have time after the dinner to discuss this matter with me and my collaborators at the Tabah Foundation?" An immensely learned scholar of Islam and a spiritually attuned man, he knew that we had touched the heart of the matter. Was a way opening up toward convergence about one of the main issues dividing Muslims and Christians?

My flight was scheduled to leave early the next morning from Dubai, an hour and a half away from Abu Dhabi. But I agreed. After dinner, we stayed up late into the night discussing the intricacies of the doctrine of the Trinity. At the center of our discussion was a simple but vexing question: "Is the claim that God is the Holy One compatible with the claim that God is the Holy Trinity?"

The oneness of God (*tawhid*) is the principle at the very heart of Islam. This is *the* central issue for Muslims disputing Christian claims about God. The reason is simple: if the Father, Son, and Holy Spirit cannot be understood as one, according to Muslim interpretations of God's unity, then Muslims and Christians do not worship the same God. With the word "God" they may be referring, in a general way, to the same divine reality—that one entity that is not the world but that created the world—but they would not be having a common God. Christians would be worshipping three gods or, at best, one true God and two idols in addition to God. This would be what Muslims call *shirk*, the unforgivable, blasphemous sin of associating other beings with God. Let's look more closely at this Muslim unease about the Trinity and use it as an occasion to elucidate how Christians understand the trinitarian nature of God.

"A Trinity of Gods?"

Recall the dispute in Malaysia about whether Christians were permitted to use "Allah" as a designation for the God they worship
(see chapter 4). Many practical issues of the coexistence of diverse
communities were at stake, but the problem of the Trinity was
central in the government's case against Christian use of the word
"Allah." Government lawyers argued that the two groups worship
different deities, because Christians recognize a "trinity of gods,"
whereas Islam is "totally monotheistic." Because "Allah" denotes
one single God, they argued, Christians should not use it to denote
a "trinity of gods."

The government's case depended on highlighting the differences between the God Christians and Muslims worship. In order
to do this, the lawyers grossly oversimplified the issue by maintaining that Christians believe in a trinity of gods, whereas Muslims
worship one God. However, the idea that Christians worship more
than one god was not merely invented to win a court case. Many
sophisticated Muslim religious scholars, even those who are familiar with Christianity and friendly to Christians, suspect that Christians aren't true monotheists. Christians *affirm* one God, while at
the same time insisting that there are three divine Persons, each
worthy of worship.

Consider the Athanasian Creed, one of the most robust Christian statements about God as the Holy Trinity, approved by the
great majority of Christian churches and read in many congrega-
tions in public worship on Trinity Sunday.[5] At the very beginning
it states plainly: "We worship one God." But it does not leave it at
that. The full first line of the section about God reads: "We worship one God in the Trinity and the Trinity in unity, neither blending the persons nor dividing the essence."

Who are the "Persons" whom Christians ought not to blend?
They are the Father, Son, and Holy Spirit. And how are they related? The "person of the Father is a distinct person, the person of

the Son is another, and that of the Holy Spirit still another." Each of the three is uncreated, each immeasurable, each eternal, each almighty; in a word, "each is God." Does the creed speak of three gods, then? It does not. Clearly and repeatedly it states what Christians have affirmed throughout the ages:

> There are not three eternal beings, there is but one eternal being; so too there are not three uncreated or immeasurable beings; there is but one uncreated and immeasurable being.... [And] there are not three almighty beings; there is but one almighty being.... [And] there are not three gods; there is but one God.

So the creed says two things at once: "Each is God" and "There is but one God." To a Muslim (or a Jewish) ear this sounds like asserting that there are in fact three gods, but calling them one! Except for the opening assertion, "We worship one God," it would seem, to quote Aref Nayed, director of Kalam Research and Media in Dubai, that a Muslim "cannot accept, and must actually reject the entire Creed"![6]

Just why must a Muslim reject what the Athanasian Creed says about God? The creed, the response goes, seems incompatible with the central Muslim claim that there is "no god but God." Moreover, the Qur'an seems to condemn directly the kinds of beliefs the creed advocates. Consider the following texts from the Qur'an:

1. "They say: 'God hath begotten a son.' Glory be to Him—nay to Him belongs all that is in the heavens and on earth: everything renders worship to Him. To Him is due the primal origin of the heavens and the earth: When He decreeth a matter, He saith to it: 'Be,' and it is." (Al Baqarah, 2:116–17)

2. "Say: 'O People of the Book! Come to common terms as between us and you: that we worship none but God; that we associate no partners with him; that we erect not, from among ourselves, Lords and patrons other than God.' If then

they turn back, say ye: 'Bear witness that we (at least) are Muslims (bowing to God's Will).'" (Al 'Imran, 3:64)

3. "They do blaspheme who say: God is one of three in a Trinity: for there is no god except One God. If they desist not from their word (of blasphemy), verily a grievous penalty will befall the blasphemers among them." (Al Ma'idah, 5:73)

4. "They do blaspheme who say: '(God) is Christ the son of Mary.' But said Christ: 'O Children of Israel! Worship God, my Lord and your Lord.' Whoever joins other gods with God—God will forbid him the garden, and the Fire will be his abode. There will for the wrong-doers be no one to help." (Al Ma'idah, 5:72)

5. "They take their priests and their anchorites to be their lords in derogation of God, and (they take as their Lord) Christ the son of Mary; yet they were commanded to worship but One God: there is no god but He. Praise and glory to Him. (Far is He) from having the partners they associate (with Him))." (Al Tawbah, 9:31)

Obedient to the Qur'an, Muslims, so it seems, must reject what Christians appear to affirm: that God has a son, that other gods should be joined to God, that God is one of the three divine beings, and that it is appropriate to worship those other beings in addition to God. From this vantage point, it looks as if Christians worship false gods.

Muslims are not alone in doubting the legitimacy of Christian monotheism. Many Jews also hold a similar view. To take one prominent example, Maimonides (1138–1204), the profoundly influential medieval Jewish thinker, seems to have considered Christians idolaters and their affirmation of the three Persons of the Trinity a form of polytheism, for they "declare unity," but "assume plurality."[7] Judaism and Islam more or less agree in considering the Christian claim to monotheism spurious.

Responses

Maimonides did not have extensive contact with Christians, and he did not give reasons for his position. The founder of Islam, however, did have contact with Christianity, and as we have seen above, the Qur'an contains explicit references to and criticism of Christian views. So let's take up the central claims of the Qur'anic passages above and see how each relates to what Christianity's creeds and great teachers mean when they speak about the trinitarian nature of God.

1. *Objection:* The God who creates the heavens and the earth by the power of the Word cannot be said to have begotten a son or anyone who is strictly like God.

   Response: The issue here is the meaning of the word "begotten," not the substance of our understanding of God. Christians do *not* think of "begetting" when applied to God as a physical act between male and female divinity. Speaking for the whole of the Christian tradition, Gregory of Nyssa (d. 385 or 386), one of the most prominent Eastern church fathers, wrote: "The divine is neither male nor female (for how could such a thing be contemplated in divinity)?"[8] Moreover, "begetting" in God does not result in an offspring spatially distinct or in any way independent from God, a godlike being or another god. "Begetting"—or "eternal generation," as the technical term goes—is a *metaphor* used to express the idea that the Word, which was from eternity with God, is neither a creature nor some sort of lesser divinity, but is the very uncreated God. The exact point of using the term "begotten" and distinguishing the generation of the Son from an act of creation—"begotten, not made," as the Nicene Creed affirms—is to insist that the eternal Word or Son is not a being next to God, but is of one essence with God.[9]

2. *Objection:* God cannot have an associate joined to God, any equal or lesser divinity next to God.

   Response: Exactly right. When Christians speak of "Father, Son, and Holy Spirit," writes Archbishop Williams, summarizing traditional Christian convictions, they "do not mean one God with two beings alongside him." There are not three divine beings, but one divine being—"the Living and Self-subsistent, associated with no other."[10]

3. *Objection:* God is not one of three divine beings in the Trinity.

   Response: Again, exactly right. When Christians speak of the three in God, they do not mean "three gods of limited power," writes the archbishop.[11] The Athanasian Creed makes the same point by saying the divine essence is "not divided." To divide the divine essence in any way is to slip into polytheism, which Christians reject.

4. *Objection:* God cannot be "Christ, the son of Mary," because then God would be a creature, in need of food and shelter, not the sovereign creator of heaven and earth, beyond all needs.

   Response: Christians generally do *not* say that God was Christ; I know of no significant classical theologian who makes that claim.[12] Instead, Christians say that "Christ was God" (or, to use New Testament phrases, "God was *in* Christ" [see 2 Cor. 5:19] or the eternal "Word became flesh" [John 1:14]). The two claims—that God was Christ, and Christ was God— seem similar, but are in fact very different. Christians believe that Christ was fully human, and therefore in need of food and shelter, as well as fully divine, and therefore of one undivided essence with God.[13]

5. *Objection:* Christians worship persons they associate with God in denigration of the one true God.

   Response: Christians agree that anyone who worships a

human being does so in denigration of God; that person is an idolater. Christians reject worshipping Christ or anyone else *in place of* God. In worshipping Christ, whom they consider to be fully divine, they are worshipping the one and undivided divine essence.

The critical issue in all these objections is this: Do Christians, their explicit statements to the contrary notwithstanding, divide the divine essence in the way they speak about God? The great medieval Muslim commentator Fakhr al-Din al-Razi (1149–1209) thought that Christians did just that. With the doctrine of the Trinity, he said, Christians are "actually affirming the existence of several 'self-subsisting essences.'" This is, from the Muslim perspective, "pure unbelief,"[14] he insisted. "Pure unbelief" at the heart of the Christian faith! That's just about as far apart as two religions could be, despite all their similarities. And yet, contrary to al-Razi's opinion, I suggest that there is actual agreement on this very issue.

Even from the Christian perspective, affirming the existence of multiple self-subsisting divine essences is polytheism and "pure unbelief." That is why the Athanasian Creed unambiguously and repeatedly states that "dividing the divine essence" is unacceptable. A basic rule for Christians as they speak about God is this: "Never divide divine essence." This rule must not be broken when talking about God as the Holy Trinity. A positive way to make the same point would be to say that Christians affirm the "numerical identity of the divine essence." This is the phrase I used in my conversation with Sheikh al-Jifri, and he immediately recognized it as addressing the crux of the tension between Christian and Muslim conceptions of God's unity.

Recall the crisply formulated conclusion that Nicholas of Cusa reached after examining Muslim and Jewish critiques of the doctrine of the Trinity: "In the manner in which Arabs [Muslims] and Jews deny the Trinity, assuredly it ought to be denied by all."[15] The Christian creeds and the great Christian teachers reject dividing the divine essence no less adamantly than do Muslims and Jews. Seyyed Hossein Nasr, a preeminent contemporary Muslim scholar, agrees: "The doctrine of the Trinity certainly does not negate Divine Unity in mainstream Christian theology."[16]

Now, there is a difference—sometimes even a great difference—between tenets of normative religion and the actual beliefs of ordinary people. All religions are beset by such discrepancies, and Christianity is no exception. The beliefs of some Christians can be contrary to what Christian creeds and the great Christian teachers advocate. As with all religions, some Christian believers are religiously illiterate or simply mistaken; they know as much about their faith as the average nonscientist knows about astrophysics or neuroscience. In statements that address the doctrine of the Trinity, the Qur'an may well be targeting the beliefs of such Christians,[17] for what the Qur'an rejects in this regard, Christians ought to reject as well.

Undivided Acts

"False victory!" a Muslim critic may cry out. "The agreement you have sketched about God's unity is nothing but mere words. Just listen to the way you talk about how God acts in the world, and the agreement will disappear like dense fog under the sun's warm rays. If you claim that the 'Son' was incarnate, but the 'Father' was not, then have you not in fact divided the Trinity? At best, you are confused; you say you reject dividing the divine essence, but you actually divide it by your belief that Christ was both God and man. You are simultaneously saying two contradictory things, namely, that the divine essence is undivided and that the divine 'Persons' are distinct. At worst, you are disingenuous; to soothe your guilty monotheistic conscience (or maybe even to mislead Muslims and Jews), you put up a good front by insisting that God's essence cannot be divided. But behind the scenes, you actually believe in three gods. Come clean! Either give up on God's unity or reject the Trinity. You can't have it both ways."

Clearly, it is one thing to reject dividing the divine essence, and another thing actually to avoid dividing it (just as it is one thing to condemn sin and another thing not to commit it). So how do Christians actually keep the divine essence undivided? In addition to stating clearly that there is only one "numerically" identical divine essence, they note that the "Persons" are tied and intertwined together in a most intimate manner, more intimate than any relation between creatures could ever be.

There are two related ways of understanding this intimate connection between the divine Three who are indivisibly one. First, when God acts "toward the outside"—creating, redeeming, and bringing the world to completion—*God's acts* are *undivided, inseparable*. Every act of one "Person" is always caused by all three. If this were not the case, then, as Augustine put it, "the Father [would do] some things, the Son others and the Holy Spirit yet others."[18] And this would be utterly unacceptable, he explicitly states. It would verge on polytheism.

The second way to think how the divine "Persons" are tied together is their *mutual indwelling* or, in technical terminology, *perichoresis*. Again, as Augustine put it, "they are always in each other" and never "alone."[19] One divine "Person" is what it is, not simply in virtue of being distinct from others, but in virtue of the presence of the other two "Persons" in it. The Father and the Spirit are always "in" the Son; to be the "Son" *is* to be indwelled by the Father and the Spirit. Two consequences follow:

1. With regard to the *identity* of divine Persons, you cannot simply say, "To be one is not to be the other," as you can say of creatures, including human beings. When it comes to God, "not to be the same" does not mean "to be other," and "to be other" does not mean "not to be the same," as Nicholas of Cusa rightly noted (see chapter 2).
2. With regard to the *activity* of divine Persons, you cannot say that the act of one is the act of that Person alone, as you must say of human beings. When it comes to God, the act of one

Person is always done by all three, because the other two are
always "in" the third. When human beings act together, they
join forces, each acting separately toward the common goal
(as when three persons are pushing a car). It is different with
God. The three divine "Persons" never need to join forces,
because when one acts, the other two are in that "Person" and
act through it.

For al-Razi the proof that Christians putatively "affirm one
[divine] essence," but in reality posit three divine "essences," is
that "they deem it possible for one of these essences to inhere in
the person of Jesus and of Mary."[20] If Christians truly considered
the divine essence to be indivisible, then it could not be that one
"Person," the Word, would have become incarnate in Jesus Christ;
rather, all three would have become incarnate. To have the incarnation of just one of the Persons, argues al-Razi, you need more than
one divine essence. Incarnation is therefore an irrefutable proof of
Christian polytheism.

Is his argument valid? Not if we affirm that the three "Persons" mutually indwell each other or that God's acts toward all
that is outside God are undivided. These affirmations resolve the
problem of dividing the divine essence. It is not that one divine
"Person" inheres in Jesus, while the other two continue to remain
together in "heaven." Rather, the one God, in the "Person" of
the Word, becomes incarnate. According to John's Gospel, "the
Word became flesh," the Word, that is, which both "was God"
and was "with God" (John 1:1–2, 14). And yet it was not "the
Word" alone that dwelled in Jesus. Using metaphorical terminology of "fatherhood" and "sonship," in John's Gospel Jesus claims:
"The Father is in me and I am in the Father" (10:38). The same is
true of the Spirit, who is said to "remain" on, and therefore act in
and through, the Incarnate One (see John 1:33–34). Though only
one Person is incarnate, all three Persons are present and act in
that one Person who became incarnate. This is the consequence
of saying that the "Persons" of the Trinity "mutually indwell"

one another. Thus, the incarnation doesn't require any division of God's essence.[21]

Beyond Concepts

Much of the confusion about the Trinity is terminological; it concerns the words we use to describe God, who is in many ways beyond words and beyond thought. The problems with the terms "begetting" and "Son"—which suggest that God might have a carnal offspring—to which I referred earlier, are two examples. "Person" is another.

Christians use the term "Person" to describe the Father, the Son, and the Spirit. This is a *very* different use of "person" than in our ordinary language. By "persons" we ordinarily mean individuals who are separate, but related to other individuals; in al-Razi's terminology, human persons are "self-subsisting essences." No such separation is conceivable in the one God! Divine "Persons" are not like human persons, only magnified to superhuman proportions. To avoid confusion over precisely that issue, many theologians counsel against the use of the word "Person" to refer to one of the three in God.[22] We might be able to put it this way. Christian tradition uses the word "Person" not because it expresses exactly what Christians believe, but because there is no word more adequate to speak of the three in God. So we use the word, knowing we must mentally adjust its meaning when it refers to God.

A Muslim critic might respond: "Those are just the kinds of difficulties you get yourself into when you affirm the Trinity; then you have to use words like 'begetting,' 'Son,' and 'Person,' but can't use them properly like everybody else does." But now it may be my turn to suggest that this would be a false victory, for our difficulties in speaking of God would not go away if God were not the Holy Trinity. *All* words we use of God—such as "sustainer" and "master" or "gracious" and "merciful" (Al Fatihah, 1:1–4)—are inadequate. Why? Augustine explains: "Because the total transcendence of the godhead quite surpasses the capacity of ordinary speech."[23] The words paint a picture or tell a story, so to speak, but the picture or the story is always more dissimilar than it is similar to who God truly is.[24] God is uncreated and infinite. Therefore God is inexpressible, beyond our concepts, beyond our language.

The talk of "Persons" captures something important about God, but is inadequate to express the full reality, because God transcends the notion of "person," as we have seen. The same is true of "essence," "goodness," "love"—all to varying degrees correct and true when referring to God, but all also deeply inadequate. The very reality of God is such that God always remains inconceivable, a mystery that can never be properly named or puzzled out. And yet we speak of God—guided by God's self-revelation. We have true knowledge of God, but we are capable of understanding much better what the divine Mystery is *not* than what that Mystery is.[25] Important strands in all three Abrahamic faiths agree on this.[26]

Beyond Numbers

When I was a student of philosophy at the University of Zagreb, then still in Communist Yugoslavia, one of my professors was an atheist philosopher and a critic of Christianity. He was a well-known intellectual, but not a very profound thinker. In one of his lectures he engaged Christian convictions about God, and my nineteen-year-old ears could not believe that anyone with any knowledge of the Christian tradition would actually say what he said.

"It's very simple," he said, trying to display the absurdity of the doctrine of the Trinity and clinch his argument. "One plus one plus one can never be one." The audience was nodding with self-satisfied approval. I've heard Muslim critics make the same argument. But for my professor, Christian "bad math" was yet another indication that the God in whom Christians believe does not exist; whereas for a Muslim critic it does not invalidate the claim that God exists, but merely serves as proof that the doctrine of the Trinity is false.

"Right," I thought sarcastically. "If I just hadn't skipped kindergarten math, I'd now be counted among the smart ones who reject the absurdities of Christianity."

And yet, I could not brush aside my professor's simplistic remark that easily. I thought of my nanny, a simple and uneducated Christian woman who radiated saintly joy. If I had asked her, "Teta (Aunt) Milica, you and I believe that God is one and that God is the Holy Trinity. But how can one plus one plus one be one?" she would have simply shrugged her shoulders in lightly embarrassed but unperturbed simplicity and said, "It's a mystery. We won't know the answer until we see God face to face."

In refusing to try to account for such paradoxical arithmetic, did she simply prove my professor's point? She did not. What she could not fully appreciate and my professor failed to note is how different God is from any creature, how profoundly mysterious God is. Recall the argument of Nicholas of Cusa that God is not just beyond concepts, but also *beyond numbers*. "One" and "three" do not apply to God the way they apply to human beings or to any other thing in the world. Denys Turner, a philosopher and historian of medieval thought, puts it this way:

> Suppose, in the conduct of some quite lunatic thought-experiment you were to imagine counting the total number of things that there are, have ever been, and will be, and you get to the number n. Then I say: "Fine, that's the universe enumerated, but you have left out just one being, the being who made all that vast number of things that is the universe, namely, God," and, because you are not an atheist, you agree that this is so. Do you now add God to the list? Is that what I am asking you to do? Does the total number of things that there are now amount to n + 1?[27]

The answer is no. "God's oneness is not such that God is one *more* in any numerable series whatever."[28] God is not one thing among many other things in the universe, not even one supremely important thing without which none of the other things could exist. Instead, God is unique and categorically different from the world. We always go wrong when we employ numbers with regard to God the way we employ them with regard to created things.

Yet you can't remove math from God entirely. To say that there is one undivided divine essence excludes, for instance, the option that there are eighteen gods, the number of Titans in the Greek pantheon. But "one" does not mean that, instead of there being eighteen gods, there is only one god belonging to the same category as all eighteen would, if they existed. Then we would be reducing the one true God to an idol—a unique idol, but an idol nonetheless—because God would still be one "entity" in the world. Monotheism would be then indistinguishable from idolatry. Instead, to affirm that that there is one God means that there is only one, unique, and incomparable divine being, on a different plane of existence from everything that is not God.[29]

Consider, now, the "three" in God. To say that there are three "Persons" in the Trinity excludes, for instance, the option that there are twelve, the number of Olympians in the Greek pantheon. It excludes also the option that there is only one. But it does not say that, instead of there being either twelve or one distinct and separate individual essences in God, there are exactly three such individual essences, for, in fact, there are *no* individual essences *in* God. Instead, to say that there are three "Persons" in God means only that there are three eternal, inseparable, and interpenetrating agencies; in each, the other two are present, and in each, the single divine essence is present.

Numbers don't work the same way with regard to God that they do with regard to created realities. And if we try to make them work in the same way, we gravely distort our conception of God. That's as true of "one" and it is of "three." And it's as true for Muslims as it is for Christians.

The Same God, Without the Trinity?

I hope that the arguments presented so far will be plausible to Muslims and Christians alike. With regard to Muslims, however, my purpose here is not to persuade them that God indeed is the Holy Trinity. I have not offered a single argument in favor of this cardinal Christian belief. My purpose is more modest: to demonstrate that the rejections of the "Trinity" in the Qur'an do not refer to normative Christian understanding of God's threeness, and that the Christian doctrine of the Trinity does not call into question God's oneness as expressed in Muslims' most basic belief that there is "no god but God." What the Qur'an may be targeting is misconceptions about God's nature held by misguided Christians.

The discussion above is directed not primarily to Muslims, but to Christians. This entire book is about what Christians should think about the issue, not what Muslims should think. My goal is to remind Christians that Muslim objections to the doctrine of the Trinity and the uncompromising affirmation of God's oneness from which these objections stem are not, in themselves, good enough reasons for *Christians* to think that they have a radically different understanding of God than Muslims. Unity of God doesn't separate Muslims from Christians; it binds them together.

In short, with regard to God's unity:

1. Christians deny what Muslims deny. And together with Muslims they can say there is "no god but God" (Muhammad, 47:19), because the first of the Ten Commandments says, "You shall have no other gods before me" (Exod. 20:3).
2. Christians affirm what Muslims affirm. And together with Muslims they can say, "God is one and only" (Al Ikhlas, 112:1), because Jesus, echoing the Jewish Shema (Deut. 6:4), affirmed that "the Lord our God, the Lord is one" (Mark 12:29).

But Muslims—even those who believe that Christians do not compromise God's unity—still reject the claim that God is the Trinity. Without coming to agreement on the question of the divine trinitarian nature, can we truly say that the God Muslims and Christians worship is the same God?

Let's rephrase the question to make it more general. If those with whom Christians share the belief in God's oneness fail to affirm that God is the Holy Trinity, do they still believe in the same God as do Christians? Consider religious Jews. They deny the doctrine of the Trinity. Moreover, many Jews think, as the great Maimonides did, that Christians are idolaters because they are trinitarians. They therefore conclude that Christians do not have the same God as the Jews do.[30]

Do Christians likewise conclude that Jews do not have the same God they do? Overwhelmingly they do not. Neither Jewish rejection of the doctrine of the Trinity nor the accusation that Christians are idolaters has led Christians to assert that Jews believe in a different God! That would turn *Jews* into idolaters. But how could Christians possibly accuse the Jews of idolatry? New Testament writers, mostly Jews, assumed consistently that the God of the Hebrew scriptures and the God of their fellow Jews was the very same God they worshipped. Similarly, throughout Christian history, only declared heretics taught that the true God was different from the God of the Hebrew scriptures, as in the case of the Marcionites and the Cathars.[31] From the Christian side, the debate with Jews was about how to describe God properly (whether to do so in trinitarian terms or not) and how to worship God truly (whether God should be worshipped through Christ or not). The debate with Jews was *never* whether Jews and Christians worshipped the same God.

Let's shift now from Jews to Muslims. Religiously speaking, Christians generally relate to Muslims differently from the way they relate to Jews. But my question here is a narrow one: If Muslims deny that God is the Holy Trinity, does it follow that they therefore worship a different God from Christians? The Muslim critique of the doctrine of the Trinity is no more radical than the Jewish critique. Moreover, on the whole, Muslims are more hesitant than Jews to describe Christians as idolaters and to contest the idea that Christians worship the same God Muslims do. The Qur'an states clearly that the God of all the People of the Book—Muslims, Jews, *and* Christians—is one and the same (Al 'Ankabut, 29:46). Christians should treat the Muslim rejection of the Trinity the same way they treat the Jewish critique. If, as I have argued in chapters 5 and 6, we have other good reasons to believe that Muslims have a common God with Christians, then their denial of the Trinity doesn't provide sufficient grounds to say that Muslims don't believe in the same God. Instead, by rejecting the Trinity, Muslims, we might argue, are misunderstanding the true nature of God. That's why this debate about the question of the Trinity, though important, is not as fundamental for Christians as it is for Muslims.

Is, then, the doctrine of the Trinity an optional add-on to other, more essential convictions about God—like a set of extras on a car? Do Jews and Muslims have a stripped-down, unitarian version of God, while Christians have a "fully loaded" trinitarian version of the same God? No, that doesn't work. The doctrine of the Trinity is central to the Christian account of God and to the Christian faith as a whole, not an optional extra. Take away the trinitarian nature of God, and the Christian belief about Christ as the incarnation of God collapses, and, with it, the whole Christian faith. The most representative and widely used creed among Christians in the past and today is the Nicene-Constantinopolitan Creed (381). It is fully and normatively trinitarian—the result of centuries-long debates precisely on how to hold together the undivided unity of divine essence while affirming the trinitarian nature of God. The Trinity is not an add-on; it is the full reality of the one God who, Christians affirm, can be worshipped, but only inadequately without reference to God's trinitarian nature.

Those very debates about God and God's trinitarian nature may provide something of a model for how to handle the disagreements between Muslims (and Jews) and Christians about the Trinity. The early Christian trinitarian debates were *not* about which of the following different gods is the true God and worthy of worship:

1. Sabellius's God: the one who is a single being with three divine names and three modes of divine manifestation, Father, Son, and Holy Spirit.[32]
2. Arius's God: the one who, as the Father, has created the Son to mediate between the One and the universe.[33]
3. Athanasius's God: the one existing as the Father, the Son, and the Spirit, in three ways of being, which are genuinely distinct, but share the same divine substance.[34]

Different as these description are—some of them, like that of Arius, are not too far from what Muslims believe about God— they were not considered to be descriptions of three different gods. Rather, they were considered three different, and hotly contested, descriptions of one and the same God. In other words, the debates were not about which god was the true God, but which description of the one true God was correct.

I suggest that we understand the debates between Muslims and Christians about the nature of God in a similar way. They are about how to describe truthfully the one God in whom both believe.

Why the Trinity?

In the course of that late evening at the Tabah Foundation, after Sheik al-Jifri, his colleagues, Professor Ford and I had explored the unity of divine essence and how the distinctions between divine "Persons" are related to it, Sheikh al-Jifri wanted to know why. Why not embrace the grand and elegant simplicity of the unitary God as believed by Jews and Muslims? Why do Christians affirm the three divine "Persons"—and then have to contend with complications of still holding on to the one undivided divine essence?

At one level, the answer is simple. Christians have come to

believe that God was in Jesus Christ reconciling the world to its divine source and goal (see 2 Cor. 5:19). If you embark on the path that starts with this simple claim, it will ultimately lead to the affirmation of the trinitarian nature of God. Whole libraries have been written about various stages along that path. I need not rehearse here the history of that slow and painstaking doctrinal progress, with many stops, detours, and returns to places already left behind.[35] Here, what matters is that Christ as the self-revelation of God is the reason why Christians affirm the trinitarian nature of God. Once you put it that way, you see how essential the Trinity is to the Christian faith.

I have noted briefly what gave rise to the doctrine of the Trinity. Let's push the question of why just a bit farther, by exploring what is at stake in affirming it. At stake, above all, are two things. The first concerns the *knowledge of God*. To know God truly, it does not suffice to have accurate information about God, to be able to describe God adequately. We need to encounter God at a level deeper than the cognitive one. It takes two things for this to happen:

1. God, while in no way compromising God's divinity, has to *come* to human beings *as* God.
2. Human beings, limited as they are, need to *perceive* God *as* God.

Only God truly knows God. Only God can reveal God adequately. Only God can perceive God adequately. From these simple observations some great Christian thinkers, like Søren Kierkegaard[36] and Karl Barth,[37] have concluded that authentic revelation has a trinitarian structure. Without ceasing to be God, the infinite and sovereign God comes to humanity in Jesus Christ; and through the power of the Spirit, people are able to recognize in Jesus Christ the self-revelation of God. As we have seen in chapter 4, Nicholas of Cusa offered a version of this argument. So what is at stake in affirming the trinitarian nature of God is the reality of God's self-revelation.

The second thing is the matter of *God's love.* "God is love" (1 John 4:16) is one of the bedrock claims of the Christian faith. Not "God loves the creatures God has made," which is certainly true, but "God *is* love." But how is God to be love before there were any creatures to love? Only if, in God's own very being, God loves and is love. "The doctrine of the Trinity," writes Archbishop Williams in the text that Sheikh al-Jifri so highly praised, "is a way of explaining why we say that God *is* love, not only that he shows love."[38] For love, you need more than the sovereign and solitary one, another point made eloquently by Nicholas of Cusa (see chapter 2).

In the next two chapters, I explore further the character of God as love.

CHAPTER EIGHT

God's Mercy

Much of the public discussion about Islam revolves around the problem of violence. In the minds of many Christians, Islam is associated with terrorism, and they see the God of Islam as a fierce deity, a war God, spurring Muslims to irrational violence. The problem of violence was at the heart of the controversy about the Danish cartoons, some of which portray Muhammad as a wide-eyed brandisher of a scimitar or a bearded suicide bomber with a lit fuse in his turban. The satirical message was this: as was Muhammad, so is Muhammad's God, and so are Muhammad's followers. Similarly, in the Regensburg address, Pope Benedict XVI zeroed in on the illicit use of force on the part of Muslims and offered an explanation: unlike the God of the Christian faith, who is reason and love, Muhammad's God is an irrational and therefore violent deity. The common theme? Muslims and their violent God (see chapter 1).

The accusation that violence is inherent in Islam is not new. For centuries, Christian and non-Christian Westerners have linked the two. As we have already seen, in the fifteenth and sixteenth centuries Pope Pius II thought that Islam was founded on pleasure and maintained by force rather than devotion or reason (see chapter 2). The Protestant Reformer Martin Luther—himself anything but a mild-natured man, to say the least—thought similarly; he believed that, unlike the Christian faith, which relies on the power of the proclaimed word, Islam expands by the power of the sword (see chapter 3). Over the centuries and today, in much of the Christian and non-Christian Western imagination, the God of Muhammad is seen to have "terror on his mind."[1]

For many Christians the contrast between the God of Islam and the God they themselves worship is sharp. Four stark polarities are typical:

1. The God of arbitrary will and wrath *versus* the God of reason and love;
2. The God who demands unconditional submission *versus* the God who invites a free response of faith;
3. The God who commands the enforcement of harsh and unbending laws regulating all of life *versus* the God who enjoins love of neighbors and respect for their freedom;
4. The God who is unbendingly hostile toward any infidel and all enemies *versus* the God who demands love for all people, including one's enemies.

Two different Gods! Two distinct ways of life! Two alternative arrangements of social relations! Incompatible and clashing! This is the impression in the minds of many Christians. But is it correct?

Let's be clear about our question. It is not whether there are Muslims who believe that God demands unconditional submission to unbendable and inhumane laws and is hostile toward unbelievers. There are such Muslims, and some of them are a major threat to fellow Muslims and non-Muslims alike. But there are such Christians as well; they might *say* that God is love, but they believe first and foremost in the Mighty Warrior. Filled with resentment and hostility and drawing on selected portions of their sacred books, religious people from all traditions have crafted God into their own deeply insecure and violent image.[2] It is important to study the religious convictions of such people and understand how they function to justify and motivate their actions, private and public. But this is not my task here.

I am not inquiring about the God of a small band of terrorists and warmongers, but about the God of the great Christian and Muslim teachers, the God of the millions of ordinary religious people. I am interested in what normative Islam and Christianity have to say about God, not in what some of the worst Muslims and Christians believe about God. Threat comes from the terrorists, but hope comes from "saints," men and women of pure heart who seek to love God and neighbor.

Love Versus Violence

It was, in fact, largely to counter a portrayal of Islam as a violent religion that "A Common Word" was written (see chapter 1). Addressed above all to Pope Benedict XVI in the wake of his Regensburg address,[3] it states clearly and unequivocally that at the heart of Islam lie the two greatest commandments as stated by Jesus in the Gospels: "Love God!" and "Love neighbor!" (see Mark 12:29–31). "A Common Word" insists that Islam isn't about mere submission to an arbitrary divinity and obedience to an unbending law, whereas Christianity is about love of God and love of neighbor. Islam too is about love of God and love of neighbor. Like Christianity, Islam is a religion of love. Indeed, many of the signatories would argue that in practice Islam is *much more* a religion of love than Christianity because, over the course of its history, they believe, it has been less violent than Christianity.[4]

Let's assume that the signatories of the "Common Word" are correct that love of God and neighbor is central to Islam. After all, they are some of the most prominent Muslim leaders in the world, its "popes," "archbishops," and "great theologians" (to translate their roles into rough Christian equivalents). Where does this leave the contrast between the Qur'an's God of imposing law who insists on submission and the New Testament's God of self-giving love who calls us to a way of love? Is the contrast just a caricature?

Not so fast. Both Christians and Muslims may be commanded to love, but do they love the same thing? And how is justice related to love? This takes us back to our original question. Who is God? What is God's nature? Is God something like a Supreme Legislator and Commander in Chief? Or more like a Loving Parent, comparable to the devoted mother of whom the Prophet Muhammad spoke when he said, "God is [even] more merciful to His servants than is this woman to her child"?[5] And if God is a loving God, what is the nature of God's love?

When the "Yale Response" to the "Common Word" was published in 2007[6]—endorsed by many leading Christians across the world—a vigorous debate ensued. At issue was whether the God Muslims are commanded to love is the same as the one Christians are commanded to love. This was the right question to press. Most of the actual discussions, however, centered on the cardinal Christian convictions of God as the Holy Trinity, God's incarnation in Jesus Christ, and Christ's role as the Lamb of God, who, dying on the cross, takes away the sin of the world. These convictions are central to Christians, since they define Christian identity, yet, critics complained, the "Yale Response" was silent on them all.

What such critics failed to realize, however, was that their own discussions, focused so narrowly on Christian identity, essentially skirted the key issue in Christian-Muslim relations today: the problem of violence. As we have already noted, it was concern about violence that drove the framers of the "Common Word." Thus, in replying to the "Common Word," those of us writing the "Yale Response" aimed to focus on that same issue. When we took up the question of God, rather than delving into theological concerns that are important but not directly pertinent to the issue of violence, we concentrated instead on the relation between God and love.

Do Muslims and Christians agree not just that we should love God, but that God is a loving God or, as Christians would put it, that God *is* love? The "Yale Response" sketched a Christian stance on these issues—insisting above all that God *is* love, that God's love is unconditional, and that even the ungodly are its objects. A sketch is not a full picture, however. In this chapter and the next, I want to fill in the outline presented in the "Yale Response," drawing a more complete depiction of the Christian view of God as love. Writing from a distinctly Christian perspective, I am asking a simple question: How much common ground is there between Muslims and Christians about these themes?

Does God Love?

A very important and very contested matter can be settled quickly: both Muslims and Christians believe that God loves human beings. True, if one pays attention specifically to the use of the word "love," God's love is less obvious in the Qur'an than in the Bible, but Christians can nonetheless find it affirmed as a basic characteristic of God's activity. Let me explain, starting with a Christian stance.

Nothing is more basic to the Christian faith than the claim that God loves. Consider the most memorized verse of the most widely disseminated portion of the Bible, the Gospel of John: "For God so loved the world that he gave his only Son . . ." (3:16). Another verse, not as famous but equally central, echoes the same thought: "God's love was revealed among us in this way: God sent his only Son into the world so that we might live through him" (1 John 4:9). God loves. And because God loves, God creates and sustains all things, God delivers the needy from affliction, God forgives the sins of evildoers, and God grants eternal life. None of this God does out of necessity; all of it God does in the complete freedom of God's infinite love.

At first glance, Islam seems different. Even though the Qur'an explicitly states that God loves certain things and certain kinds of human beings, over the centuries some influential Muslim theologians have either refused or hesitated to speak about God's love.[7] Now, in Islam, theologians do not play nearly as central a role as they do—or used to—in Christianity. Jurists are much more influential with regard to the practice of the religion. But the religious sensibilities of a great many scholars and common believers alike have been, and continue to be, shaped above all by the Sufi masters.[8] As we will see, they don't hesitate at all to talk about God's love. But let's stay for a while with theologians.

Some Muslim theologians think like this. God creates and sustains, and God rules and commands, but God doesn't strictly speaking love (unless love is simply identical with God's will, so that it can be said that whatever God wills God loves). Though this may seem alien to Christians, from one angle the position of such Muslim theologians isn't significantly different from a Christian one. It all depends on what you mean by love.

So, what do we Christians mean by love? First, let's consider what we *don't* mean. Plato's *Symposium* is likely the most influential text about love in the whole of Western literature. In it, Socrates argues that to love is to desire something one does not have and considers to be good.[9] Apply this definition of love to God, as some Muslim theologians do, and you immediately see the difficulty. God lacks nothing that is good, and God has no needs. So God cannot desire anything God doesn't have. Therefore God cannot love—in Socrates's sense of the word. Now, Christians *agree* with Muslims who think this way. All responsible Christian theologians insist that God doesn't love in this "needy" kind of way; such love wouldn't be worthy of God.

Does it follow, however, that God doesn't love at all? We use the word "love" in another sense—not just to designate desire for what we lack, but commitment to give of what we have and of who we are. This is the main sense in which the Christian tradition speaks of God's love. "For God so loved . . . that he *gave,*" reads the famous verse about God's love quoted earlier. When God loves, God doesn't long to get something, but undertakes to impart something. God *gives* when God creates; God *gives* when God delivers; God *gives* when God forgives; God *gives* when God grants eternal life. God gives, and in giving God loves. All of God's works are done out of generosity, none out of acquisitiveness.

Would Muslims agree about God's generosity, even if they don't specifically use the word "love"?[10] In fact, many of what the Qur'an calls the "Beautiful Names" of God[11] speak of divine giving—of God's compassion for those who are in any way needy, whether in an ontological or existential sense ("The Merciful" and "The Compassionate"); of God's forgiveness of those who have transgressed ("The All-Forgiving"); and of God's generosity and benevolence ("The Generous" and "The Benevolent"). And among the Beautiful Names of God in the Qur'an is "The Loving" (see Al Buruj, 85:14; Hud, 11:90). The great eleventh-century Muslim master al-Ghazali's commentary on this name makes clear the intimate connection between God's loving and God's giving. As "The Loving One," al-Ghazali explains, God bestows "honor and blessing . . . favor and grace" on creatures.[12] Indeed, al-Ghazali insists that, were it not for the gifts of God, human beings "would never have emerged from behind the curtain of non-existence into the visible world."[13]

"Mercy" sums up all such divine giving in the Qur'an. In a central and much discussed verse we read that God has "inscribed for Himself (the rule of) Mercy" (Al An'am, 6:12). One of the early and most famous commentators on the Qur'an, Muhammad ibn Jarir al-Tabari (838–923), wrote the following in his comments about this verse:

> When God created the heavens and the earth, He [also] created a hundred mercies, [the extent of] each mercy can fill that [space] which is between the heaven and the earth. He has [kept] ninety-nine mercies with Him and divided one mercy amongst [His] creatures. By this [mercy] they are affectionate toward one another and by it [all] the animals and birds [are able to] find water to drink. On the Day of Resurrection, God will restrict this [mercy] to the God-fearing and He will give them in addition the [other] ninety-nine [mercies].[14]

These comments are particularly significant, as al-Tabari is here quoting Salman al-Farisi, one of the companions of the founder of Islam. Ninety-nine mercies are the ninety-nine Beautiful Names of God. God's whole being, turned toward creation, is but one infinite and multifaceted mercy.

Some Muslims do not use the world "love" to describe God's

action toward creatures, and most hesitate designating God's very being as "love." And yet, on all those innumerable occasions when they speak about God's mercy, Muslims affirm that God loves. In the next chapter, I have more to say about some differences in how Christians and Muslims understand God's love, differences, in fact, so important that some Christian theologians thought that they marked the line between the true faith and false varieties (e.g., Martin Luther; see chapter 3). But no matter how crucial, these differences don't cancel out deep and important commonalities; they presuppose them.

Love and Justice

If God loves in all these ways, what happens to God's justice and God's laws? Do they disappear in the vast ocean of God's love? Christians and Muslims affirm together that God is just and condemns wrongdoing. The Qur'an calls God "The Holy One" (Al Hash, 59:23), which is also one of God's Beautiful Names. Some of God's other names are "The Just" and "The Arbitrator." And God's laws famously regulate much of the lives of pious Muslims and are enforced in many majority Muslim societies. This emphasis on abiding by laws is what most Christians would expect to encounter in Islam.

Those who know anything about the Christian Bible know that justice is not absent from it either. On the contrary, it is central. Innumerable are the places where God is described as being just, as issuing binding commands, and as judging people and their deeds. Some see the New Testament as a book of love in contrast to the Hebrew scriptures as a book of law. But the New Testament describes God as just (see Rom. 3:26; 1 John 1:9) and even as being wrathfully set against "all ungodliness and wickedness" (Rom. 1:18).[15] The texts in the New Testament that speak most of divine love—the Gospel and the Letters of John—distinguish sharply between light and darkness (1 John 2:8), love and hatred (2:10–11), truth and lies (2:21), justice and unrighteousness, good and evil (3:12). God affirms one and condemns the other. And Jesus, who for Christians is the very incarnation of divine love, was hardly shy about bringing up the topic of eternal damnation! So we don't have a God of spineless sentimental love on the Christian side and the God of stern and unbending law on the Muslim side. We have a loving and just God on both sides—though, again, with differences.

We can take the argument a step farther. Over the centuries, religious teachers from both camps have struggled to hold together what seem to be contradictory qualities of "love" and "justice."[16] Now, there are certainly a number of teachers on both sides who would contest this claim, but many from both faiths agree that God's love precedes and encompasses God's justice. If there are differences of opinion on this matter, these are as much differences within each camp as they are differences between camps. Thus, a third commonality between Christian faith and Islam in understanding God's love is the widely held belief in the priority of God's love over justice.

For Christians, the basis for this prioritization comes from the Bible itself. Although the Bible famously states, and does so twice, that "God is love" (1 John 4:8, 16), it never states that God is justice. It does, however, repeatedly underscore that God is just and acts justly. Justice, although essential, is an aspect of divine love—of God's care for human beings and intention to establish the right relations among them.

Similarly, mercy, as we have seen, is one of the key ways in which the Qur'an speaks of God's gift-giving love. All except one of the Qur'an's 114 chapters begin by invoking God as "Most Gracious, Most Merciful," and pious Muslims repeat these words many times every day as part of their daily prayers. According to a well-attested saying of Muhammad, "When God created the world, He wrote above His Throne, 'My mercy precedes (or prevails over) My wrath.'"[17] As we have already seen, in the opinion of some of the most important Qur'anic commentators, God's mercy "regulates" all of God's relations with creation.

Now, of course, Muslims do believe that God rewards good and punishes evil; but that very activity of God is a form of mercy intended to either lead to restoration or curb further injustice. Because God is "Oft-Forgiving" and "Most Merciful," often when justice demands wrath because a wrongdoing has been committed, God's mercy overrides it. And so, as it says in the Qur'an, God's "mercy encompasses all things" (Al A'raf, 7:156; see also Al Ghafir, 40:7)—from the emergence of all things from behind the veil of nonexistence to the gift of eternal life; from punishments to forgiveness.

With regard to God's love, Muslims and Christians share the following three convictions:

1. God loves.
2. God is just.
3. God's love encompasses God's justice.

Should We Love?

In a sense, "Should we love?" is a nonquestion. Muslims love. Christians love. *All* human beings love—well, almost all. As Augustine maintained, to be human is to love (though not necessarily to love the right things and in the right way).[18] And yet we need to inquire what the two faiths *do* with human love, especially the love for other human beings. Do Islam and Christianity encourage it? Do they steer it? If so, how and in what direction? It is one thing to love, and it is another thing to love well. And one kind of love is love for, say, cake (which a person with a sweet tooth wants to devour), and another is love for a child (for whom good parents would sacrifice their lives).

The Bible is clear on the matter: "Beloved, let us love one another, because love is from God; everyone who loves is born of God and knows God. Whoever does not love does not know God" (1 John 4:7–8). To love means to give, bestow benefits, as I wrote earlier.

God loved, so God gave. The same holds true for human love—despite the fact that, unlike God, human beings love with a needy kind of love as well. "How does God's love abide in anyone who has the world's goods and sees a brother or sister in need and yet refuses help?" the writer of the same letter asks rhetorically (1 John 3:17). Love abides in us when we give. More generally, the way to love our neighbor is to follow the Golden Rule: "In everything do to others as you would have them do to you, for this is the law and the prophets" (Matt. 7:12).

The Golden Rule has an important echo in Islam, as we have seen earlier (see chapter 1). The Qur'an does not mention it, but both of the most authoritative *hadith* collections (collections of the sayings of Muhammad and his companions) contain a version of it: "None of you has faith until you love for your brother what you love for yourself," and, "None of you has faith until you love for your neighbor what you love for yourself."[19] Love here is not a mere sentiment, a sincere wish of the heart unaccompanied by the movement of the hand. It includes sacrificial actions as well. The Qur'an calls the faithful to "spend of your substance, out of love for Him, for your kin, for orphans, for the needy, for the wayfarer, for those who ask, and for the ransom of slaves" (Al Baraqah, 2:177; cf. Al Balad, 90:4–17; Al Duha, 93:6–11). The "Common Word" sums up the Muslim position: "Without love of neighbor there is no true faith in God and no righteousness."[20]

So we can add a fourth point of agreement between Muslims and Christians to the three above:

4. Human beings should love their neighbors as themselves.

However, that's not the end of the discussion on the relation between God and love in Muslim and Christian sacred texts and the writings of the great teachers. In many ways, that's just the beginning of it. We need to zoom in and examine more closely what it means to "love" and who the "neighbor" is. That path will take us back to God and God's love.

But before I enter this exploration in the next chapter, let's pause for a moment. I want to examine from up close the fine texture of one aspect of love in Islam and Christianity to illustrate how similar their understandings of love can be. I'll make the exploration a bit personal.

Making Manifest What Is Beautiful

When I first read al-Ghazali's *The Ninety-Nine Beautiful Names of God,* I was struck by how deeply saturated the text is with love—with God's love, with love for God, with love for neighbors. Early on, commenting about the second and third Beautiful Names, al-Ghazali describes God's mercy as perfect and inclusive:

> Perfect inasmuch as it wants to fulfill the need of those in need and does meet them; and inclusive inasmuch as it embraces both deserving and undeserving, encompassing this world and the next, and includes bare necessities and needs, and special gifts over and above them. So He is truly and utterly merciful.[21]

That is God's mercy. Human mercy is similar. The whole book rests on a simple conviction central to al-Ghazali and many who, like him, embrace Sufism, the mystical tradition of Islam: human perfection consists in "conforming to" and "adorning" oneself with "the meanings of His attributes."[22] So from the reality of God's mercy follows the "counsel" to practice the same kind of mercy.

As I was reading the book for the first time, I still had a lingering sense of Islam as a religion of "law" in contrast to Christianity as a religion of "love." One passage in particular jarred memories from childhood and made me question the validity of the contrast. It was al-Ghazali's commentary on the fifteenth Beautiful Name of God, *al-Ghaffar,* which means "He who is full of forgiveness." God "makes manifest what is beautiful and conceals what is ugly," al-Ghazali writes, replicating the meaning of that Beautiful Name.[23] Sins are among these ugly things. God conceals them "by letting a cover fall over them in this world, and refraining from requiting them in the next."[24] So to forgive is to conceal, an echo of "covering" as a dominant metaphor for forgiveness in the Bible (see Ps. 32:1; Rom. 4:7).

After exploring the Beautiful Name *al-Ghaffar,* al-Ghazali offers the "counsel": "Whoever overlooks the ugly and mentions the beautiful is one who shares in this attribute."[25] It then dawned on me where al-Ghazali's comments were going. I was so locked in on forgiveness as "concealment" and the commonality with the Christian tradition it represents, that I failed to notice the significance of "manifestation." To forgive is not just to "conceal" in the sense of not seeing the wrong and therefore not counting it against the wrongdoer. That is radical enough, and yet there is more. To forgive means to highlight the good, rather than merely hiding the bad. Which was, of course, the first thing al-Ghazali mentioned about the forgiving God: God is the one "who makes manifest what is beautiful." He tells a story from the life of Jesus—an apocryphal one—to illustrate his point:

So it is told of 'Isa [Jesus]—may God's blessings be upon him—that he and his disciples passed by a dead dog whose stench was overpowering, and they said: "How this carcass stinks!" Yet 'Isa—may peace be upon him—said: "What beautiful white teeth he has!"

This brought to mind memories from childhood.

If they could help it, my father and mother would never speak ill of anyone, even of those we all knew were doing us harm (like the government informers who were creating mischief in my father's church). If we as children steered the conversation the wrong way, they would admonish us. If adults were involved, they would suffer it with quiet unease or mention a good quality or two of the person in question. "What a killjoy household I live in," I would think as an adolescent, "where you can't even have the pleasure of exposing evil for what it is, let alone indulge in a little sweet gossip!" When my sister and I grew up and our parents would sit at our tables, if anyone's faults were discussed, my father would find a reason to leave. He wasn't only concerned about others being unjustly maligned; he was concerned that they, our neighbors whoever they were, were not being loved. Love "covers a multitude of sins," the Bible says (1 Pet. 4:8). Love celebrates the good; it makes manifest the beautiful and "rejoices in the truth" (1 Cor. 13:6).

I am fifty-three years old as I write this, and I have traveled the world. Except from the pulpit of my father's church, I don't remember hearing a sermon on this aspect of love. I haven't seen many modern Christian theologians urge people to make manifest the good even of those who deserve condemnation; Søren Kierkegaard's profound comments on the matter in *Works of Love* and *Upbuilding Discourses*[26] are more the exception than the rule. I know a few people, especially one beautiful, saintly friend, who consistently practice that particular virtue, but they are rare.[27] And now I read a compelling exposition of this virtue in a book by a Muslim scholar—and not just a maverick thinker, but one of the highest repute among Muslims? Was al-Ghazali not supposed to practice a religion of harsh law rather than a religion of love?!

My father, a Pentecostal minister, would have rejoiced, and doubly so—not just because someone insisted that love requires speaking well of others, but because a Muslim did so. As a young man, he was a confectioner, working in confectioneries owned by others. One of the owners, and his boss, was an Albanian Muslim. "He was the best man I have ever worked for," I heard my father say many times with great admiration.

There are affinities in the way Christianity and Islam understand the fine texture of goodness and of love. Similarities in their understanding of God are the reason why these affinities exist. But there are differences as well, though not as deep and not as plentiful as many think. I discuss them in the next chapter.

CHAPTER NINE

Eternal and Unconditional Love

Some time ago, I was driving with my son, who was then four. It was a long trip, so I needed to entertain him. I had gone to New York the night before to see Mary Zimmerman's play *Metamorphoses*. I thought that the action of the play—the transformation of everything King Midas touched into gold, the morphing of Alcyone and Ceyx into seabirds, and Zeus and Hermes disguising themselves as humans—might be of some interest even to a four-year-old. So I started telling him about it.

"What is meta . . . ?" he asked.

"Met-a-mor-pho-sis." I helped him out with the big word. "Well, metamorphosis is when you get transformed into something else." He knew a lot about "transformation," because of his extensive experience with the Transformers—toy cars that can be transformed into robotic monsters and then back into cars.

"In the play," I continued, "there is a story called *The Golden Ass* . . . I mean *The Golden Donkey*."

"A golden donkey?"

"What happens is that there is this man by the name of Lucius who really wants to see and practice magic. One day he sees a woman practice her witchcraft and transform herself into a bird. He is amazed, so he tries to do the same. But he accidentally turns himself into a donkey, a dumb and stubborn little creature, with big shaggy ears, a funny tail, and all."

My son was quiet for a while, and then he asked me a question I had not expected. "Daddy, would you love me if I became a donkey?"

I don't care much for donkeys, so I responded, very philosophically and very foolishly, "Well, if you turned into a donkey, you would no longer be Nathanael, and then I would not love you, but the donkey. In fact, if I loved that donkey, I would not . . ." In the rearview mirror, I saw horror on the face of my son. He did not fully understand my reasoning, but he got the drift. It never occurred to him that, if transformed, he would, at the core, not remain himself.[1] Changing radically while remaining yourself is what transformation is all about! He sensed that, and it was only my dislike of donkeys and a temporary shutdown of my emotional intelligence that made me forget it for a while.

After the horror had passed, the tears came streaming down. He was inconsolable until I stopped the car and took him into my arms. He could not bear the thought that his father might stop loving him under any circumstances—whatever happened to him and whoever he became. Love is love, and it never changes—this he felt in the core of his being. He did not have the words to describe the character of true love. His tears were eloquent enough.

My son was yearning to find in my love a reflection of divine love, unchanging no matter what changes we undergo, completely unearned but freely given. When Christians speak of God's love, it's this kind of love that they have in mind. In evaluating the potential similarities between Christian and Muslim understandings of God, Christians will always want to know what normative Islam thinks about the utterly gratuitous character of God's love. To explore this issue adequately, though, it is not enough to inquire about how God relates to creatures, as I did in the previous chapter. We must go behind God's actions to the character of God's being. It will be a journey—at points a difficult journey—toward the luminous heart of the Christian faith.

Is God Love?

Christians and Muslims agree that God loves, if by love we mean the compassionate desire to give of what we have rather than acquire what we lack. This is what I argued in the previous chapter. But for Christians it is not enough to say that God loves. We insist that God *is* love. The difference seems small, but the whole character of the Christian faith depends on it. Can Muslims embrace this idea? Some strenuously object. Others come close to it.

To say that God is love is not just a passive or a plodding way of saying that God loves. It is not merely to describe the nature of God's activity toward the world. It is to name the character of God's eternal being, to describe the fountain from which the river of divine loving flows. God's very being is love—so much so that the great church father Augustine could, perhaps a bit too daringly, invert the statement and write: "Love is God."[2] Not just any kind of love, mind you. Not, for example, love as a mere relation between human beings[3]—as though Augustine had anticipated Ludwig Feuerbach, the nineteenth-century critic of Christianity whose influential method consisted in transmuting all claims about God into claims about humanity.[4] Love properly understood *is* God—the font of all creation and the ultimate goal of all desires; God properly understood *is* love.

As we have seen in the previous chapter, if by "love" we mean compassionate beneficence and benevolence, all Muslim teachers without exception insist that God loves—that God is "The Merciful One" and "The Loving One," caring for all creatures and forgiving human sins. But do Muslims affirm that God *is* love or at least that love is an eternal attribute of God? In answering this question, it is important to distinguish between perspectives of Muslim theologians and Muslim spiritual masters, mainly Sufis (who, as I noted in the previous chapter, are much more important in shaping Muslim religious sensibilities than theologians). Reza Shah-Kazemi, a Muslim scholar who himself argues that love has "a principal or ontological priority within the divine nature,"[5] notes the unease of Muslim theologians about describing God in terms of love. They "debated the very legitimacy of ascribing love to God in any essential manner."[6] This will raise the eyebrows of many Christians—what matters to them the most about God is strenuously contested by many Muslim theologians! But Shah-Kazemi adds immediately, "This is only one side of the story."[7] So let's look at the other, perhaps more important, side of the story.

Some Muslim scholars take the very verse I quoted in the previous chapter—about God prescribing for himself "mercy"—as proof that in Islam love is an eternal attribute of God, for the verse speaks of God's prescribing—or inscribing—mercy on God's very self.[8] This is the view of many great Sufi masters.[9]

For those who doubt that love is God's essential attribute in Islam rather than just God's face turned toward creatures, the best "proof" comes from Ahmad ibn Taymiyya (1263–1328).[10] He is the spiritual and intellectual ancestor of contemporary Salafis, members of one of the most conservative movements within Islam, and the major influence on Muhammad ibn Abd al-Wahhab (1703–93), the founder of modern Wahhabism.[11] Ibn Taymiyya argues strongly that God loves apart from creation and that God's love is therefore an essential aspect of God's eternal being. He was led to the conclusion by considering the implications of God's love for creatures, something that is clearly affirmed in the Qur'an (see Al Buruj, 85:14).

Here is a rough sketch of his argument. Since God is perfect, God's love for creatures cannot be a consequence of a deficiency on God's part. That excludes two reasons for loving creatures. First, God doesn't love creatures because God needs them; that would be incompatible with God's self-sufficiency. Second, God doesn't love creatures simply for their benefit; that would mean, in Ibn Taymiyya's view, that God loves them for no reason and that God's love is whimsical.[12] He therefore concludes that God loves creatures because God first of all loves God's own self![13] So God first loves God's own self, and this eternal divine love is the fountain of everything pertaining to creatures. God's self-love is the reason God created the world, and God's self-love is the source of all other loves—of God's love for human beings and of human love for God and for neighbors. The bottom line of the argument is that, if it weren't for God's essential and eternal self-love, there wouldn't be any other love, either divine or human.[14]

Notice where we have arrived with the discussion of God's love in Christianity and Islam. We have left popular opinions based on prejudice (rooted in the distorted practices of some Muslims) that the Muslim God is a God of unbending laws with "a heart of stone," whereas the Christian God is a God of tender love whose heart is as wide as an ocean.[15] Instead, we are discussing differences between two faiths that concern the fine texture of divine love. These differences matter, as we will see, but they in no way invalidate widespread convergence. And although these differences may be crucial when it comes to human standing before God (salvation), they are less important when it comes to the ability of Muslims and Christians to live together peacefully in one world—a primary interest in this book.

Self-Love and Love of the Other

Christians too have maintained that love within the eternal God is the source of creation and of all other loves. Like Ibn Taymiyya, Christian theologians also say, as did the great Thomas Aquinas (1225–74), that "God loves Himself."[16] But Christians interpret this divine self-love in a trinitarian way, as love among the three divine "Persons" who are the one God of undivided essence. We can see inklings of the connection between God's love within the Trinity and God's love directed toward the world in John's Gospel. The "Father" loved the "Son" before the world was created (17:24), and the "Son" loves the "Father" (14:31). It is because there is love between the "Father" and the "Son" that God loved the world and sent the "Son" (3:16). Augustine gave the idea a full-blown, and now classic, expression in *The Trinity,* the most important book on the subject ever written.[17] So we have returned to the debate about the Trinity—a topic I discussed in chapter 7. Christians affirm God's self-love, but understand it in a trinitarian way, as love among the three "Persons" of the one God. Muslims too affirm God's self-love but, given their rejection of the Trinity, understand it in a unitary way, as love of God for God's own self. We have come far on our journey exploring the character of God as love in Christianity and Islam. To get a sense of why the exploration matters, we need to press a bit farther. And here, for a stretch, the path becomes steep.

In 2010 I gave a talk at the National Prayer Breakfast in Washington, DC, about the utterly unconditional character of God's love. The next day, I had lunch with a friend whose daily milieu is the world of business and politics. Though not a religious scholar, he has a deep interest in reconciliation between Muslims and Christians. He liked that I was writing a book on Christian responses to the God Muslims worship, so I started telling him about it. At the time, I was working on the chapter on the Trinity, and I began to explain the fierce debates between Muslims and Christians about the "undivided divine essence" and how there can be "other" in the one God. After only a few sentences, I could see his eyes glaze over. He suffered me for a while and then said, "You know, Miroslav, God is a mystery that we can never fathom." "True enough," I thought. Along with many other great Christian theologians, Augustine would have agreed, but that did not prevent him from writing a whole thick book on the Trinity.

My friend's impatience was really a way of asking: Why does this matter? Does anyone care about discussions about God's unity and Trinity besides theologians? What's at stake here when it comes to living in the real world as family members, friends, or citizens? When it comes to God's eternal love, does the affirmation of the Trinity make any difference? It does.

If God is not internally differentiated as the Holy Trinity, then you have a unitary divine self who loves himself as the being most worthy of love. God's love for creatures and creatures' love for God

and for one another are all enveloped in this original and origi-
nating divine self-love. Two consequences are likely to follow: (1)
the purest form of love is self-love, and (2) creatures are ultimately
unreal. That's what al-Ghazali thinks, and he is in many ways the
most representative Muslim thinker you'll find, from any period.

Since the love of the eternal and perfect God cannot be a needy
kind of love, God cannot love any other, but can only love God's
own self, al-Ghazali reasons. At the same time, the Qur'an says
explicitly that God loves people (e.g., Al Ma'idah, 5:54). How can
we put together these two claims—that God loves people and
that God does not love another? Al-Ghazali answers: "God does
indeed love them [people], but in reality He loves nothing other
than Himself, in the sense that He is the totality [of being], and
there is nothing in being apart from Him."[18] The two consequences noted above follow. (1) All love is God's self-love. God
loves people in that God gives them the ability to love God, and
that love for God is nothing else but God's own self-love. God
loves God's own self through people. (2) Creatures are illusory.
In God's self-love, the absolute unity of all reality is affirmed as
identical with the unity of God; all individuality, all multiplicity
is then ultimately an illusion.

For the most part, Christians strenuously resist speaking about
the unreality and illusoriness of creatures. As monotheists, they are
able to do so coherently partly because of the doctrine of the Trinity, because they believe that the one God is internally differentiated and that from the "beginning" God loves "the other." If God
is the Holy Trinity, then there is already "other" in the undivided
essence of the one God (the "other," as we have seen earlier, who
is not simply "not the same"; see chapters 2 and 7). Moreover, the
kind of love that is at the foundation of all reality, then, is not love
that ultimately redounds to the self. Instead, it is a love that gives
to the other as well as receives from the other. From this standpoint, God's creating to benefit creatures is exactly what God's love
does—it gives to the other for the other's sake, and not merely for
one's own sake. God confirms God's own being as love in giving to

others—to other "divine" Persons and to creatures. And all that is not out of need, but out of a sheer abundance of love.

With regard to God's love, the debate here is about what kind of love is ultimate: self-love or love of the other. And that has much to do with God's relation to the world, with the world's coming into existence, and with the affirmation of the world's full integrity in distinction from God, and with the character of proper human love. A basic metaphysical intuition of many great Christian thinkers is this: only if divine love is, from the beginning, a love for the "other" *within* God does it make sense for God to create and love the world—the other *outside* of God.[19] And only if "other" is already in God, does it make sense for the creation not to "collapse" into God. So the issue is this: Does "creaturely difference" have sufficient integrity before God?[20]

Does God Love the Ungodly?

"Daddy, would you love me if I became a donkey?" My son did not ask whether I would love his newly acquired "donkeyness" or whether I would like the fact that he turned into a donkey. He asked whether I would love *him* even if he turned into a donkey. I am here asking the same kind of question. It is not whether God loves ungodliness, but whether God loves *the ungodly*—a conviction central to the Christian faith.

As I noted in the previous chapter, in both traditions God does not love injustice, wrongdoing, evil, or any other form of ungodliness. Indeed, both traditions speak about God's wrath against ungodliness. Here is only one example from each. In the Bible it is written: "The wrath of God is revealed from heaven against all ungodliness and wickedness of those who by their wickedness suppress the truth" (Rom. 1:18). Similarly, the Qur'an speaks of apostates as those who follow "that which called forth the wrath of God" (Muhammad, 47:28).

God's rejection of ungodliness is a given for both traditions.

Does it follow that God doesn't love the *people* who engage in ungodliness, "the ungodly"? For Christians, it most definitely does not. God loves even the ungodly. The most famous verse in the Bible, to which I keep returning in these reflections on God's love, says: "For God so loved the *world*" (John 3:16)—the "whole world" and each and every person in it (see 1 John 2:2). God's love for the world doesn't merely refer to God's providential care for all people, to God's letting the sun "rise on the evil and on the good" and sending rain "on the righteous and on the unrighteous" (Matt. 5:45).[21] It refers also to God's saving love, to God's desire to give eternal life to all (1 Tim. 2:4) and God's saving actions on behalf of all (2 Cor. 5:14; Rom. 5:8). Some Christians, the so-called hyper-Calvinists, contest that God's saving love is universal. Building their case on biblical passages like Romans 9:13—"I have loved Jacob, but I have hated Esau" (quoting Mal. 1:2–3)—they contend that God loves only the elect. But the hyper-Calvinists are a small minority even among Protestants. The great majority of Christians believe that, as creator and redeemer, God loves all with preserving and redeeming love—the good and the evil, the godly and the ungodly, Christians and non-Christians.

How is it possible to hate ungodliness, but love the ungodly? There's a tension between the two, as most who have tried to love those who have harmed them will attest. Three important convictions explain the stance, one about human beings and two about God.

First, Christian theologians distinguish between the *doer* and the *deed,* between the person and the work.[22] It's a very simple distinction. Those who love make the distinction, like a mother who loves a child even when the child seriously misbehaves. Those who want to be loved make that distinction as well, as my son did when he asked me his donkey question. Similarly, every time we forgive, we draw a line between the doer and the deed. In William Shakespeare's *Measure for Measure,* judge Antonio has condemned Claudio to death for making Claudio's lover pregnant. Isabella, Claudio's sister, comes before the judge to plead for her brother's life. She tells the judge: "I have a brother is condemn'd to die. I do beseech you, let it be his fault, and not my brother."[23] In essence, she is asking the judge to separate the doer from the deed, and "condemn the fault but not the actor of it," as Angelo puts it a few lines later.[24]

Second, Christians believe that God's love is *creative* rather than merely *reactive*. In his famous *Heidelberg Disputation,* Martin Luther explains the difference between divine and human love: "The love of God does not find, but creates, that which is pleasing to it. The love of man comes into being through that which is pleasing to it."[25] Typical human love is a desire for what is pleasing to a person or what a person considers to be good. Love is a response to qualities in others that the lover deems desirable. Divine love is different, argues Luther. God's love is not a reactive desire, dependent on people's changing qualities; such love would not be worthy of God, as Muslim theologians have also noted. God's love is a creative power, independent of people's qualities. God doesn't find what is pleasing and then desire it; instead, even when God encounters what is displeasing, God creates what is pleasing out of it. God loves, and seeks to creatively transform an ungodly person into a godly one. God loves, and in loving God brings forth from the unlovable creature the beloved object of God's delight.

Third, in God's own essential being, *God is love,* as we have seen earlier. As a consequence, God cannot but love. Now, since with God "all things are possible" (Mark 10:27), it is always risky to claim that God cannot do something. But the writers of the Bible do occasionally make such claims. For instance, "God cannot be tempted by evil" (James 1:13). Just as God cannot be tempted by evil, because God is goodness itself, so God cannot fail to love, because God *is* love. God's love is eternal and unchanging, as the being of God is eternal and unchanging.

For Christians, God's eternal and unchanging love is the foundation stone on which everything else is built—the gift of creation with its myriad delights, the gift of God's coming into the world to redeem humanity from evil, and the gift of eternal and glorified life. The critical test of whether we have understood God's love correctly is whether we affirm that God loves the ungodly—those who are unlike God and even those opposed to God. Let's apply this test to the God of the Qur'an and of the great Muslim teachers.

Conditions of Love

A casual reading of the Qur'an gives a picture of a world divided in two—those whom God loves and those whom God doesn't love. Reza Shah-Kazemi notes that the Qur'an lists eight categories of people whom God loves:

> those who do good (Al Baqarah, 2:195)
> those who turn to God constantly (Al Baqarah, 2:222)
> those who keep themselves pure and clean (Al Baqarah, 2:222)
> those who act rightly (Al 'Imran, 3:76)
> those who are firm and steadfast (Al 'Imran, 3:146)
> those who put their trust in God (Al 'Imran, 3:159)
> those who judge in equity (Al Ma'idah, 5:42)
> those who fight for God's sake (Al An'am, 61:4)

In contrast to those whom God loves, the Qur'an also names eleven categories of people whom God *does not* love, among whom are the following:

> transgressors (Al Baqarah, 2:190)
> creatures ungrateful and wicked (Al Baqarah, 2:276)
> those who reject faith (Al 'Imran, 3:32)
> those who do wrong (Al 'Imran, 3:57)
> the arrogant, the vainglorious (Al Nisa', 4:36)
> one given to perfidy and crime (Al Nisa', 4:107)
> the wasters (Al A'raf, 6:141)
> the treacherous (Al Anfal, 8:58)

The line between the loved and the unloved ones is drawn depending on their stance toward God (believers versus unbelievers) and their moral qualities (righteous versus unrighteous). Shah-Kazemi concludes that, on such a casual reading of the Qur'an,

> the outside observer might infer that for Muslims, God's love is conditional, contingent upon particular human acts and qualities, rather than being an essential aspect of God, manifested in a manner at once universal and unconditional. God's love appears to be given as a reward for the righteous and denied as a punishment for the sinners.[26]

On this level, the love of the God of Islam seems very different from the love of the God of Christianity.

But we need to look beneath the surface of these verses. Before we do so, let's be clear about the issue at hand. It is not whether, in *some sense,* God's love is conditional or not. The Qur'an says, "If you do love God, follow me [i.e., Muhammad]: God will love you and forgive your sins; for God is Oft-Forgiving, Most Merciful" (Al 'Imran, 3:31). We have here a clear condition: *if* you love God, *then* God will love you. But there are similar conditions surrounding God's love in the Bible (though, obviously, these do not involve the founder of Islam). The famous verse in Exodus prohibiting idolatry speaks of God's punishing those who reject God, but "showing steadfast love to the thousandth generation of those who love [God] and keep [God's] commandments" (20:6; see also Ps. 103). Here too there is a clear condition: *if* you love God, *then* God will love you. And this is not just true of the God of the Hebrew Bible. It is not merely a feature abrogated by the revelation of the unconditional love of God in Christ. In the Gospel of John, Jesus urges his disciples to "abide in [his] love" and then he adds: "If you keep my commandments, you will abide in my love" (John 15:9–10). Again, we have a condition.

For both Muslims and Christians, then, there are conditions on God's love. The central question is this: What happens to those who fail to meet the conditions? Are they unloved? In one sense yes, but in another sense no. Let me explain.

The Loved and the Unloved?

First, look at the New Testament. Although it is true that Christ will love those who keep his commandments, the opposite is not true; when the disciples fail to keep the commandments, Christ does not cease loving them. Human disobedience never cancels out God's love. Instead, God's love remains constant but, faced with disobedience, can take the form of displeasure or even wrath, so as to restore people to the good from which they have fallen. If disobedience could cancel out God's love, God's love would be a reward and not a free gift; it would be reactive and not creative; it would be changeable and not eternal. How should we then understand the conditions of God's love? We can put it this way: when people do God's will, God loves the doer and the deed; when people fail to do God's will, God loves the doer, but not the deed. God's love for the doer, for the person—anyone and everyone, for the good and the evil—is always an unadulterated and unchanging gift; it is never anything but a gift.

As we have seen in chapter 3, Martin Luther proclaimed the good news of God's gift-giving love with volcanic vehemence. In the most profound depth of God's heart, he said, God is "pure, unutterable love."[27] Indeed, he insisted that you *dishonor* God if you want to earn God's love (as you dishonor the generosity of a giver if you insist on paying for the gift). Luther was a reformer, and many of his Catholic contemporaries opposed him for varied reasons, but none among the profound, past or contemporary, disagreed or disagrees with that central point. All are loved, and no conditions are imaginable under which God would cease loving any person.

How do things stand in this regard in the Qur'an? A sharp division between those whom God loves and those whom God doesn't love is not the whole story of the Islamic understanding of God's love either. Shah-Kazemi highlights two important convictions widely embraced by Muslim spiritual masters. First, mercy is the overarching way God relates to creation. According to the Qur'an, God's mercy "extends to all things" (Al A'raf, 7:156). Second, Shah-Kazemi maintains that love is an essential attribute of God, inscribed on God's very self, and not merely a quality of God's action toward creatures. According to the Qur'an, God "has inscribed for Himself . . . Mercy" (Al An'am, 6:12). As I noted earlier, this view is shared by Muslim thinkers as diverse as al-Ghazali and Ibn Taymiyya.

Love for the divine self and mercy in relating to all creatures—this is the large framework into which we have to place the division in the Qur'an between those whom God loves and those whom God does not love. God is merciful to all people, because God's nature is "loving mercy." Whether through kindness or severity, God's mercy seeks to bring back to God even those who, according to the Qur'an, are not loved by God. In this version of Muslim teaching, God is then merciful even to the ungodly. To the extent that Muslims agree with this understanding of God's mercy, there is significant common ground on this matter of crucial importance to Christians.

Still, a Christian might feel both gratified and a bit uneasy. It is not just that Jesus Christ, who is God's mercy incarnate, has not been mentioned at all.[28] That's what one would expect from Muslims, who consider Jesus a messenger from God and even a Word from God, but not the "God-from-God" who became flesh to dwell among mortals. It is, rather, that all love is now self-love, *divine* self-love. Might self-love that seeks something for itself become a threat to mercy, which always imparts something to the other? What happens to those who stubbornly refuse to know God, which is what divine self-love seeks? What happens when they persistently spurn God's mercy? Do they continue to be loved? For Christians, that's where the trinitarian nature of God comes in. From eternity to eternity, God's love is not self-love, but a self-giving love. It is God's nature to give. That's why God gives even to the unrighteous. Love for the ungodly is the shape that God's love for the divine "other" takes when faced with godlessness.[29]

"Love Your Enemies"

God's love for the ungodly and human love for enemies are inextricably tied together. Over the centuries, Christians have not been very good at loving their enemies, to say the least. We have left a trail of blood and tears as we marched through history. Still, human disobedience doesn't annul the divine command, especially not a command that is so close to the center of the gospel and so bound up with the nature of God. That's why even those who transgressed egregiously the command to love enemies still felt compelled to try to reconcile their conduct with the command. For example, in a letter to Sultan Mehmet II after the Ottoman leader had sacked Constantinople (1453), Pope Pius II noted, "We are hostile to your action, not to you. As God commands, we love our enemies and we pray for our persecutors."[30] At the same time, the pope went on organizing a crusade against the mighty sultan—which is not, in my judgment, the way to love an enemy (see chapter 2).

Consider the famous text from Matthew's Gospel, to which I alluded earlier:

> You have heard that it was said, "You shall love your neighbor and hate your enemy." But I say to you, Love your enemies and pray for those who persecute you, so that you may be children of your Father in heaven; for he makes his sun rise on the evil and on the good, and sends rain on the righteous and on the unrighteous. For if you love those who love you, what reward do you have? Do not even the tax collectors do the same? And if you greet only your brothers and sisters, what more are you doing than others? Do not even the Gentiles do the same? Be perfect, therefore, as your heavenly Father is perfect. (5:43–48)

God's love is a model for human love. True, we are not God. We cannot love exactly like God does. In our human and limited way, however, we should strive to imitate God's love even for the ungodly by loving our enemies.

The passage from the Gospel speaks of the sun and the rain and appeals to God's life-giving care for all creatures without distinction, including evildoers. The New Testament letters speak of Christ's death on the cross and appeal to God's forgiveness of sinners: "Live in love, as Christ loved us and gave himself up for us" (Eph. 5:2). We should not repay evil for evil or abuse for abuse, but, "on the contrary, repay with a blessing" (1 Pet. 3:9). We should forgive, "as God in Christ has forgiven" us (Eph. 4:32).

The point of loving one's enemies—of "repaying" persecution with blessing, and wrongdoing with forgiveness—is not to put up with evil. It is to resist being "overcome by evil" and to "overcome evil with good" (Rom. 12:21). Martin Luther makes the point eloquently. The followers of Christ are supposed to

> grieve more over the sin of their offenders than over the loss or offense to themselves. And they do this that they may recall those offenders from their sin rather than avenge the wrongs they themselves have suffered. Therefore they put off the form of their own righteousness and put on the form of those others, praying for their persecutors, blessing those who curse, doing good to the evildoers, preparing to pay the penalty and make satisfaction for their very enemies that they may be saved. This is the Gospel and the example of Christ.[31]

The ultimate purpose of loving one's enemies is clear: "that they may be saved" from their evildoing and that goodness may triumph.

Surprisingly perhaps for some, an apt, even radical, illustration of Luther's idea that we forgive for the sake of the transgressor's salvation is found in a story of a famous Muslim, a Persian Sufi by the name of Abu Yazid al-Bistami (804–74). He was at the public bath when a thief stole all his clothes. Abu Yazid went out to catch the thief, and when the thief saw him, he began to run faster. Abu Yazid called out to him, "Stop, I'm not going to do anything to you." So the man stopped. And Abu Yazid said, "I just wanted to tell you that you can have the clothes." Hamza Yusuf Hanson, the influential U.S. Muslim to whom I owe this story, explains Abu Yazid's generosity: he did not want the thief to have the wrong action on his soul and on his account on the Day of Judgment.[32]

A Just Struggle Against Enemies?

In New Testament times, Christian communities were a persecuted minority with no aspirations to become a political or military power. If any fighting were to be done to protect these communities or if any retribution were to be exacted to avenge the injuries they suffered, God was the one, *not* them, to fight and to exact retribution (see Rom. 12:19; Rev. 19:2). Violence against enemies was displaced onto God. God fights; Christians do not—neither in their own name nor in the name of God.

The cultural-political context of the Qur'an is closer to that of the Hebrew Bible than the New Testament. The believers, even as a small band, were from the start a "political" community with military forces. Believers fight their enemies, protecting their boundaries and avenging injustices committed against them. They wage wars alongside God and in God's name. In the Qur'an we read about battles, about "terrific onslaughts" (Al 'Imran, 3:125), and about "striking terror into the hearts of enemies" (Al Anfal, 8:60). This fits with the image of God as one who loves some people and does not love others.[33] None of this justifies contemporary terrorism, of course, let alone anything like suicide bombings, for in Islam affairs of war, as any other righting of wrongs, must be conducted with justice. Both the cause and the conduct of war must be just (for instance, defensive wars fought with proportionate response and without the killing of noncombatants).[34]

Are we left with the contrast between "love of enemies" (in

Christianity) and "just struggle against enemies" (in Islam)? Such a contrast would be a crass caricature. Many Christians, notably Augustine, have affirmed the legitimacy of just war and have developed criteria to assess which wars are just and what conduct in war is just.[35] They have insisted that war against the enemy is compatible with the command to love enemies, for we wage war out of love for those who have suffered serious injustice and whose lives are threatened; and, motivated by love, we engage in war to establish peace between enemies.[36] Some Christians strenuously disagree. They insist that Christ's call for love for enemies requires the practice of nonviolence. But whichever view one takes, there is no doubt that the "just war" position is not just tolerated as legitimate within Christianity, but is in fact the dominant position.[37] In either case, however, love of the enemy is the overarching virtue; justice is subservient to it.[38] Could Muslims see a just war—and more generally, the use of force to right wrongs—as a form of the love of enemies?

Many Muslims refuse to draw this conclusion, including the signatories of the "Common Word." "As Muslims," they write, "we say to Christians that we are not against them and that Islam is not against them—so long as they do not wage war against Muslims on account of their religion, oppress them and drive them out of their homes."[39] Muslims are "not forbidden" from "dealing kindly and justly" with those who are "just" toward them (Al Mumtahinah, 60:8). Muslims can be kind to non-Muslims as long as they are not against Muslims. But Muslims *are* against those who wage war against them. This is an understandable stance, and it is compatible with the requirements of justice. But that's not love for one's enemies as Christians understand it. To love, we have to be *for* someone. That is the teaching and the example of Christ. For Christians, this is not just a noble way to live out one's faith, a supererogatory act, but an explicit and repeated command of God. Whether Christians act in kindness and forgive or act with severity and engage in a just struggle, they are commanded to act in their enemy's favor, as the "Yale Response" to the "Common Word" underscores.[40]

There is a powerful tradition of Muslim spirituality in which kindness even to the enemy is highly praised. This is not quite as definitive as the Christian *command* to "love the enemy," but it is nonetheless important. In his still popular manual on Sufism, Abu al-Qasim al-Qushayri (986–1074) gives an illustration of what kindness means. It is a story about a Muslim tailor and his Zoroastrian client who would pay for the services with false dirhams:

> The tailor would [always] take them. One day, when he had business away from his shop, the Zoroastrian came and paid counterfeit dirhams to his assistant, who would not accept them, and so the Zoroastrian paid in authentic dirhams. When the tailor returned, he asked, "Where is the shirt of the Zoroastrian?" When the assistant related what had happened, he said, "What evil you have done! He has been treating me like that for some time, and I've borne it patiently, casting his counterfeit money in a well, lest another be harmed by it."[41]

Christians can recognize in this story love for neighbors and perhaps even love for enemies.

Same God, Different Love?

Let's sum up the conclusions reached about God and love in this chapter and the previous one. If sacred books and great teachers of both traditions are our guide, we can say that Christians and Muslims (roughly) agree that:

1. God loves creatures in a compassionate, gift-giving sort of way.
2. God is just.
3. God's justice is an aspect of God's love for—or mercy toward—creatures.

4. Human beings are called to love all neighbors as they love themselves.

These agreements, though incomplete, are significant. True, they do not nullify the sense of many Muslims and Christians that the moral character of the God they worship is also different. But that is because the spectrum of opinions about God among both Christians and Muslims is wide. When some Christians, for instance, insist that Muslims worship a violent deity bent on war whereas they worship the God of love, this may be true with regard to a specific group of Muslims (say, the *takfiris*[42] and the jihadists). But this is not true with regard to the God of the Qur'an as interpreted by the great Muslim teachers throughout history. The difference between the God of the Muslim and Christian normative traditions is not "God of war" or "God of justice" versus "God of love."

However, there are differences, places where Christians would want to push Muslims to go farther than many seem able to go. The comments below highlight the primary areas of difference and are intended as an invitation to explore the possibility of greater Christian-Muslim agreement on aspects of the understanding of God that matters most to Christians:

1. Christians affirm unequivocally that *God is love*. All Muslims affirm that God is loving in the sense of being merciful toward creatures, and most are willing to say that love is an essential characteristic of God's eternal being. Most are, however, unable to say that God *is* love.

2. Most Christians say that God's eternal love includes love of the other, the divine other within the triune godhead and, derivatively, a creaturely other. When Muslims speak of God's eternal love, they affirm God's self-love and see in it the foundation of divine love of creatures.

3. Christians affirm unequivocally that God, though condemning all ungodliness, loves "the ungodly" with a saving love and not just providential care. God is love, and

therefore loves all human beings unconditionally and without exception, the godly and the ungodly. To Christians, for whom this is one of the bedrock tenets of their faith, it seems that the sharp distinction in Islam between those whom God loves and those whom God does not love suggests that divine love must be "earned" by human obedience to God's precepts. They will want to hear that the primacy of God's love and mercy in the view of many great Muslim teachers makes the need to earn God's love superfluous and, indeed, inappropriate.

4. Christians affirm unequivocally that God commands people to love even their enemies. As God loves the "ungodly," we should love our enemies. Though Muslims insist that we should be kind to all, including those who do us harm, most reject the idea that the love of neighbor includes the love of enemy.

Do these differences undermine the argument that Muslims and Christians have a common God? More than anyone else I can think of, Martin Luther would have been inclined to say that they do. For the unconditional love of God who is nothing but pure love was at the core of his reformation. Catholics missed that, he argued. So did Jews and Muslims. And yet even Luther did not think that Jews, Muslims, and Catholics worshipped a God different from the one worshipped by right-believing Christians. He held that they worshipped the same God, but had a seriously distorted understanding of the one and only God.

Although I agree with the basic thrust of his "same God, different understanding" thesis, unlike Luther, I am more struck by the similarities in Christian and Muslim understandings of divine and human love than by the differences. He highlighted critical differences partly because his primary concern was the standing of a human person before God, salvation of the soul. I can elevate pervasive similarities, because my primary concern is the ability of Muslims and Christians to live a peaceful, well-ordered life in this

PART IV
Living Under the Same Roof

CHAPTER TEN

The Same God, the Same Religion?

The bottom line of my argument so far? Muslims and Christians have a common God and partly overlapping understandings of God and God's commands—above all that God is one and that God is benevolent and commands us to love God with our whole being and our neighbors as ourselves. Does this make any difference for the way Muslims and Christians relate to one another? Some say, "None whatsoever." Obviously, I disagree. Otherwise I would have been merely shadowboxing in this book. So let's first briefly examine the arguments of those who dismiss the importance of similarities, and then, in the remainder of the book, we'll explore what difference "a common God" makes for relations between Islam and Christianity as faiths (chapters 10 and 11) and for the civic life of Christians and Muslims as citizens in the same state and inhabitants of the one world (chapters 12 and 13).

Many Christians and Muslims are keenly concerned with the question of eternal salvation. They might wonder whether having a common God means having a common eternal destiny. A quick and inadequate answer is, "Not necessarily." But for the time being, I have to leave it at that. Important as this issue is, this book is not about eternal salvation, whether in a city that "is pure gold" (Rev. 21:18) or in "gardens beneath which rivers flow" (Al Baqarah, 2:25). My concern here is more mundane, the earthly coexistence of Christians and Muslims.

God: A Marker of Identity?

In an earlier chapter (chapter 4), I referred to a proposal about how to determine whether Muslims and Christians have a common God. As it is with money, so it is with God, the proposal went. If you find even the slightest difference between two banknotes, one of them is false; and you know that it's false, because it differs from the genuine one. Since Muslim convictions about God are partly different from Christian convictions, Christians must conclude that Muslims' God is false. But that argument is no good, I contended. If the argument were good, Christians would have to say that the God of the Jews is false, and Catholic Christians would be forced to say that the God of Orthodox Christians is false, and so on. Indeed, two people sitting in the same pew or prostrating in the same mosque could each rightly accuse the other of having a false god, for none of us has exactly the same convictions about God as someone else. The reason is simple: the infinitely rich God is very much unlike a banknote. It is enough, I argued there, that our beliefs about God and practices in obedience to God be *sufficiently similar* to be assured that we have a common God.

But do these similarities in beliefs and practices make any difference in real life? Again, some argue they don't. As it is with flags, so it is with God, they suggest. The flags of the United States and of Malaysia are remarkably similar; they both have red and white stripes with a blue rectangle in the upper left corner. The difference is that there are fewer stripes in the Malaysian flag than in the U.S. one and that the blue rectangle in the Malaysian flag has a waning crescent and a yellow star instead of the fifty white stars. The similarities between the flags of these two countries are striking and obviously greater than the differences. And yet the similarities are of no consequence at all. A flag is a symbol of national identity. It demarcates one nation from another no matter how much or how little it differs from another flag.

Some suggest that God is like a flag, a symbol of the identity of a religious community. The great German philosopher Georg W. F. Hegel expressed the position well: "Religion is the place wherein a people gives itself the definition of what it holds to be true. . . . Thus the representation of God constitutes the general foundation of a people."[1] It would be as absurd to say that two groups of people have a common God as it would be to say that two nations share a flag.[2] Worship of a God—that is, a religion—marks a community as distinct from another community. Any similarities in religious rituals or in beliefs about God are irrelevant. Different flags for different nations; different Gods for different communities.

Examples of religion serving as a marker of identity are not hard to find. When Serbia won the European basketball championship in 1995, the entire team flashed the "three-finger salute" (the right arm raised with the thumb, index finger, and middle finger extended). They weren't making a botched victory sign with a thumb sticking out when it should have been folded in; they were brandishing a genuine religious symbol. The Orthodox Serbs use three fingers to cross themselves; a popular Serbian rhyme goes that you cannot cross yourself validly without using three fingers (*Nema krsta bez tri prsta!*). The three outstretched digits stand for the Holy Trinity, and the two fingers stand for the two natures of Christ. The most important mysteries of the Christian faith are expressed in that simple gesture. But in using it, the victorious basketball players were not thinking about these profound principles of the Christian faith. As one of the players, Saša Djordjević, explained: "That's Serbia, that's us, that's me—nothing else. It's my pride."[3] The point was to mark identity; the salute's deeper meaning was irrelevant at that time. Instead of flashing the three fingers, the basketball team could have waved a flag.

Just as, in the basketball scenario, the three fingers was an empty symbol, so some believe that God, as a marker of identity, is an empty symbol. "We believe in the Holy Trinity," then, means no more than, "That's 'us' as opposed to the nontrinitarian 'them.'" Or maybe it's better to say that the symbol is emptied of its genuine religious meaning rather than that it is empty, for a community does infuse "God" with life and value. God is then the god *of* a given community, an embodiment of its own sense of its character as a community, and it separates that community from all other communities. As communities compete or fight, Gods compete and fight—our God against yours. The result is a clash of communities. Understood as a marker of identity, God is a source of difference and conflict, never a resource for reconciliation.

But God is not a flag—at least Muslims and Christians, who inherited the one true God of Israel, should not treat the Creator of the Universe as a flag. If you turn God into a marker of identity, then you replace the one God, creator and redeemer of all humanity, with the many gods of diverse nations. The living God, who is above all creatures, morphs into an idol stitched together by human imagination from the stuff of this world, an empty receptacle of a community's sense of itself. For both Christians and Muslims, God infinitely transcends any community; God is the source of everything that is truly valuable, including any given community in fellowship with all other communities. Rather than God's being an expression of a community's aspirations, Christians and Muslims believe that all people and all communities ought to align their aspirations with God's character and demands. God should be a *maker* and not a marker of identity. For Christians and Muslims alike, God is the *source* of worshippers' deepest values. That's why two communities can have a common God. And that's why having a common God can be the foundation for unity rather than a cause of division.

If God is a marker of identity, then the Gods of two communities must be different, and any similarities between them are immaterial. It is very different if God is the source of worshippers' deepest values. In general, if communities worship different deities who have very little in common, the values of the communities will collide, and their beliefs about God will deepen conflicts between them. Inversely, if communities have a common God and if their beliefs about God are similar, they will share values, aspirations, and motivations. More important, to the extent that they give ultimate allegiance to God, these shared values, aspirations, and motivations will trump values, aspirations, and motivations derived from their respective group identities.[4] The one common God is the God of all human beings, whether they recognize God as God or not, commanding all persons to aim higher than the kind of life defined for them by society or even the religious community to which they belong.

Muslims and Christians have a common God, I argued. And, notwithstanding important differences in their beliefs, they think of God in remarkably similar ways. What difference might this make in the way they relate to each other as religious groups?

The Same God, the Same Religion?

If Christians and Muslims pray to the same God, doesn't this make Christianity and Islam the same religion? "Religion" is a contested term, so much so that some scholars think that "religion" as a separate sphere of human activity was invented at the dawn of modernity.[5] But the basic idea behind my question is simple, and I can state it without using the term "religion." If Muslims and Christians have a common God, are not Islam and Christianity just two versions of the same thing? Progressives, on the whole, celebrate this possibility, seeing in it the hope of mitigating conflicts generated by religious differences. Conservatives, on the whole, fear this possibility, suspecting that those who embrace it are not concerned about the truth of God's revelation and the dangers that a dissolution of religious identity represents.

Gotthold Ephraim Lessing, a major figure in the Western Enlightenment, set the tone for the way in which many modern people think about relations between religions. Let's return to his *Nathan the Wise,* a play about the relation between Judaism, Christianity, and Islam. The play is set in Jerusalem and contains the story of the three rings. At one point in the play Sultan Saladin asks a Jewish merchant by the name of Nathan which religion "makes most sense" to him, pointing out that "only one can be the true religion."[6]

Caught between the alternative of betraying his own faith or offending the ruler, Nathan tells a story of a father who had three sons and a special ring, which had the mysterious power of making whoever wore it agreeable to God and human beings. Since he loved all three equally, he promised each that, upon his death, the ring would be his. When his days were nearing their end, he was at a loss for what to do. So he had two additional rings made, identical to the original one, and on his deathbed he fulfilled his promise, giving one to each. Immediately the sons started to quarrel about which of the three rings was genuine. "The true ring was indistinguishable" from the false ones, Nathan said to Saladin. Then, after a pause to let Saladin absorb the point, Nathan added, "almost as indistinguishable as the true religion is to us."[7] Saladin protested. Religions are different, he said, and their differences are visible even in the dress codes. Nathan was undeterred. In outward rituals and customs, the three religions are different, he said, but "in their foundation" they are indistinguishable.[8]

The story implies that there is a true religion, but that we just can't tell which one it is. Yet for Lessing, it seems, the truth of religion was not at issue, at least not the truth in its usual sense of our beliefs somehow matching up to the divine reality. Lessing was interested in the *fruit* of religion—love of neighbor. The religion with the higher yield in generosity is the truer one.

For many today in the West, all religions, though not the same, are roughly on par with one another, versions of one and the same thing. Some consider them equally useful, equally efficient ways to promote human values. Others consider them, in addition, equally true, each a culturally conditioned version of one essential truth.[9] To people who hold one of these positions, the claim that Muslims and Christians have a common God merely states the obvious: that Christianity and Islam are different versions of the same thing— two variants of the same basic orientation of human beings toward the same mystery at the heart of being.

But are Islam and Christianity basically one religion in two versions? More important for our purposes here, does having a common God make them variants of the same thing? It does not, as the self-understanding of the majority of Muslims and Christians would attest. It is possible to believe in the same God as another person and yet to belong to a different religion.[10] Compare again relations between Christianity and Judaism. Almost universally, Christians consider the God of Israel to be the same God as the one they worship (even if many Jews beg to differ with them for reasons that I briefly explored in chapter 7). But Christians don't consider Judaism and Christianity to be the same religion. Christianity emerged as a sect within Judaism, but there was an eventual parting of ways (scholars debate why it came about and when exactly it occurred[11]).

Return now to the relation between Islam and Christianity. The differences between the two are greater than the differences between Judaism and Christianity. The connections with Christianity at Islam's origin are looser, as Islam did not emerge as a sect within Christianity or Judaism; it was a distinct way of life from the start. We have, therefore, all the more reason to conclude that the common God does not erase boundaries between Christianity and Islam as religions.

In many ways, however, it does not really matter whether Islam and Christianity are the same *religion*. Commenting about "religion," Denys Turner notes, "I know of no one at all who actually practices 'religion.' For sure I don't. I am a practicing Catholic Christian."[12] A practicing Christian who doesn't practice "religion"?! To many this makes no sense. If you are a practicing Christian, you practice religion, Christianity being one of the world's great religions. But "religion" is an abstract concept; a person does not follow "religion" in general, but always a specific one. Though it is a useful term in some regards, "religion" tells you little about what Christians, Muslims, Buddhists, or Hindus actually believe and practice. We can discard the term "religion" and not lose anything of the living reality of a community's life with God in the world.

If neither Muslims nor Christians practice "religion," why should it matter whether Islam and Christianity are one religion or two? The similarities and differences in Muslim and Christian beliefs and practices are important, not whether you designate Christianity and Islam one religion or two. Nicholas of Cusa thought that all "religions," maybe especially Islam and Christianity, are versions of a single faith (see chapter 2). Martin Luther, I suspect, would have been aghast at that suggestion, prone as he was to think in terms of "either/or" rather than "both/and" (see chapter 3). But for Nicholas, no less than for Luther, it was crucial which beliefs and practices you embrace.

Does the doctrine of the Trinity imply division in God? Is God love? Is Jesus Christ the incarnation of the Word, which was in the beginning with God? Did Jesus die on the cross for the salvation of the world? Was Muhammad the "Seal of the Prophets"? Does God love the ungodly, and does God command us to love our enemies rather than to love just our friends or neighbors? Questions such as these would remain whether we designated Christianity and Islam one religion or two religions. How Muslims and Christians answer them shapes the life of each community and relations between them. The conviction that Muslims and Christians have a common God does not prejudge correct answers to these questions. But it should motivate Christians and Muslims to engage in a common search for answers, including through vigorous arguments. After all, these questions concern the character and the actions of the One to whom both give ultimate allegiance.

A Christian and a Muslim at the Same Time?

In his famous article "The Clash of Civilizations?" Samuel Huntington suggests that civilizations clash partly because they are based on different religions. Religions, he notes, define nearly exclusive identities: "A person can be half-French and half-Arab and simultaneously even a citizen of two countries. It is more difficult to be half-Catholic and half-Muslim."[13] More difficult, maybe, but far from impossible! We live in a world of interdependent and intermeshed peoples in which individual choice reigns supreme. It's a mix-and-match world, and that applies to religions as well. Jubus, people who seek to combine Jewish and Buddhist forms of spirituality, are the most famous example of such hybrid religiosity. The number of those who blend elements of various religions into unique forms, tailor-made for them or their small community, is growing. Today many are abandoning the religious prix fixe menus of traditional faiths in favor of new cafeteria-style forms of spirituality.[14]

Not surprisingly, people have created "religious dishes" by combining Islam and Christianity. Ann Redding was an ordained Episcopal priest. She was moved by Muslim spirituality—by the act of prostration in total surrender to God and by a chanted prayer. God was inviting her, she felt. She responded by saying the Shahada, the profession that there is no god but God and that Muhammad is God's messenger. She was now a Muslim—*and* an Episcopal priest! In her car, she hung a cross made out of clear crystal beads and next to it a heart-shaped leather object etched with "Allah" in Arabic. "For me, that symbolizes who I am," Redding explained. "I look through Jesus and I see Allah."[15]

Although supporters defended her actions, her bishop defrocked her in accordance with the canons of the Episcopal Church. The explanation? She "abandoned the Communion of the Episcopal Church by formal admission into a religious body not in communion with the Episcopal Church." In her mind, however, membership in a religious body should not have decided the matter. Her ultimate allegiance should have determined her status in the church. "Both religions say there's only one God, and that God is the same God. It's very clear we are talking about the same God! So I haven't shifted my allegiance."[16] She was 100 percent Christian and 100 percent Muslim, she insisted.[17]

In the controversy, the issue was Redding's priesthood, not her Christian faith. She was defrocked, not excommunicated. While claiming to be 100 percent Muslim, she remained a member of the Episcopal Church. Many would have excommunicated her as well, for in Christian circles the reigning consensus over the years has been that one cannot be simultaneously a Christian and a Muslim.

This consensus has been recently unsettled, however. Now a spirited debate rages around it, especially in evangelical circles. It centers primarily on Muslims who insist that they can be followers of Christ without abandoning Islam. In an article on Muslim-background believers, Joseph Cumming tells of such a person:

> Ibrahim was a well-respected scholar of the Qur'an, a hafiz [a person who has memorized the entire Qur'an]. When he decided to follow Jesus, he closely examined the Qur'anic verses commonly understood as denying the Trinity, denying Jesus' divine Sonship, denying Jesus' atoning death, and denying the textual integrity of the Bible. He concluded that each of these verses was open to alternate interpretations, and that he could therefore follow Jesus as a Muslim.[18]

Again, 100 percent Muslim and 100 percent Christian—or so Ibrahim would claim.

Rules for Blending Religions

Can we legitimately blend Christianity and Islam in the ways Redding and Ibrahim want to? Let's be clear on what this issue is *not* about. (Here, as throughout this book, I am writing from a Christian standpoint; Muslims will have their own ways of approaching the matter.)

1. The issue is not whether a person has *the right to combine elements* of two faiths. All people have the right to believe whatever they please, whether what they believe fits with normative Christianity and Islam or not, and whether what

they believe even makes sense or not! Error may have no rights, but human beings have the right to err. On account of their beliefs, people may be denied membership in a given religious community, but their right to decide what they believe is sacred. One either believes freely, or one doesn't believe at all.

2. The issue is not whether it is appropriate to *adopt cultural forms*—such as dress, food, or language—associated with another faith. The Christian church was born on the day of Pentecost when the Spirit fell on the disciples and they spoke in the languages of the peoples from different cultures assembled in Jerusalem (see Acts 2:1–13). From the start the Christian message was translated into idioms and cultural forms other than Jewish ones.[19] The Christian faith doesn't have a sacred language; neither Latin (for centuries the language of Roman Catholic liturgies) nor Old Slavonic (used in some Orthodox churches) is a sacred language. Translatable as it is, the Christian faith can be completely at home in any culture (though it will partly change that culture from within).[20]

3. The controversy is not whether it is legitimate to *take over religious practices and spiritual insights* from one faith into another. Each faith has a repertoire of beliefs and practices.[21] At a given time or place, a faith will foreground some themes in its repertoire and background others. Currently, for instance, "submission to God," Islam's central theme, is not a favorite "melody" of many Christians in the West;[22] it runs counter to Western egalitarian cultural sensibilities. But it's an essential and often performed part of the historic Christian repertoire. After all, Christians believe that God is the sovereign Lord. It would be fully legitimate, and maybe even desirable, for Christians in the West, partly nudged by Muslims, to rediscover "submission to God" as a key dimension of spirituality. In addition to foregrounding various themes from the existing repertoire, new elements can be legitimately added to the Christian repertoire from outside sources. These

just need to fit with the basic content of the Christian faith. Christmas celebration is a trivial example. December 25, the day on which, according to legend, the pagan sun god Mithra was born, was adopted as the date for the feast of the Nativity. What would then prohibit the act of prostrating and saying, "Glorified is my Lord, the Exalted!" from being adopted by Christians? Merely the fact that it is a Muslim practice?

4. The issue is not whether it is legitimate to *acquire a new religious identity or discard the old one*. Religious identities are fluid and mean different things to different people at different times. In some circles in the West, you can deny the divinity of Christ, think Mahatma Gandhi was a more authentic messenger of God than was the apostle Paul, and be an exemplary Christian. If that's what "Christian" means, there is no reason why Redding, while fully embracing a traditional Muslim understanding of Jesus Christ as a great prophet, could not be 100 percent Christian. Religious labels are useful because they help avoid confusion, but in a deep sense they don't matter. The first followers of Jesus Christ were not Christians—until *outsiders* called them by that name (see Acts 11:26). The name and religious identity are unimportant; the reality of following the Christ as the Lord is.

What, then, is the critical issue in attempts to blend Christianity and Islam? It is people's allegiance, practices, and beliefs, all three taken together. Redding zeroed in on the allegiance to the same God. If the God of Christians and Muslims is the same, then embracing Islam is no shift in allegiance, and therefore it is only a slight shift in beliefs and practices, she suggested. This is true, but it disregards an important consideration. The Christian faith is not simply about allegiance to the right God; it is not even about allegiance to the God whose character was fully revealed by Jesus Christ. Christian faith in its normative expressions is about the *right worship of God through Christ*. The right worship consists above all in receiving the gift of God's own self given in Christ apart from any human qualifications—apart from belonging to a particular community, apart from persons' moral qualities. Paradoxically, the only condition for receiving the gift is not trying to satisfy any conditions. The gift is utterly free. That was Martin Luther's point when he, in debates with Islam, insisted that everything in the Christian faith depends on the conviction that God was in Christ and that Christ "died for our sins, that he was raised for our life, that justified by faith in him our sins are forgiven and we are saved."[23]

When it comes to blending elements of Islam with Christianity, the central questions for Christians are the following:

1. Were you baptized in the name of the triune God?
2. Do you confess that Jesus Christ, in whom God dwelled in human flesh, is the Lord?
3. Have you received the divine gift of new life given freely through Christ?

If your answers are yes, then you are 100 percent Christian (or, if you prefer, a follower of Christ). You might be a bad Christian, in saintliness more like the thief on the cross than like St. Francis of Assisi; or you might be an underinformed Christian, with an understanding of faith more like my eight-year-old son Aaron than like Augustine. But you are still 100 percent Christian.

Now imagine that you also fasted on Ramadan, prayed five times a day by prostrating and saying Al Fatihah (the first surah of the Qur'an, the seven lines of which sum up the human relation to God in contemplation and prayer),[24] and believe that Muhammad was a prophet (not "the Seal of the Prophets," but a prophet in the way in which we might designate Martin Luther King Jr. "a prophet"). If your answers are still yes to the three questions above, you would still be 100 percent Christian.[25]

In holding many Muslim convictions and engaging in many Muslim practices, you can still be 100 percent Christian. Can you be 100 percent Muslim if you have answered the three above questions with yes? That is not for Christians to answer. Muslims must answer it.

In a sense, hybrid religiosity—wanting to be 100 percent Muslim and 100 percent Christian or mixing the two in some other proportion—is a *good problem* to have. If there is an error in the attempt, it is born of attraction to the beauty of the other faith, possibly even of love for those who practice it, and not generated by disdain and malice. The most pressing problem among religions today is not the blurring of boundaries by mixing and matching; it's the propensity to engage others with disrespect, hostility, and violence. These often manifest themselves in deep-seated prejudices and aggressive forms of mission—the subject of the next chapter.

CHAPTER ELEVEN

Prejudices, Proselytism, and Partnership

With their tips reaching into the heavens and their foundations dug in the earth, steeples and minarets symbolize the spiritual elevation of flesh-and-blood human beings toward God. Nothing seems controversial about such symbolic representations of love of God. And yet controversies over them abound. As a result of a referendum in 2009, construction of minarets (though not mosques) has been banned in Switzerland.[1] In many majority Muslim countries, if new churches are allowed to be built, they often do not even have a plaque, let alone a steeple, to mark them visibly as Christian houses of worship.[2] Why the prohibitions? Steeples symbolize *Christians'* love for God, whereas minarets symbolize *Muslims'* love for God. And that difference, made publicly visible, generates conflicts.

Steeples and minarets are a public witness to the presence of Christianity and Islam in a community or a nation, to the claim of these religious groups to be recognized as shapers of public space and discourse, and to their desire to spread themselves into new territories. They keep before people's eyes three highly explosive issues: (1) the relation of strangers and minorities to communal and national identity, (2) the distribution of political power, and (3) the right to engage in mission and to expand.

In some ways, the issue of mission and expansion is the most critical one; both the presence of a group in a community and its power depend on it. A no to minarets is above all a no to Muslim expansion. In the campaign before the Swiss referendum, the opponents of minarets created a poster on which a Swiss flag is pierced by minarets portrayed as missiles. A poem that landed Recep Tayyip Erdogan, present prime minister of Turkey, in jail in 1998 was widely circulated in support of the poster's imagery: "Mosques are our barracks, the domes our helmets, the minarets our bayonets, and faithful our soldiers." Similar resistance to expansion is palpable in the Muslim opposition to new churches in many majority Muslim lands; a no to new churches—or a no to the *visibility* of new churches—is a no to Christian expansion and Christian mission.

Public religious symbols do not just express the aspirations of believers; they communicate those aspirations to outsiders. But what insiders want to communicate and what outsiders actually hear and see may be two very different things. Who is it actually that's "invading" our space? As of the writing of this book, Imam Faisal Abdul Rauf has undertaken to build a Muslim center with a mosque—Cordoba House—in close proximity to Ground Zero, the place where the Twin Towers stood before Muslim terrorists destroyed them. The stated goal of Faisal Abdul Rauf is to contribute to the atmosphere of interfaith tolerance and respect between Muslims, Christians, and Jews. Though city officials have rallied behind the project, many New Yorkers and many Americans more broadly are fiercely opposed to the project. The terrorists were Muslims who acted in God's name.[3] A Muslim house of prayer near Ground Zero would be an insult to the attack's three thousand victims, they feel. Their unstated assumption is that Islam is inseparable from terrorism. But who is right, Imam Faisal Abdul Rauf or his opponents? Is he dissimulating, smiling on the outside but cursing on the inside, or are his opponents passing off demeaning and dangerous prejudices as incontestable verities? As public symbols of Islam, mosques are repositories of conflicting interpretations of Islam as a religion. A new mosque in a non-Muslim land, such as Cordoba House, raises the question of the proper knowledge of the other.

In this chapter I take up these two problems: mission by the other and knowledge of the other. I argue that a common commitment to love God and neighbor should lead both Christians and Muslims to seek (1) to know themselves and others truthfully and (2) to spread faith respectfully. I end the chapter by noting that the two faiths may have a common mission in the contemporary world. Steeples and minarets, I said at the beginning, are symbols of human elevation toward God. This elevation, understood by each faith differently, is their joint mission—to bear witness that a life of true human flourishing is possible only when we resist the pursuit of mere pleasure and in love turn toward God and neighbor.

Against Prejudice

Prejudices are errors born of ignorance, self-absorption, resentment, and fear—all stances incompatible with the active love of neighbor enjoined on Muslims and Christians alike by their common God. The best way to fight prejudice is by knowledge—not just knowledge of peoples' beliefs and practices, but knowledge of their feelings and hopes, their injuries and triumphs as well.

"To understand" is not necessarily "to agree with." No amount of study of the ideology of extremists is likely to make me believe that issuing death threats against the Dutch feminist activist Ayaan Hirsi Ali, who wrote the screenplay for the short film *Submission,* is an acceptable way to respond to her criticism and rejection of Islam. "To understand" is also not necessarily "to excuse." Empathetic understanding of the Moroccan Muslim who killed Theo van Gogh, the director of *Submission,* will not make me believe that his behavior was somehow excusable. But understanding will prevent me from concluding: "Issuing death threats and killing people for advocating views deemed unacceptable proves that violence is at the heart of Islam." Instead, I will more likely conclude that people with violent proclivities and beset by fear use Islam to justify violence or erroneously think they are defending Islam by being violent. The same holds true for terrorist acts more generally committed by Muslims.[4]

Acquiring knowledge of the other is a complicated affair. For one thing, our lives are saturated with information, and it is hard to pick out "knowledge" from mere opinion. Second, "knowledge" always comes bearing somebody's stamp on it; knowledge is acquired from one perspective rather than another and motivated by one set of interests rather than another. Perspectives and interests sometimes clash, and then knowledges collide. Knowledge of one person can be the prejudice of another, and then truth and falsehood, two polar opposites, merge.

In *Exclusion and Embrace,* a book that treats conflicts involving group identities, I suggested a way of keeping apart knowledge and prejudice, truth and falsehood. I called for "double vision": for seeing things *from here* as well as *from there,* for inspecting things from our vantage point as well as from the vantage point of others.[5] It takes little effort to see things from our vantage point; that's what we do all the time. To see them from the vantage point of others is an achievement. Here is how you do it:

1. Register how you see the other and yourself.
2. Step imaginatively outside yourself and into the world of the other.
3. Observe yourself as well as the other with the eyes of the other.
4. Return to yourself and compare the findings.
5. Repeat the process.

The goal? Not necessarily full agreement. The question at this stage is not who is right—for example, Muslims who reject that Jesus Christ is the Son of God who died on the cross, or Christians for whom this is the central pillar of their faith? The question is, rather, the one that we must ask before we can explore who is right, that is, what does each party mean—what do Muslims mean when they reject that Jesus is the Son of God, and what do Christians mean when they affirm this conviction. The goal is a common understanding, the presence of each belief in an undistorted way in the understanding of the other. The double vision is a way of coming to know the other truthfully, an application of the command to love the neighbor to how we seek knowledge of the neighbor.

Two Persons, Four Images, One God

Double vision is needed, because even the most ordinary encounter between people is a complex matter. It has been said that in every encounter between two people, between you and me, *four* are always involved, not just two. Two of these four are, obviously, you and me. But also present in the encounter are my image of you and your image of me. Our encounter is truthful when my image of you matches who you truly are and your image of me matches who I truly am. If I, as a Christian, say that the God of the Qur'an is a violent deity who pushes Muslim men to inflict unimaginable cruelty on women, I distort the beliefs and practices of many Muslims (and I do so even if I cannot fully agree with the genuine Muslim understanding of God or with the status and the treatment of women in Islam). Similarly, if you, as a Muslim, say that Christians believe in three gods or that Christian faith encourages empty hedonism rather than other-regarding saintliness, you distort the beliefs and practices of many Christians.

The match between the image and reality will never be complete. All our knowledge is partial. And yet I will strive to adjust my image of you to your reality. My distorted image of you dishonors you; I do you injustice by clinging to it. Prejudice is injustice.[6] If I care for you, I will want my image of you to do you justice. I will seek to know you as you are (while recognizing that I will never be able to achieve such knowledge fully).

The "encounter of four" approach would take us a long way in combating prejudices in relations between Christians and Muslims. However, the approach isn't quite complete. I would propose that in every encounter *seven* are involved. There are you and I, and my image of you and your image of me—the obvious two and the other, somewhat surprising, two. But there's also my image of myself (which may not be true to who I am and may be unlike who you think I am). Correspondingly, there's your image of yourself (which may not be true to who you are and may be unlike who I think you are). So that makes six in one encounter.

The consequence? I have to learn to see myself as I truly am, not just expect that you see me as I see myself. If I don't learn this, I might experience your truthful description of me as prejudice. For instance, as a Christian, I may cling so tightly to the idea of Christianity as a religion of love that I completely shut out the persistent history of violence associated with it; or I might so readily embrace freedom of religion that I forget that it was only in the course of the last century that the Catholic Church embraced the idea.[7]

Similarly, you have to learn to see yourself as who you truly are, not just demand that I see you as you see yourself; otherwise you might experience my truthful description of you as prejudice. For instance, as a Muslim, you may think that harsh punishments against apostates are appropriate and miss the fundamental disregard for a person's conscience that the punishments represent, or you may fail to notice the contradiction between punishments for apostates and the claim that there is no compulsion in religion (see chapter 12). To combat prejudices effectively, we need to remove distortions in our image of ourselves and not just in our image of others.

I spoke of *seven* in every encounter. Who is the seventh? In every encounter there is also another one present—the categorically unique and utterly incomparable One, the absolutely truthful and infinitely loving One. God is present in every encounter between Christians and Muslims, their common God. As the truthful Judge, God sees each person truthfully rather than distorting their identities. As infinite love, God cares for each and therefore desires for each to care for the other in all their dealings with each other. Being truthful about the other as well as about ourselves is part of care for others.

If God is always involved in any encounter, then the seventh one is really the First One—not first among others, but the first who makes all others and their undistorted encounters possible. For Christians and Muslims, combating prejudices starts with joint allegiance to the absolutely truthful and infinitely loving God.

Mission: War by Other Means?

Mission is an explosive issue in relations between Muslims and Christians. Prince Ghazi bin Muhammad, in charge of religious affairs in Jordan and the main force behind the "Common Word" initiative, named "fear and resentment of the massive missionary movement launched from the West into the Islamic world" as one of the top three roots of tensions in Muslim-Christian relations—immediately after the conflict in Israel/Palestine and the Iraq war.[8]

Ever since Jesus sent his disciples "to proclaim the kingdom of God and to heal" (Luke 9:2), Christians have engaged in mission.[9] All four Gospels report that the last words of Jesus to his disciples included a commission to proclaim the good news. When Christians engaged in mission well, they did not try to spread the "Christian religion," let alone to establish a "Christian culture" or expand the "Christian sphere of influence"; they were bearing witness to Christ in word and deed, as Christ himself instructed them to do (see Acts 1:8). As witnesses, Christians were at their worst when zealous preachers followed in the wake of expansionist traders, businessmen, and conquering soldiers (for example, in 2003 evangelical preachers arrived in Iraq immediately after the soldiers[10]). At the same time, missionaries have consistently been among the most dogged critics of aggression and exploitative business practices of their countrymen.[11] As bearers of the good news, Christians have a somewhat mixed track record. But mission and the Christian faith are inseparable.

Many Muslims see Christian mission as war by other means. Muslims' fears of Christian mission are fed by a sense that the West, often mistakenly described as "Christian,"[12] has subjected Muslims to "humiliation and disgrace" for "more than eighty years," as Osama bin Laden put it in his first tape after al-Qaeda brought down the Twin Towers and attacked the Pentagon in 2001.[13] What was he referring to by pointing to the early years of the twentieth century? The Ottoman Empire was defeated in 1918, a final act of its steady decline, which started in 1683 when the Turks were repelled from Vienna. With the demise of the Ottoman Empire, the Muslim world was divided between the four European colonial powers: Britain, France, the Netherlands, and Russia. As in Western imagination at the time, so also in Muslim perception today— the fall of the Ottoman Empire was the conclusion of the Crusades, triumphant for the West and humiliating for the Muslim East. On December 11, 1917, the British-led force overcame the Turkish defenders of Jerusalem and ended eight centuries of Muslim rule over the Holy City of Jerusalem.[14] Is this an accurate and nuanced portrayal of relations between Muslims and Christians from the First Crusade to the beginning of the twentieth century? In my judgment, it is not. But this is how many Muslims see things, and it shapes the way they perceive Christian mission.

Muslim disgrace continued after decolonization in the aftermath of World War II. Western hegemony changed character, but continued unabated—at least in the experience of many Muslims. The United States, presently the dominant Western power, exerted its hegemony in two ways. First, it lent political and military support to oppressive and partly secularized regimes in the majority Muslim nations. It also propped up Israel, which is seen as occupying Muslim holy sites, and it engaged in direct wars against majority Muslim nations. Second, the United States is the force behind "globalization," a dirty word in the vocabulary of many Muslims, because it is associated with exploitation of people and destruction of Islamic culture. Globalization is but the continuation of colonialism, many of them believe.

Recently, I discussed Christian mission in majority Muslim lands with a Muslim friend. He was passionately opposed to it, unimpressed by the arguments for the right to bear witness to one's faith and the right to choose one's faith freely. He remained unswayed in his antagonism toward Christian mission even by the record of missionaries' consistent critique of military and cultural aggression against Muslims. Western soldiers kill Muslims' bodies with their sophisticated weapons; Christian missionaries kill Muslims' souls with their sleek evangelism techniques and material inducements, he insisted. To strip Muslims of religious identity is to kill them as Muslims. Christian mission is war. Mission, colonialism, and globalization feed off each other to the detriment of Muslims.

Christians have their own set of complaints against Muslims. Just ask African Christians, and they will tell you that for every misdeed of Christian evangelists, you will find one on the Muslim side, and more.[15] On the whole, however, the main Christian complaints are concerned less with *da'wa*—the Muslim call to faith—and more with freedom of religion and the laws against apostasy enforced in many majority Muslim countries. I discuss these issues in the next chapter about living together in the same state. Here, in a chapter about relations between two religious communities, my topic is the clash between the Christian obligation to witness and visceral Muslim opposition to it. Does having a common God and overlapping understandings of God help? It does. But how?

A Common Code of Conduct

Some suggest that having a common God makes all Christian evangelism—as well as Muslim *da'wa*—superfluous. Our attitude about this matter, argues Seyyed Hossein Nasr, one of the leading Muslim thinkers in the world today, "will change if we realize not only theoretically, but also concretely, that we belong to the same family of religions, worshipping the same God."[16] Both evangelism and *da'wa,* which in his view amount to trying to "destroy each other," should give way to vying "with each other in goodness" (Al Ma'idah, 5:48).[17]

Christians will appreciate the sentiment, but most are likely to reject the proposal. As I have argued earlier, the Christian faith is not simply about allegiance to God. It is about worshipping God through Christ, the Word become flesh (see chapter 10); Christ reveals the true character of God, and Christ makes the true worship of God possible. Having a common God doesn't cancel the need for witness to Christ as the way to God.

Many Muslims feel similarly about *da'wa,* as Muhammad was sent "as a universal (Messenger) to men" (Saba', 34:28). For a small minority of Muslims this implies obligation to wage war until all have submitted to the call of Islam, for Muhammad said, "Fight with them until they bear testimony to the fact that there is no god but God and Muhammad is his Messenger."[18] In this interpretation of *da'wa,* rejected by all leading Muslim scholars today,[19] war is a legitimate and obligatory means of *da'wa;* faith is spread by the sword. In contrast to this marginal view, the great majority of Muslims insist on the obligation to call people to the proper understanding and true worship of the one God. Grand Ayatollah Muhammad Fadlallah, the late leader of Lebanese Shi'a Muslims, spoke for them:

> Islam is a religion of *da'wa* addressed to all people. Islam works through those who believe in it to bring all people into the circle of faith in God, his Messengers and his messages, and [to bring about] a practical commitment in all of this. It takes the view that God's guiding of any person to Islam constitutes the highest value in loving God—indeed that it is higher than every other intellectual value in human effort. In the scope of its activity, Islam makes no distinction between a pagan or atheist society and a religious one—Jewish, Christian, Zoroastrian or adherent to other religions, such as Buddhism and the like.[20]

Like Christians, most Muslims are not ready to give up on *da'wa* simply because the God of Christians is the same as theirs. Grand Ayatollah Fadlallah explicitly states that the call to Islam should be directed not just to pagans and atheists, but to Jews and Christians as well.

I suggest that having a common God is neither here nor there when it comes to mission. But a joint affirmation that God is a loving God and that God enjoins people to love their neighbors as they love themselves is critical, for it provides a basis to work out a *common code of conduct* as Christians engage in evangelism and Muslims in *da'wa*. Here is a very brief sketch of such a code of conduct.

Imagine being guided in mission/*da'wa* by the Golden Rule, which explicates, in the tersest possible way, what love of neighbor means. If we consider some of the worst conversional practices throughout the history of both Christians and Muslims—conversions at the point of the sword, snatching small children from parents and raising them in the other faith, "bribing" people to convert, to name just three—the idea might seem radical. And yet the Golden Rule clearly applies, for its scope is universal. Jesus explicitly commanded: "In *everything* do to others as you would have them do to you" (Matt. 7:12). "Everything" includes mission.

Two basic rules for witness in word and deed follow:

1. Witness to others only if you are prepared to let them witness to you.
2. Witness to others in the way you think others should witness to you.

These two basic rules need to be carefully fleshed out. For instance, the second rule could be amplified in the following ways:[21]

1. It is wrong to coerce others to accept faith; the recipients have to be able to receive or reject faith in freedom, rather than be forced to cave in under the pressure of a superior power.
2. It is wrong to bribe or seduce others to embrace faith; the faith has to be offered as valuable and attractive in itself, rather than on account of its "packaging" or the extrinsic rewards associated with it (money or status).[22]

3. It is wrong to compare the best practices of one's own faith with the worst practices of the other faith.

For the common code of conduct to be of use in concrete situations, more is needed than good rules. Concrete situations are too complex for any rule to be sufficient. The application of the rules that express love of neighbor should be guided by the supple wisdom of that same love.

These basic rules are formulated from a Christian perspective. Muslims will have their own sense about the implications of love of neighbor for their own *da'wa* as well as for Christian witness. What would happen if Christians and Muslims discussed the issue, guided by shared allegiance to a common God who loves and commands us to love one another? I would be surprised if the result were not a *common code of conduct* to which each could hold the other accountable.

A common code of conduct is for those who agree that Christian witness and Muslim *da'wa* are obligatory, a sacred religious duty. As I noted earlier, for some Muslims—and some Christians as well, I should add—to witness is to shoot to kill. Would a shared allegiance to a common God who loves and commands us to love one another help in this case? It would, but indirectly. The two disagreeing parties would now likely not be able to appeal to the common commitment to love, because to "love" in this case would mean two different things for them. From the perspective of Muslims who oppose Christian witness, to love them would require not to witness, as it is difficult to see how "killing or destroying" a person (which they consider witness to be) could be an act of love. From the perspective of most Christians, on the other hand, to love is to bear witness—to give people an opportunity to hear the truth of the most important kind and make up their minds. The same holds true in the opposite direction, for Muslims who advocate *da'wa* and Christians who oppose it. Two people both intending to practice love—and clashing! Does this bring us to an impasse?

Not really. Disagreements about the nature of love are common.

We have seen that Christians and Muslims differ about the scope of love of neighbor. For Christians love of neighbor includes love of enemy; for most Muslims it does not (see chapter 9). Now we see a possible difference in what it may mean concretely to act in a loving way (though a difference that cuts across Muslim and Christian communities). How would a shared allegiance to a common God who loves and commands us to love one another help? It would prod us to dig deeper and find the roots of our differences (maybe diverging understandings of freedom and of the importance of group belonging for identity) and ways of bridging those differences. It would also nudge us to design workable ways to live together notwithstanding these differences.

Muslims and Christians: Shoulder to Shoulder

From what I have written so far in this chapter and the previous one it may seem as if Muslims' and Christians' biggest problem is the one that each presents for the other—attempts at conversion, prejudices, mixing and matching of the two faiths, or collapsing them into a single religion. Yet this is not the case. When Christians and Muslims turn from each other and look around, they quickly realize that the problems they face together are bigger than the problem they present to each other—abject poverty of millions, scarcity of freshwater, irreparable degradation of the environment, widespread disease, and more. Instead of merely facing each other to quarrel or reconcile, can we stand shoulder to shoulder to tackle together these grave ills of humanity?

To have a common God, creator and lover of the world, translates into commitment to care for the common world and all human beings. Christians and Muslims are both called to care for one another and for the world; there is no reason why they should not join forces and care together. In *Acts of Faith* Eboo Patel offers a powerful rationale for Muslims and Christians, along with those of other religions, to collaborate in stemming the relentless and rising tide of human misery.[23] Similarly, there is no reason why they cannot work together against the degradation of the environment.[24]

Tackling a common task often creates a common bond. The repair of ruined interfaith relations often progresses from "hand" to "heart" to "head," as Ruth Turner, the executive director of the Tony Blair Faith Foundation, has aptly put it—from working to solve a common problem, to sympathy for the other, to deeper understanding of one another.[25] Of course, the "hand" is never without the "heart" and the "head." If the hand were alone, it would be a robot's hand, not a human hand, and engaging the hand could never lead to mutual affection and deeper understanding. We work together because some human bond connects us—even if it is a mere recognition that each empathizes with the plight of those who suffer—and because the work we undertake fits with our understanding of humanity and how God is related to it. So "head" and "heart" always inform the "hand." Still, joint projects often keep the virtuous spiral moving; working together we discover deeper common affections and convictions, which in turn propel us to further joint projects.

For Muslims and Christians, one joint project seems particularly apt, if it is true that we have a common God and together believe that love of God and love of neighbor are the two greatest commandments. The joint project I have in mind doesn't so much concern the well-being of the body as it concerns the fundamental orientation of the soul and a major driving force of contemporary culture.

The Love of Pleasure and the Pleasure of Love

A major cultural disease is spreading through many nations today, especially those highly integrated into the global economy. It is not a new disease, and paradoxically it is also a reason for the economic vibrancy of these nations, which is lifting many out of poverty. The disease? For many (*not* for all), the vision of the good life, the dream of flourishing as a human being, has shrunk to the pursuit of mere pleasure. The pleasure itself is, well, wonderfully pleasurable—the sound of a child laughing, the smell of freshly baked bread, the touch of the beloved's lips, the taste of a vine-ripened strawberry, or the sight of the sun's rays falling through the trees after the rain. Such simple and primal pleasures of our senses count among the finest delights of life. And yet the pursuit of *mere* pleasure is a problem.

Today, we increasingly live for pleasure, for things and experiences that gratify us, we hope without a deferral. The point is not that we are self-indulgent, hedonistic, or possessive, whereas in the past people were altruistic, virtuous, and generous. Human nature has not changed much. Throughout history people have been self-indulgent, hedonistic, and greedy. The saying, "Let us eat and drink, for tomorrow we die," recorded in the Bible some three thousand years ago (Isa. 22:13; cf. 1 Cor. 15:32; Luke 12:19), is just one ancient expression of putting pleasure at the center of human life and embracing it as hallmark of the good life.

In the past great religions and philosophies have all sought to humanize and channel desire. Even the Epicureans, the most well known of sophisticated hedonists, did so. Though Epicurus (341–270 BCE) considered pleasure the goal of human life, he argued that attainment of happiness required moderation.[26] Today market forces and libertarian notions of freedom have colluded to stimulate desire and give it free reign; increasingly, we want desires gratified, not shaped, redirected, moderated, or deferred. We even craft religion as a servant of our pleasure, with God conceived of as not much more than a "divine butler."[27] As Philip Rieff noted in *The Triumph of the Therapeutic* more than half a century ago (1966), contemporary culture is a culture of the managed pursuit of pleasure, not a culture of sustained endeavor to lead the good life as defined by sacred narratives or philosophical convictions.[28]

The pursuit of mere pleasure is problematic, first, because it is ultimately self-defeating. We value pleasure so much that we do not want it to point beyond itself (as when pleasure of sex is an expression of a deeper reality of mutual love). When pleasure for pleasure's sake is the goal—when it is not placed into a structure of meaning—melancholy emptiness is often the result.[29] Our pleasure is truly human and therefore genuinely satisfying when it is an expression of something more important and enduring than the pleasure itself. The laughter of a child is pleasurable not just as a sound, but because it signifies freshness, immediacy, and innocence, for which we long. The smell of freshly baked bread and the taste of a ripe strawberry are enhanced when they are sacraments of a relationship between friends. As to the kiss, most of its pleasure comes because the lips are the lips of the beloved. Desire is fulfilled when love of pleasure gives way to the pleasure of love.[30]

True personal happiness is not the only casualty of the pursuit of mere pleasure. Civilization might be as well. Recall the work of Sigmund Freud, that great twentieth-century master of the human psyche. In his view, a human being is caught in a deep tension. On the one side are instinct and desires (the id), either an energizing life instinct or a death instinct that seeks release and rest. On the other side is the structured reality of our conscious lives (the ego), which tries to meet the desires of the id while maintaining a rational balance. Working to influence the ego is the superego, through which social repressions—cultural norms—are internalized. In the life of every person, native pulsating desires of the id are colliding with the learned regulatory mechanisms of the superego.

Freud is known for his therapeutic work, in which he sought to diminish the power of guilt and shame and open up more space for desire and the pursuit of pleasure. One thing was clear to Freud, however: management of instinctual satisfaction through repressive social norms is a condition of personality. Even more, he saw clearly that such management of pleasure seeking is a condition of civilization as well.[31] No repression, no self; no repression, no civilization. In this regard, Freud fits in the long line of philosophies and religions that always both affirmed desire and sought to control and channel it. Today, we are losing the ability to control desire effectively.

To have life revolve around the pursuit of pleasure represents a major cultural crisis. The problem is mainly visible in Western "civilization," but it is carried to all four corners of the world on the wings of globalization processes (just as much good is carried on those same wings!). Muslims and Christians can be allies in exposing the futility and destructiveness of the pursuit of mere pleasure as well as in making plausible that a life marked by love of God and neighbor is both deeply human and truly pleasurable.[32]

Al-Ghazali begins his small book *The Alchemy of Happiness* with the following words: "Know, O beloved, that man was not created in jest or at random, but marvelously made and for some great end."[33] What is that great end for a being whose spirit is "lofty and divine," even if its body is, as al-Ghazali thought, "mean and earthly"? Here is how he describes it:

> When in the crucible of abstinence he [man] is purged from carnal passions he attains to the highest, and in place of being a slave to lust and anger becomes endued with angelic qualities. Attaining that state, he finds his heaven in the contemplation of Eternal Beauty, and no longer in fleshly delights.[34]

Al-Ghazali's little book is all about "turning away from the world to God," from the pleasures of the flesh to the incomparably higher pleasures of the love for God. Contemporary readers may stumble over his polemic against "carnal passions" and his praise of the "contemplation of Eternal Beauty." But for many centuries, Christians would not have put things much differently. They would have spoken of Christ as the way to God. And yet, what people should turn away from ("being a slave to lust and anger") and what they should ultimately desire ("contemplation of God") would have been expressed very much the way al-Ghazali does.[35]

I don't necessarily suggest that we emulate all aspects of the spirituality of al-Ghazali and of the many Christians who agreed with him. But the agreement is nonetheless significant. Think of it this way. Muslims share with Christians the basic idea underlying

Augustine's *City of God,* one of the most important works of all time about Christians' relation to the outside world. The whole of humanity is divided into the city of this world and the city of God, one dedicated to the love of self and the other to the love of God and neighbor. Muslims and Christians can be allies in promoting a vision of human flourishing centered on love of God and love of neighbor.

Granted, Muslims and Christians each have their own versions of that vision; they even contest the validity of each other's vision to the point of excluding the other from belonging to the city of God. The debates between Christians and Muslims on this very issue are fierce, and rightly so. And yet, why could not each see the other as engaged in a common cause of trying to persuade people that lives and cultures centered on the pursuit of mere pleasure are in the end futile and unsustainable?

A steeple is not a minaret, and a minaret is not a steeple. Though each points differently toward the common and similarly under-stood God of Christians and Muslims, both point away from the pursuit of mere pleasure as the hallmark of the good life. Push-ing back together against what both Christians and Muslims find harmful is better than fighting over what each believes is the most beneficial.

CHAPTER TWELVE

Two Faiths, Common God,
Single Government

In 2008, Prime Minister Tony Blair and I started teaching a course at Yale titled "Faith and Globalization." Our assumption is that religious faiths and globalization are among the most powerful forces shaping the world today. The future of the world will depend greatly on the relation between these two forces, which partly collide and partly reinforce each other. Throughout the course, at the center of our attention are two great issues: (1) conflicts between faiths as a result of globalization, pushing people of different faiths more tightly together and rapidly changing their worlds, and (2) the need to infuse globalization processes with a greater sense of justice and solidarity and steer them to better serve human flourishing and the global common good.

The very first session of the course was held on September 11, seven years to the day after the terrorist attack on the Twin Towers and the Pentagon. Our theme was "The Ambivalence of Faiths." We explored how faiths can inspire people to horrendous acts of violence (e.g., terrorism) as well as motivate them to engage in sustained acts of kindness designed to "mend the world" (e.g., Jubilee Year efforts at debt relief for the Global South). After my introduction and Mr. Blair's lecture, the discussion ranged broadly, mirroring a spectrum of concerns that a diverse body of students brought to the class. But the very first question posed during that first session stayed with us throughout the entire course.

Yasir Qadhi, a Muslim graduate student, was first to raise his hand. "Certain elements of faith are by definition exclusivist, whether we would like them to be so or not," he said. "For example, large segments of Christianity believe very strongly that unless you accept Jesus Christ as your personal Lord and savior, you are basically excluded from God's grace. That very belief is, of course, anathema to Muslims. So the question arises: [Since] we are not able to change these fundamental beliefs, how can we make people genuinely love and care about one another when they believe that that person, who is outside their faith tradition, is outside of God's grace?" Mr. Qadhi singled out Christians. Many Muslims display the same exclusivity, a sense that Islam is *the* true religion, and other religious groups do so as well.

Mr. Qadhi's question was not merely about interpersonal relations, about our ability as private individuals to care for neighbors whom we consider outside God's grace. It was about politics. He was mainly inquiring about the ability of people who belong to exclusivist faiths to advocate equal treatment of all people in a given state. "How can we be expected to treat someone with whom we think God is displeased the same [way] as someone with whom God is pleased?" Secular and religiously impartial states mandate just that: equal treatment of all, of those who do what is deemed pleasing to God and of those who do not. But God does not seem to treat all equally. Does loyalty to God then clash with loyalty to the state? If so, religious exclusivism leads straight to political intolerance!

In response, Mr. Blair immediately recognized that the problem of exclusivism is, in my words, the eight-hundred-pound gorilla sitting in the space where, pushed by globalization, faith meets faith. It is crucial, he insisted, to find "a way that people could really be comfortable, while they believe that they have the truth, with the truth of somebody else."[1] The second time we taught the course, early on the same issue surfaced, and again it stayed with us throughout the course.

Can religious exclusivists, adherents of different religions, live comfortably with one another under the same political roof? What kinds of political arrangements would be necessary for this to happen? Can belief in the one common God support such political arrangements? Or is the belief in one God the major source of religious exclusivism and therefore a cause of unending political strife? These are the key questions with regard to the public role of faith in an interconnected and interdependent world.

Let's start with the last question: Is monotheism by its very nature religiously and politically exclusive?

The True God Against the False Gods

Jan Assmann, an Egyptologist who has written extensively about the historical emergence of monotheism, argues that the basic monotheistic idea is not that there is only one supreme God. Many enlightened polytheists thought the same. It is, rather, that *the one God is the true God* and that *all other gods are false.*

Parmenides, the great early Greek philosopher who influenced Plato and with him the whole of Western thought, strictly distinguished between "truth" and "falsehood" in the realm of knowledge. Moses, argues Assmann, was the Parmenides of religion. He was the first to make a distinction between truth and falsehood in the realm of religion. As truth is opposed to falsehood, so the one true God is opposed to all other gods (idols) and to all false opinions about the one God (heresies). Monotheism, Assmann argues, is always "theoclasm," an endeavor to destroy all other gods and all alternative opinions about God.[2] Now, *that's* religious exclusivism!

Historically, monotheism was not just an exclusivist religious idea. It was also a political vision. One influential version of this vision goes like this. The indivisible power of a single earthly ruler should mirror the indivisible power of the one God. And since God's power extends through the whole cosmos, the power of the earthly ruler, God's representative, should extend to the ends of the earth. According to this view, the belief in the one true God makes the centralized power of a single ruler imperialistic.[3] In sum, monotheists are out to destroy all religious convictions other than their own and to subdue all disagreeable peoples! One God—one religion and one rule in the whole world! That's religious exclusivism underwriting political expansionism.

If aggressive exclusivism were in the DNA of monotheism, how could Muslims' and Christians' allegiance to the one God lead to the common good? Indeed, how could they live together without pervasive conflict? With Christianity and Islam, we would have two monotheistic religions, each religiously exclusive and each politically imperialistic. The aggression of one would feed on the aggression of the other. Unless Christian and Muslim understandings of God were completely identical (which they are not), how would having a common God help? At best, one group would see the other as heretics and be implacably opposed to them in the name of the full truth about God and God's ways with humanity. The more each was attached to God, the worse things would get between them.

Defenders of monotheism have some ready responses.

Response no. 1: *Monotheism is no worse than polytheism.* Polytheistic societies of the ancient world were not known for their peacefulness. When they went to war, their gods marched alongside them.[4] Jumping to today, even though some Hindu thinkers argue that polytheism promotes decentralized "liberal pluralism," whereas monotheism promotes a state-centered society intolerant of all pluralism,[5] it is not clear that in contemporary India polytheistic Hindus are less aggressive and more pluralistic than monotheistic Muslims or Christians.

Let's assume that this response to the critique of monotheism is persuasive (as I think it is). Even so, it doesn't get us where we need to be; it's a victory in a small skirmish, not in a decisive battle. We need monotheism to be socially beneficial, not merely less detrimental than polytheism. Since our goal is to promote the common good in societies with Muslims and Christians living side by side, we need to show not that polytheism is as aggressive as monotheism, but that monotheism is not necessarily socially and politically exclusive.

Response no. 2: *Monotheism is democratizing.* It is true, the defenders of monotheism concede, that monotheism was used to support centralized and top-down forms of rule: one God, one (human) lord, and one religiously unified and expanding empire.[6] But it is also true that in all three monotheistic faiths monotheism was used to support decentralized and bottom-up forms of rule: no lord but God.[7] When the people of Israel decided to have a king, the response of the prophet Samuel, speaking in God's name, was: "This is what the Lord, the God of Israel, says: 'I brought Israel up out of Egypt, and I delivered you from the power of Egypt and all the kingdoms that oppressed you.' But you have now rejected your God, who saves you out of all your calamities and distresses. And you have said, 'No, set a king over us'" (1 Sam. 10:18–19, NIV). God and the king are not aligned; they are alternatives.

This argument moves us in the right direction, but it doesn't get us to the goal either, for bottom-up, democratic forms of rule are not sufficient by themselves. As social "wars" in any schoolyard make manifest, the people can be as tyrannically exclusive as rulers are. The people too can prefer to live in religiously and socially homogenous spaces. If Christians and Muslims (along with other religions) are to live under the same roof, it is important for them to affirm *political pluralism* and not just democracy. The question, then, is: Can believers in one true God affirm social arrangements that include people with different religious (and nonreligious) perspectives on life on equal terms?

Response no. 3: *Monotheism is inclusive.* Because God is one, the world God created is one as well, the defenders of monotheism rightly insist. It is not divided into hostile regions by competing divine powers, it is not split into realms of light and darkness by incompatible moral visions. A single unifying truth binds all human beings, and the same demands of justice apply equally to all.[8] The correlate of "one God" is "all people." Nothing could be more inclusive than monotheism.[9]

Agreed—in part. The stress on universality is an important, even indispensable contribution that monotheism makes in today's world. Globalization processes are erasing walls that separate diverse communities and are gradually intertwining all into a single interdependent humanity. If we are not to remain mired in conflicts, we need a common set of rules as well as converging and partly overlapping visions of the global common good (see chapter 13). While honoring differences, we need to understand humanity as one. This is exactly implied in the belief in the one God.

And yet, there is a problem. Though monotheism is inclusive, *it is inclusive on its own terms.* You are "in" if you embrace the one true God, creator of the world, and if you accept God's commands as binding for all. But you are "out" if you don't. Exclusivism is the obverse of monotheism's inclusivism. Must we then conclude that Muslims and Christians, just because they give allegiance to the one true God partly differently understood, will be unable to live under the same political roof and work together for the common good?

Religious Exclusivism and Political Pluralism

The *decisive question* regarding the relation between the allegiance to the one true God and the ability of Christians and Muslims to coexist in a single state and pursue the common good is this: Can they be religious exclusivists while embracing pluralism as a political project? Let's first clarify the two crucial terms in this question, "religious exclusivists" and "pluralism as a political project."

Religious exclusivists believe that their religion is the true one. Most of them don't necessarily think that other religions are *totally* false. Though these religions are not true as ways to salvation, they may contain truth about God and moral life, some more and others less. But religious exclusivists judge the truth of other religions (and other worldviews more generally) by the degree to which those other religions conform to the exclusivists' own religious beliefs and practices. In contrast, *religious pluralists* believe that all religions are roughly equally true; they are simply different but equally "efficient" ways of scaling the same mountain.

Some Muslims and Christians are committed religious plural-ists. Most of them, however, are religious exclusivists. They are true to the basic monotheistic insight: there is no god but God, and the categories of "true" and "false" apply to religions. Equally impor-tant, a majority of those Christians and Muslims who are passion-ate about their faith's social import are religious exclusivists. That's a problem if political exclusivism follows in the wake of religious exclusivism. Each group will then want to control the public space, pushing the other out. And if it comprises a sufficiently strong ma-jority, it will insist that all who live in the land embrace its faith, submit to its rule as second-class citizens, or be forced to leave.

These are not merely theoretical options. Christian and Muslim rulers and governments have implemented them in the past and still do in many places today. The sixteenth-century Christian principle *Cuius regio, eius religio*—the religion of the ruler is the religion of the people—is one example (see chapter 13). The Muslim idea of a *dhimmi,* according to which a non-Muslim subject of a Muslim ruler enjoys protection but not equal rights, is another.[10]

But is political exclusivism a *necessary* consequence of religious exclusivism? We know that religious exclusivists cannot be *religious* pluralists; the two are polar opposites.[11] Can religious exclusivists be *political* pluralists, however? That's the decisive question. By po-litical pluralism, in its pure form, I mean the view that all religions, though not considered to be equally true by those who embrace them, are *equally welcome* in a given nation or state. There are two basic conditions of political pluralism:

1. The state does not favor one religion over the others, but is impartial toward them, indeed toward all overarching interpretations of life, whether religious or not.
2. Each religion is allowed to bring its own vision of the good life into the public arena and to do so by drawing on the resources of its own sacred books and traditions.

These are the "ideal" conditions of political pluralism. No state embodies them perfectly; they sketch a direction toward which a properly practiced political pluralism should be aiming. A state like Britain, for instance, where Christianity is an established religion, may prefer one religion to all others for historical or practical reasons and yet give full freedom to others and seek to be impartial toward them within these constraints. From my perspective, such a state would count as politically pluralistic. To achieve a successful common life for diverse groups within a polity, more is needed than pluralistic political institutions, such as the absence of prejudice and the ability to pursue the common good (see chapters 11 and 13). But pluralistic institutions are essential.

Can religious exclusivists agree to the above two conditions? More specifically, is it possible for Christians and Muslims who embrace exclusive monotheism to agree to these conditions? The answer is a simple yes, for two reasons, one factual and one theoretical.

It is an uncontested fact that many Christian and Muslim religious exclusivists endorse the impartiality of the state toward all religions and the right of each to engage in public debates. The so-called Christian Right in the United States is a good example, or at least a significant segment of it is. Those who belong to it are Christian monotheists and undisputed religious exclusivists. They are also committed to bringing their religious convictions to bear upon public life. And yet they grant the same right to religious groups with whom they strenuously disagree (even if they wish that there were no such groups in the United States). Moreover, when the preferred candidates or causes of the Christian Right lose in elections, its members stay engaged with the democratic process.[12]

In addition to many Muslims in the West who embrace liberal political institutions, an example in Islam may be Nahdatul Ulama, the largest Muslim socioreligious organization (with over 40 million members) in the most populous Muslim country in the world (Indonesia, with over 240 million inhabitants). In the words of sociologist Peter Berger, it is "avowedly pro-democracy and pro-pluralism, the very opposite of what is commonly viewed as

Muslim 'fundamentalism.'"[13] At the same time, Nahdatul Ulama is a religious revival movement deeply committed to a faith whose central tenet is monotheism.

Are these groups anomalies, at odds with Christians and Muslims who are *consistent* exclusivists—with those who are political exclusivists and not just religious exclusivists? Is it inconsistent of monotheists to embrace political pluralism rather than insisting on a unitary state in which a single ruler (the authoritarian version) or a religiously homogenous people (the democratic version) is sovereign? This takes us to the second and theoretical reason why Christians and Muslims can and should agree to the above two conditions of political pluralism.

Monotheism and Political Pluralism

My contention is that it is *not* inconsistent for monotheists to embrace pluralism as a political project. To the contrary! Two essential features of monotheism in fact *favor* pluralism as a political project. Let me put this bold thesis a bit more precisely. Two features of the kind of monotheism that Muslims and Christians arguably share (the belief in one benevolent God who commands all people to love their neighbors) favor pluralism as a political project.

I identify and explicate these two features of monotheism as they appear in the Christian faith and do so from a distinctly Christian perspective. This is in line with the approach I have taken throughout this book. I write as a Christian and offer for Muslim consideration a way of thinking about the relation between the two faiths that is both fully faithful to the Christian faith and, I trust, congenial to Muslims. I see no reason why Muslims, who believe that the command of the one God to love neighbors and act justly toward them transcends the boundaries of Muslim communities, could not follow me on the rarely trodden path I am about to embark upon.

Feature no. 1: *The belief in the one true God gave religion an essential ethical dimension*. Earlier I noted that monotheism introduced into the world of religions the distinction between "true" and "false." The result was a form of exclusivism that troubles many today. But monotheism brought something else as well, troubling for some, but immensely promising for others. With the distinction between "true" and "false" came also the distinction between "just" and "unjust." In contrast to polytheism, from which it emerged, monotheism made justice, law, and freedom into central themes of religion. Whereas polytheistic religions were primarily cultic, monotheistic religions are fundamentally *ethical* (though not only ethical!). This feature, no less than the distinction between the true and the false God, was one of monotheism's most revolutionary innovations.[14] From now on, to act justly, to show mercy, and to love neighbor *is* to serve God (see Mic. 6:8). Ritual observance without moral rectitude is worse than empty; it is a counterfeit religious coin with which a worshipper wishes to procure divine and human approval for behavior that deserves censure (see Isa. 58:3–7).

The one God, to whom Christians and Muslims owe exclusive allegiance, commands love of neighbors—to "do to others what you would have them do to you" and not to do to others what you would not want them do to you.[15] This is the principle of reciprocity, in doing what is right and not doing what is wrong. Since the one God is the God of all people, the principle of reciprocity applies to all. Acting in accordance with this principle *is worship of God,* a genuinely religious act (see chapter 6).

Feature no. 2: *Monotheism decoupled religion from the state and from ethnic belonging.* This decoupling took place in two stages.

Stage no. 1: *Decoupling of religion from the state.* From the start, monotheism was arguably connected with the liberation of Abraham's children from slavery in Egypt. It involved the *founding of an alternative form of social life* "in which human beings do not rule over other human beings but come together in freedom to place themselves under the rule of the covenant made with the one God."[16] God is the only true lord of the people; the ruler of the state does not rule in God's place. Salvation is not identical with political rule; it is a gift to a community from God.

Stage no. 2: *Decoupling of religion from ethnic belonging.* In Israel, the one God of all peoples remained attached in a special way to the Jewish people, the physical descendants of Abraham and Sarah. The apostle Paul, the great missionary to the Gentiles, sensed an unresolved tension between the universality of the one God and the particularity of a single chosen people. He insisted that all human beings, Jews and Gentiles, are included in the people of God, the new Israel, *on equal terms,* on account of God's utterly gratuitous love rather than in virtue of any natural "characteristic" or "achievement" of their own.[17] The one God of love is related to all people on equal terms and commands them to love! To us today this thought has the ring of a trite truism. In reality it is revolutionary. It has profound and far-reaching implications for the relation between religious communities and the state.

Consider these implications, again from a Christian angle. What happens when the gospel is preached to all nations in accordance with the belief that God, as revealed in Jesus Christ, is the God of all peoples? If the preaching is successful, churches will emerge as new and foreign social bodies in those nations. Nicholas Wolterstorff, a leading Christian philosopher working on political theology and philosophy today, notes a crucial feature of the Christian church:

> On the one hand, its [the church's] membership included people from other nations; on the other hand, its membership never included all from any nation. The church included more than Slavs and not all Slavs; the church is not Slavic. The church includes more than Americans and not all Americans; the church is not American. And so forth, for all nations, all peoples. The church is not the church of any nation or people. It does not belong to the social identity of any people.[18]

The presence of the church, a body of people giving ultimate allegiance to the one God, introduces a religious fissure in the citizenry of a state. This religious fissure in turn changes the very character of the state. As Wolterstorff notes, the state can no longer "express the shared religious identity of the people, since there is no such identity." He continues:

> The coming of the church undermines the political vision of the ancient Greek philosophers, that government is the highest institutional expression of the religio-ethical bonds uniting its citizenry. Wherever the church enters a society, it destroys whatever religio-ethical unity that society may have possessed. Now there is only religious pluralism.[19]

A fissure along religious lines is a direct result of the second feature of monotheism I highlighted—the decoupling of religion from the state and the ethnic community. Now add to this second feature of monotheism the first feature—doing justice and loving neighbor understood as a religious duty, a form of worship of God. The result? If we embrace both together, we have excellent reasons to affirm pluralism as a political project![20]

Since religion is not identical with the state, and since doing justice and loving all neighbors is a religious duty, we must affirm (1) the appropriateness of there being more than one religion in a given state as well as (2) the right of each religious group to pursue its own religious vision of the good life. It would be unjust and unloving to grant one religious community—our own—freedom to live according to its understanding of the dictates of the one God while denying the corresponding freedom to others.[21]

I can imagine Augustine and those who followed in his wake protesting. Basing his comments on the parable of the great dinner in which the master said, "Compel people to come in" (Luke 14:23), he argued that the impious and erring ought to be forced to comply with the truth. In *Concerning the Correction of the Donatists,* Augustine wrote:

> That persecution is just which the churches of Christ inflict upon the wicked. The Church, therefore, is blessed that suf-

fers persecution on account of justice, but those people are wretched who suffer persecution on account of injustice. The Church persecutes by loving. . . . The Church persecutes in order to correct. . . . The Church persecutes in order to call back from error. . . . The Church, finally, persecutes and lays hold of enemies until they collapse in their vanity so that they may grow in their truth.[22]

Love, and therefore coerce, argues Augustine here. But the argument disregards the simple fact that, as the apostle Paul put it, a person always "believes with the heart" (Rom. 10:10). The heart cannot and may not be coerced. Faith is ultimately a matter between God and the heart. Hence all coercion in matters of faith is excluded. Muslim legal scholar Abdullahi Ahmed An-Na'im shares this position. Faith itself demands freedom from being imposed by the state, because "people cannot truly live by their convictions according to their belief in and understanding of Islam if rulers use the extensive coercive powers of the state to impose their view of Shari'a on the population at large, Muslims and non-Muslims alike."[23]

In sum, many Christians and Muslims are committed to the following three propositions:

1. The one benevolent God relates to all people on equal terms.
2. Love of neighbor demands that we grant the same freedoms to others that we claim for ourselves.
3. There should be no coercion in matters of faith.

If Christians and Muslims accept these three propositions, they will be logically committed to political pluralism. It will make no difference whether they are religious exclusivists or religious pluralists. Religious exclusivists who embrace these propositions will be, if they are being consistent, political pluralists.

Freedom of Religion and Apostasy

Properly understood, belief in one God who commands love of neighbor requires pluralism as a political project. Such pluralism is inseparable, however, from freedom of religion. Today, after the Catholic Church followed Protestants and fully embraced freedom of religion at the Second Vatican Council,[24] Muslims and Christians tend to be deeply divided on the issue. Over the centuries, however, they have thought about it alike. And both have also thought about it wrongly, because they have missed important implications of their most basic convictions about God.

On May 30, 2007, Malaysia's highest court ruled that Lina Joy, a convert to the Christian faith, had lost her long fight to legally become a Christian, a struggle during which she received multiple death threats. Even though in her heart and daily practice she is a Christian, before the law she is and must remain a Muslim—against her stated wish and determined efforts. She will be unable to marry her non-Muslim fiancé. The law says that Muslim women can marry only Muslim men. Since she must remain legally a Muslim, her fiancé, a Christian, would have to become Muslim to marry her, though she is now a practicing Christian![25] During the decision, hundreds of Muslim demonstrators gathered in front of the federal court building, shouting, "God is great." As he gave the ruling, the Malaysian chief justice also expressed the opinion of the demonstrators when he said to Lina Joy that she "cannot at her own whim simply enter or leave her religion."[26]

According to a common interpretation of Shari'a, Muslims are forbidden to convert to another religion and converts are considered apostates. Sheikh Ali Gomaa, the grand mufti of Egypt and one of the most respected contemporary Muslim religious authorities, has argued recently that Muslims are free to change their religion; they will be accountable to God for their decision at the Day of Judgment, but are not subject to punishment in this life.[27] Other religious authorities insist, however, that a punishment for apostasy ought to be imposed in this world. For them, the debate is primarily about the proper character of the punishment, whether apostasy is punishable by death or some lesser penalty. Many Muslims agree. Muslim public opinion overwhelmingly supports the hardest possible line on apostasy laws,[28] and these laws are enforced without mercy even in countries like Malaysia, a model Muslim democracy.

Most Christians today consider Islamic laws of apostasy to be inhumane. In the light of these laws, the statement in the Qur'an that there is "no compulsion in religion" (Al Baqarah, 2:256) rings hollow. But before condemning Islam as a "wicked" religion, Christians should remember that there is no such statement in the Bible.[29] We should also look into the mirror of our own history. From early on, apostasy was considered a serious sin—so serious that during the first Christian centuries many considered it impossible for apostates to receive forgiveness.

When the Roman Empire became Christian, the religious practice of withholding forgiveness for apostasy became a civil law. Apostates were "punished by deprivation of all civil rights. They could not give evidence in a court of law, and could neither bequeath nor inherit property. To induce anyone to apostatize was an offence punishable with death."[30] In the Middle Ages, both canon and civil law classed apostates with heretics—and the harshest imaginable penalties were imposed on them. In what sense did the church embrace freedom of religion throughout most of the centuries of its history? People were free to *embrace* the faith and *enter* the church. Once in, they could neither leave it nor deviate from its basic convictions. In either case, they would be leaving the truth and undermining social order. But leaving the truth is wrong, and one can never have the right to do what is wrong.

We are back at the connection between religion and truth, which, as Assmann argues, came about with monotheism—first at the religious level (one God, one truth, one choice) and then at the political level (one God, one earthly rule, one acceptable way of life). But if my argument in this chapter is correct, we are back at a *seriously misguided appropriation of that connection*. The advocates of the laws against apostasy disregard two essential and socially revolutionary features of monotheism: the decoupling of religion and the state, and the tying of religion to loving all neighbors and to doing justice. Apply these features of monotheism to the question of religious freedom and the partiality of the state toward one religion, and the laws against apostasy must go.

The central problem of Muslims and Christians throughout their unhappy history with religious freedom was the failure to apply consistently the principle of reciprocity, a basic form of loving neighbors and doing justice. When Christians or Muslims were an overwhelming majority, they felt justified curtailing the full freedom of others to exercise their faith. When they were a minority, however, they demanded for themselves full freedom to exercise their own religion. Each was unwilling to grant to others what they claimed and enforced through the power of the state for themselves—a patently unjust and unloving stance.[31] Similarly, both Muslims and Christians engaged in missionary activity and readily accepted converts from other faiths. Yet each group severely punished both its own members who abandoned the true faith and the followers of other faiths who may have led them astray. Again, a glaring case of a lack of reciprocity—more appropriate to armies at war and how they treat defectors and spies than to religious communities committed to worshipping the one and common God who commands love of all human beings.

To be consistent in their convictions about God, Christians and Muslims must embrace two simple principles:

1. All persons and communities have an equal right to practice their faith (unless they break widely accepted moral law), privately and publicly, without interference by the state.
2. Every person has the right to leave his or her own faith and embrace another.

When Christians and Muslims deny either of these principles, they can be rightly accused of transgressing against the most basic principles of justice. Even more important, when they deny these principles, they dishonor the one God who commands them to love all people and do justice.

Identity, Separation, Impartiality

At the beginning of chapter 5, I quoted from a letter that Pope Gregory VII wrote to al-Nazir, the king of Mauretania, in 1076. Read it one more time with issues of political pluralism and religious freedom in mind.

> Almighty God, who desires all men to be saved (1 Tim. 2:4) and none to perish is well pleased to approve in us most of all that besides loving God men love other men, and do not do to others anything they do not want to be done unto themselves (cf. Matt. 7:12). We and you must show in a special way to the other nations an example of this charity, for we believe and confess one God, although in different ways, and praise and worship Him daily as the creator of all ages and the ruler of this world. As the apostle says, "He is our peace who has made us both one" (Eph. 2:14).[32]

In this letter, the pope's theological starting point and goal are close to my own: the one God who commands love is the foundation for peace between Muslims and Christians and their common witness to the world.

Would Pope Gregory VII have agreed that pluralism as a political project follows from these theological convictions? Not very likely. His dealings with both earthly rulers and Muslims suggest otherwise. He saw himself as above earthly rulers. He had the emperor of Germany, Henry IV, come to him barefoot through the ice and snow, stripped of his royal robes and clad as a penitent, and absolved him from censure only after the emperor spent three days fasting and waiting in the wintry weather in front of the closed doors of the citadel in which the pope resided. As to Muslims, his conciliatory letter to King al-Nazir was only one side of the story, a less prominent one. Pope Gregory VII tried, unsuccessfully, to organize a crusade to free the Eastern Church from the Seljuk Turks. Like many great theologians and church leaders through the centuries, Pope Gregory VII would have bristled at the idea of political pluralism.

Were those Christians who through the centuries did not embrace political pluralism (like Gregory VII) wrong? It is correct to say, I think, that they did not consistently apply the belief in the one God who commands love of neighbor to the relationship between church and state. There are many reasons for this failure, including the fact that they lived in the religiously homogenous world of medieval Europe. We live in a different world. Ours is a highly interconnected, interdependent, and religiously mixed world. As a rule, many religions inhabit a common political space. For us, it is crucial to seize the promise of political pluralism contained in Christian and Islamic (and, of course, Jewish) monotheism. If we do, the common God of Muslims and Christians will become "our peace," as Pope Gregory VII suggested to the Mauretanian ruler.[33]

In a religiously pluralistic world, how should believers in one God understand the relation between religion and the state? I'll sum up the position I am advocating in three simple principles— all three related to one another, and all three grounded in the belief in one God who commands love of neighbor.

Principle no. 1: *No identity between religion and state.* A state is the state of all its citizens who are, as a rule, divided along religious lines. God's laws, as understood by a particular religious community, are binding for that community. They are its ethical code and not necessarily the law of the land to be imposed on all citizens. In case of conflict between the communal ethical code and the law of the land, a religious community will feel obliged to "obey God rather than any human authority," as the apostle Peter said when the earliest Christians were prohibited from proclaiming that God raised Jesus from the dead (Acts 5:29). Subordinating human authority to God's authority is an inescapable consequence of giving ultimate allegiance to God. The monotheistic principle that "there is no god but God" means that God's command is above any human law.

Over the centuries Islam has been associated more with the tendency to identify religion and the state than Christianity has been (though Christianity has exhibited similar tendencies as well). Islamist thinker Sayyid Qutb, of the Muslim Brotherhood, is a modern example. For him, the sovereignty of God requires that the society as a whole be ruled by God's law, the Shari'a.[34] But many Muslims disagree, as the example of Fethullah Gülen, a Turkish religious leader with a worldwide following, shows. For him, as for many Muslims throughout the world, the aim of Islam is more spiritual and ethical than political.[35] He affirms the need for religion to influence the culture and the state, but denies the identity of religion and rule.[36]

Principle no. 2: *No complete separation between religion and the state.* Jesus Christ, famously, said to the Pharisees: "Give to the emperor the things that are the emperor's, and to God the things that are God's" (Mark 12:17). Guided by these words of Christ and mindful that Christ was crucified as a political criminal by the Romans, over the centuries Christians have had an ambivalent relation to political power. When they came to wield power after the conversion of Constantine, theirs was, in a sense "an accidental empire."[37] Fittingly, the idea of separation of religion and state was originally conceived and implemented in the Christian cultural environment.

And yet, for believers in the one God who commands love of neighbor, complete separation of religion and state will not do. For them—Jews, Christians, and Muslims alike—God is the God of all people and therefore the God of all citizens of a state, whether they believe in God or not. The commands of the Master of the Universe are the moral law for all. A religious community will therefore seek to persuade its compatriots of the rightness of its moral vision and to infuse the laws of the land with the values embodied in God's commands. Many Christians today oppose the idea of a secular state—either in the sense of a state's being detached from religions by a wall of separation or in the sense of a state's advocating a nonreligious worldview. They maintain that such a state cannot be fair toward people with robust religious convictions. They reject strict separation of religion and state and advocate the *impartiality* of the state toward all religions.[38]

Principle no. 3: *Impartiality of the state toward all religions.* The only adequate option open to Muslims and Christians as citizens of the same state is to advocate the impartiality of the state toward all religions; no religion is preferred by the state, and all religions are impartially supported. This allows Christians and Muslims to be faithful to two fundamental impulses of monotheism simultaneously—to (1) honor the conviction that God is the God of all people and (2) obey God's command to act justly and practice neighborly love toward all people.

CHAPTER THIRTEEN

The Fear of God and the Common Good

In May 2005, about a decade after the war ended in Bosnia, I was walking the streets of Sarajevo with a friend, a Franciscan priest and professor of theology. I had come to Sarajevo—which, after the war, became a majority Muslim city—for one of the annual "Building Bridges" conferences on Christian-Muslim relations organized by the archbishop of Canterbury, Rowan Williams. The theme was "Muslims, Christians, and the Common Good." In between scholarly papers (on such topics as national identity, just governance, care for the poor, and protection of the environment) and receptions at the residences of religious dignitaries, I sought the company of my friend. Alongside many of his Franciscan brothers from Bosnia he was a refugee during the war, driven out not by Muslims, but by Christian Serbs. A citizen of Sarajevo and a member of a religious community living for centuries with Muslims, he would have something to say about the search of Christians and Muslims for the common good, I thought.

"We've lost the fear of God," he told me somewhat abruptly.

"Fear of God?" I wondered out loud. He is a good theologian and a Franciscan, so I knew that by "fear" he didn't mean a paralyzing emotion that grips us when our lives are in danger or a constraining sense that all our moves must be approved by an overbearing potentate. He meant something like ultimate allegiance, total devotion, something not much different than properly understood love for God. Intrigued that he saw in the "fear of God" the

key for the coexistence of Muslims and Christians in Sarajevo, I
wanted to know more.

"New mosques are springing up left and right, and the old ones
are being restored to new glory," he explained. "Largely, this is not
a revival of deep spirituality seeking spaces for outward expression
and nurture. These building projects are political acts. Muslims are
asserting their identity and marking their territory. The war with
guns and tanks is over; the war with religious symbols has begun."
He knew that the desire to build new mosques and restore the old
ones is understandable. Destruction of religious objects was part
of "ethnic cleansing"; rebuilding them is part of ethnic restoration.
Still, he thought there was something worrisome about it.

Sacred objects as weapons in secular struggles! This is secularization of religion in the name of its restoration. If that continued,
I thought, it would only be a matter of time until the mask of religion was pulled down and seemingly religiously motivated activity
would show itself as a mundane struggle for power.[1]

"We Christians are not much better," I said out loud, though
more to myself than to him. I was not thinking of Sarajevo. I had
in mind Mostar, a city some seventy-five miles to the south.[2] In
2000, Bishop Perić erected a hundred-foot-high Jubilee cross on
Hum Hill, overlooking Mostar, "to spread the fruit of peace to all
sides of the world," as he put it, and as an expression of hope that
the "thunder of tanks and cannons will never again be heard from
Hum." That's not, however, how the majority Muslim population
of Mostar experienced the cross. It looms large over their heads
day and night (it is illuminated)—an assertion of Croatian Catholic identity made ubiquitous. As to the cannons, after 1992 it was
from that same hill that Croatian forces were shelling the Muslim
part of Mostar. For Muslims, the cross was merely a softer version
of the cannons.

"You make my point," my friend responded. "Christians and
Muslims alike use sacred objects to occupy spaces and celebrate
their own identities. They do so because they fear each other. They
don't fear God."

Religion, seen as a marker of identity (see chapter 10), has swallowed up allegiance to the common God. Even though God is on everybody's lips, religion has become godless (or maybe religion is godless partly just because God is on everybody's lips).[3] The consequence? Each community thinks only of its own injuries and hopes, pursuing only its own interests and its own good. Neither cares for the other or for the common good. It would take allegiance to God in love and fear to cure them from self-preoccupation and excessive fear of others, my friend suggested. To care for the common good, and not just for our own good, in the face of powerful impulses to protect the group and enhance its power, the God of truth, justice, and love must claim us.

My friend's suggestion was an echo of the main theme of biblical wisdom literature: the fear of the Lord is the beginning of wisdom, the foundation of leading a life of integrity and flourishing as individuals and communities (see Job 28:28; Prov. 9:10; Ps. 111:10). He just applied it to relations between Muslims and Christians in Sarajevo, to their ability to live together in the same space and pursue the common good. The fear of the Lord is the beginning of political wisdom in a multireligious state.

During a reception at the conclusion of the conference, Archbishop Williams gave a brief talk. In it he said:

> Many people have compared Sarajevo with Jerusalem. Many of us during these days have quite spontaneously said the same thing. As we walked through the streets of this city we have been aware, as in Jerusalem, of the presence of the three great faiths which take their origin from Abraham, and as in Jerusalem, we have been aware of the history of suffering and of hope that seems to be present in the very stones of the city. People go to Jerusalem on pilgrimage in spite of many centuries of suffering and tragedy; they still look to Jerusalem as a place where God has done wonderful things. Because although terrible suffering often closes up the human heart, when it does not do this it opens it wide to God.[4]

As Archbishop Williams evoked the memory of Jerusalem, I thought of the three monotheistic faiths in that divided city, of spaces they claim with their holy sites and of identities they project, of struggles over holy things with no room for compromise, of competing hopes tied to individual religious sites. I thought of hearts of stone, closed to one another by undeniable suffering and legitimate fear. I saw also faces of people with eyes soft with empathy, open to the vast horizon of God. But I thought also of my friend's comment about the "fear of God." Might the fear of the Lord, a common and similarly understood Lord, be "a fountain of life" (Prov. 14:27) as Christians and Muslims strive to live together in a world that has become much like Sarajevo and a little bit like the divided Jerusalem itself?

Under the Same Roof

Archbishop Williams and my friend are both clergy. Urging people to open themselves up to God in love and fear—the two attitudes are ultimately identical—is what you would expect from them. But will this advice help? Might it not exacerbate the problem, giving more weight to exclusive religious convictions associated with the belief in one God and adding religious fuel to conflicts? Consider the alternatives, though. None of them will work.

Alternative no. 1: *Eliminate religion.* This was the preferred solution of the great critics of religion in Europe from the seventeenth century on, thinkers like Thomas Hobbes, who wanted to eliminate religion as an independent force, and Karl Marx, who thought that it should disappear altogether. Among other things, the European wars of religion in the sixteenth and seventeenth centuries led them to see in allegiance to God, as defined by distinct religious communities, a source of strife.[5] Where did the hope of prosperity and peace lie? Not in any way in religious observance, but in the unleashed power of human inquiry, industry, and social engineering and control.

But, long after the seventeenth century, God does not seem to be disappearing from the hearts and minds of people. Even massive religious persecutions in the name of secular progress, in which millions were killed in the course of the twentieth century (e.g., in the Soviet Union under Stalin and in China under Mao), have not weakened religion. To the contrary, at the beginning of twenty-first century, the world continues to be a very religious place; there are more religious people alive today than at any other time, and the number of religious people is growing in absolute and relative terms. Peter Berger, a major proponent of the theory of increasing secularization during the 1960s, eventually changed his mind and now argues that the world is actually *desecularizing*.[6]

Conclusion: attempts to eliminate religion would be both oppressive and ineffective, and hopes are futile that it will wither away on its own in the foreseeable future.

Alternative no. 2: *Keep religious communities apart.* This option goes back to conflicts resulting from the Protestant Reformation in Europe. In the treaty called the Peace of Augsburg (1555), Catholic and Lutheran rulers agreed to the principle that the religion of the ruler is the religion of the ruled (in Latin, *cuius regio, eius religio*). Leave aside the specifics, and concentrate on the underlying idea: the condition of peace is religious uniformity within a given state; one rule, one religion.

The principle was problematic and difficult to implement even when it was originally formulated over four centuries ago; it was soon abandoned (though a very rough division of Europe into religious regions remains even today). For instance, freedom of religion consisted basically in the freedom to leave with your possessions the realm in which you lived if your religion differed from that of your ruler.[7] Even more so than in the past, today the principle of "one rule, one religion" is unsustainable. In the wake of globalization, people of different faiths increasingly share the same political space. There are still pockets of relatively homogenous religious spaces, like Christian Croatia and Muslim Oman. However, in an interconnected and interdependent world, societies are irreversibly becoming more and more pluralistic. In the future, religiously "pure" states, without a significant presence of other religions, will be an anomaly. Even today, at the beginning of the twenty-first century, more than one-third of all Muslims in the world live as minorities in non-Muslim states.[8]

Conclusion: in today's world, it is impossible to keep religious communities apart.

Alternative no. 3: *Privatize religion.* This was the option of the great advocates of liberal democracy, from John Locke,[9] one of its first and greatest theorists, to John Rawls, one of its more recent champions.[10] They advocated the "great separation" of political decision making from religious convictions based on revelation. Privately, people can believe any religion (or irreligion) they choose. Politics, on the other hand, should "remain unilluminated by the light of revelation" and should be guided by human reason alone, as Mark Lilla, professor of humanities at Columbia, put it recently.[11] Revelations are specific to a given religion, and when people obey revelations in their public lives, clashes follow. Reason is common to all human beings, and its deliberations can therefore lead to the common good. Yet the proposal to privatize religion is problematic.

First, most religious people in the world live in democracies of one sort or another, and many of them increasingly embrace democratic ideals. What do religious people who live in democracies do with their religious convictions? They bring them into politics.[12] This is especially true of Christianity and Islam, faiths in which everything in life is oriented toward the one God. If Muslims and Christians kept religion out of politics, would they not risk betraying their own deepest commitments by letting the state determine significant aspects of their lives? Might they not end up serving two gods, the "house" god of their private lives and the "state" god of their public lives? And if the state were to *mandate* that they keep politics "unilluminated by the light of revelation," would it not be depriving them of basic rights?

Second, it is evident that there is no such thing as common or "generically human" reason, certainly not when it comes to the nature of human beings, to relations between them, and to questions of morality and the purposes of human life. Everybody is part of a specific tradition of reasoning, not just religious people.[13] To prohibit religious people from drawing on their traditions and therefore on revelation in their political engagement is to discriminate against them.

Conclusion: religion cannot and should not be privatized.

Now that I have eliminated plausible alternatives, let's return to the suggestion that the "fear of the Lord" is a key to Muslims' and Christians' joint pursuit of the common good. Christians and Muslims who embrace a faith that shapes public life and are committed to democratic ideals will increasingly live side by side under a single roof of common governments and in a single interconnected and interdependent world. God is at the center of their faith. The way they understand God shapes how they see the world, themselves, and their relation with outsiders. Earlier I argued that Muslims and Christians have a common God and partially overlapping understandings of the common God. Consider the consequences for the pursuit of the common good:

1. For both Christians and Muslims, God is not a tribal deity; since God is one, God is never "our" God as opposed to "their" God. If possessive pronouns are appropriate at all, "our" God is as much "theirs" as "ours."

2. Both Muslims and Christians agree that their common God is just and merciful and requires human beings to be just and merciful in all their dealings.

I argued earlier that when religion is understood as a marker of identity and enters the realm of politics, it separates people of different religions and deepens their conflicts (see chapter 10). It is different with the "fear of God"—the common God and the similarly understood God of Christians and Muslims. Allegiance to that God will elevate worshippers above mere group interests and motivate them to seek the common good. It is not hard to see how the fear of *that* God, the common God, may be the beginning of political wisdom. The recipe is simple. Take the idea of having a common God and add the fear of that God, and you'll have Muslims and Christians pushed to pursue the common good. That's my thesis in this chapter.

Critics might respond that with this approach we gain little and lose much. They worry about both central claims of the thesis—that having a common and similarly understood God is important and that allegiance to that one God really matters. Instead, they argue (1) that the affirmation that Muslims and Christians have a common God doesn't necessarily foster peaceful coexistence and agreement on the common good, and (2) that the allegiance to a single God breaks communities apart because monotheism is by its very nature exclusive. I already dealt with the second argument in the previous chapter. There I showed that monotheism as understood by normative Christianity and Islam in fact favors political pluralism rather than reinforcing exclusivism. Here I turn to critics' first argument.

Socratic Warnings

How far does affirming allegiance to a common God and embracing similar understandings of that God get us in fostering the pursuit of the common good? In Plato's dialogue *Lysis,* Socrates discusses the nature of friendship. He dismisses two commonly held opinions about what draws people together to become friends. His discussion of these is useful in assessing how significant "commonalities" might be for social concord and the pursuit of the common good.

Opinion no. 1: *"Like must love like,"*[14] or, as we sometimes put it, "Birds of a feather flock together." Socrates is unimpressed with this saying, mainly because he doesn't think that the principle applies to bad people, "for the more a bad man has to do with a bad man, and the more nearly he is brought into contact with him, the more he will be likely to hate him, for he injures him; and injurer and injured cannot be friends." The real meaning of the saying is, he suggests, "The good are like one another, and friends to one another."[15]

Apply these considerations to Muslim and Christian convictions about God. The mere fact of *having* a common God and similar convictions about God will not do much to promote the common good; after all, Muslims and Christians have had a common God all along. Bad people, with no intention of doing good, can think alike about God, and that won't prevent them from being at each other's throats. But *fear* of the one and common God—the God who loves and commands love of neighbor—would make a difference. Fear of that God will nudge Muslims and Christians to emulate God and therefore to pursue the common good, for, by definition, the common God to whom they are accountable is the God of both as well as the one Lord of their common world. Muslims and Christians will then have partially overlapping visions of the good and will share the commitment to pursue the good. Now, how vigorously they in fact pursue the common good will depend on many factors, political and economic, cultural and institutional, and others. But all else being equal, fear of the common God will foster the pursuit of the common good.

Opinion no. 2: "*Like is the greatest enemy of the like.*"[16] The argument in favor of this opposite view is that those who are most alike "are most full of envy, strife, and hatred of one another, and the most unlike [are full] of friendship." Again, Socrates goes on to debunk the opinion. "Is a just man the friend of the unjust, or the temperate of the intemperate, or the good of the bad?" he asks rhetorically. Opposites may sometimes attract, but do not always make friends; inversely, being alike does not necessarily create enmity. Socrates's provisional conclusion: "Then neither like and like nor unlike and unlike are friends."[17]

Are Muslims and Christians often enemies because they are *too similar* rather than because they are too different? Might not highlighting the similarities heighten the enmity? More than a century ago, Sigmund Freud coined the phrase "narcissism of minor differences."[18] It designates the need to take pride in small differences that set us apart from people who resemble us and to harbor negative feelings toward them just because they resemble us. And yet, even if we grant Freud's point, it doesn't follow, as Socrates notes, that "the most opposed are the most friendly."[19] And that conclusion certainly doesn't follow if the differences concern ultimate values. If Muslims and Christians worshipped different Gods, they would have different and largely opposing ultimate values, and their ability to live together in the same state and in the same globalized world would be diminished significantly.

But does having common values translate into pursuing the common good? Return once again to Socrates, this time to his discussion of enmities among gods and among humans in a dialogue called *Euthyphro*. Socrates asks, what differences "make us angry and set us at enmity with one another"? The answer is that "this happens when the matters of difference are just and unjust, good and evil, honorable and dishonorable."[20] It is over these things that people fight and go to war. Euthyphro, who prides himself in knowing everything about gods and piety, counters that both humans and gods agree that a murderer should be punished; there are no differences of opinion about that. Socrates grants the point, but reaffirms his argument: mostly people do not argue about what deed is evil and whether or not the evildoer should be punished, "but they argue about the fact of who the evildoer is, and what he did and when."[21] And that takes us to the third Socratic warning.

Opinion no. 3: *Common values lead to agreement*. Socrates disagrees. Gods and humans agree that murder is bad and that it ought to be punished, and yet quarrels and enmities persist concerning whether a deed counts as a murder and whether a person has committed it.[22] Analogously, having a common God and overlapping understandings of the character and demands of God will not by itself settle disputes and calm enmities. Many disagreements that touch our civic life may remain, even profound disagreements about the nature of human beings and relations among them.

However, we do gain something important through joint affirmations of the common God understood in a similar way. We gain a common set of ultimate commitments and foundational moral injunctions on the basis of which to work through any disagreements about common life. Without such common commitments, which for Muslims and Christians derive from their worship of God, it would be difficult for them to engage in fruitful moral debate. For Muslims and Christians, belief in a common God maps a common moral universe, a space in which it makes sense to pursue the common good and in which it is possible to carry on public debates as to what that common good is.[23]

Granted, even with common moral convictions in place, it is possible for a reasoned public argument about the common good to turn into an antagonistic shouting match. A country can be deeply polarized not because people do not inhabit the same moral universe, but because groups insist on pursuing only their own interests. Breakdowns of public moral argument can happen among people of the same religious persuasion (as between "conservative" and "progressive" Christians in the United States) or they can happen between distinct religious groups (as between Muslims and Christians in Nigeria). Here again, for Muslims and Christians, the fear of God—placing allegiance to the common God above allegiance to one's own group—may be the beginning of political wisdom. For those who fear God, what ultimately matters is not to win an argument or "occupy more political territory," but to do what is right in the sight of the Final Judge.

Blasphemy

Consider the bearing of the "fear of God" on one significant issue in relations between Muslims and Christians (and more broadly non-Muslim Westerners)—that of blasphemy.

When Danish cartoonist Kurt Westergaard came to give a lecture at Yale in the fall of 2009, he triggered a storm of controversy.[24]

He acquired worldwide notoriety and fame in 2006, when he depicted the Prophet Muhammad in a turban morphing into a bomb with a lit fuse. With a few lines of his deft pen, Westergaard desecrated a cherished religious symbol and deeply offended more than one billion people. Critics of Westergaard's visit accused the person who invited him of giving a platform to a hate monger.

Westergaard saw himself and his cartoon rather differently. During the lecture he echoed the position of Flemming Rose, the cultural editor of *Jyllands-Posten,* the paper that commissioned the cartoons. Rose defended his decision to solicit and print the offensive images with the following argument. In liberal democracies people have many rights, but the one right they do not have is the "right not to be offended (by others)." The right to offend, a corollary of the absence of the right not to be offended, includes the right to desecrate religious symbols, he argued. As far as the rights guaranteed by laws are concerned, in liberal societies there is a 24/7 open season for offending and desecrating. From this perspective, to prohibit Westergaard's caricature of Muhammad from being published or to not allow him to speak at Yale would have been to deny him a basic right—the right to free speech.

America is a liberal democracy, and Yale is deeply committed to the freedom of speech. The possession of the right to free speech was not the only relevant issue, however. The other relevant issue is the *responsible exercise of that right.* Citizens of liberal democracies have certain rights and embrace liberal ideals, but should they actually do everything they have the right to do? Should Christians or Muslims, who share a common God who commands us to love our neighbors, do everything they have the right to do? They should not. Allegiance to the God who loves and commands love of neighbor will nudge them to let *care for others* govern their actions.[25]

In the case of the cartoons, care would introduce at least two considerations into public debates in addition to concern for freedom of expression. The first is *safety.* More than one hundred lives

were lost in the violence that ensued after the publication of the
Danish cartoons, not just in the Middle East, but above all in Nigeria. Though this violence was utterly unjustified and indefensible, it
was still a consequence of the publication of the cartoons, the most
offensive of which was Westergaard's. Would he have published
the caricature had he known that lives would be lost, some students
asked him after his lecture? Westergaard remained unrepentant.
Others, not he, committed the violence. In his judgment, the exercise of his right trumped any consideration of the real-world effects
of his action. To many in the audience this seemed strangely self-
absorbed.

The second consequence of care is concern for *civility*. Though
gratuitously offending others may be our right as citizens of liberal
democracies, the exercise of that right hardly counts as a mark of a
well-lived life. At issue is not the appropriateness of expressing one's
opinion and arguing for one's position; rather, at issue is the *respect*
or *lack of it* with which we express our opinions and argue for our
positions. One student put the point unforgettably. Addressing
Westergaard, he said: "I grew up in Omaha, Nebraska. My father
taught me to be honest with others, but never to be mean. Your
caricature was honest, in that you said what you thought. But did
it have to be mean?"

Westergaard responded that he was provoked by the terrorist
attack on the World Trade Center.

"So is it morally noble for one reprehensible provocation to elicit
another?" asked another student incredulously.

The exchange between Westergaard and the students ended in
a stalemate. He was resting his case on "Danish values" and on his
right to draw the caricature. The students, though not contesting
the right, worried about the safety of third parties and respect for
Muslims. Had both parties owed allegiance to the common God
who commands love of neighbor, would this not have helped resolve the stalemate?[26]

God, Religion, and the Common Good

Early in his career Karl Barth (1886–1965), one of the greatest twentieth-century religious thinkers, rebelled against religion. His whole theology, profound and voluminously expounded, is one massive rebellion against religion. Not against God! Against religion reduced to "culture" and a certain kind of morality, religion twisted into a cultural resource and used as a marker of group identity. Here's what turned this Swiss village pastor into a world-famous rebel.

In August 1914, Germany's Kaiser Wilhelm II declared war on Russia and France. After the war began, he asked the great liberal theologian Adolf von Harnack to help him draft a speech addressed to the German nation. Harnack complied. Later, along with another liberal theologian by the name of Wilhelm Hermann, Harnack also signed the famous petition by ninety-three leading German intellectuals in support of the German cause. German militarism is a protector of German culture, they declared; the land of Kant, Goethe, and Beethoven will thrive only if it doesn't shy away from using its weapons.[27] Both Harnack and Hermann were Barth's teachers. Barth was a Swiss citizen with a bit of distance from German affairs, and he was deeply disappointed in his teachers, not just personally, but with their version of the Christian faith. It was nothing but a Christianized version of German culture and Enlightenment morality, now turned aggressive. He rejected it as "mere religion"—a self-aggrandizing and dangerous betrayal of the true faith parading as the gold standard of morality and enlightened religiosity.

True faith, Barth insisted, is not a servant of a "culture" or of an "ethnic identity"; its essence is not mere morality or an elevated feeling of awe before the great Mystery. At the heart of faith is the "fear of the Lord."[28] The Bible has only *one* all-encompassing interest, and that is the "interest in God himself."[29] God is God, and therefore demands our *"entire* obedience." God, Barth insisted, "cannot be grasped, brought under management, and put to use; he cannot serve. He must rule."[30] All genuine religious beliefs and practices are merely pointers to God, nothing in themselves, and something only in the virtue of directing people to God. They are like the figure of John the Baptist in the famous sixteenth-century painting of Matthias Grünewald—standing in the corner and with an outstretched arm and finger extended, pointing away from himself to Christ.

It might appear to some people that Barth's turn to God was utterly otherworldly, detached from history, culture, politics, and the common good. It was not. It was a battle cry against the idol of religion and against the world for which it provides a sacred canopy[31]—the world of group identities, national interests, and "cleansed" territories; the world of exclusions, enmities, and aggressions. When the idol of religion is smashed and God is acknowledged as God, the world appears as a unity and the search for the common good can begin.

Nearly a century after Barth's initial rebellion, Christians and Muslims may be in a situation similar to Barth's during World War I. The thunder of wars in which Muslims and Christians are involved continues unabated, and tensions between the two run high in the West as well as in majority Muslim countries. Religious leaders and combatants both invoke religion in support of their causes. The terrorists who flew the planes into the Twin Towers were instructed in their manual: "Remember, this is a battle for the sake of God."[32] As I have noted earlier for for the influential televangelist and former U.S. presidential candidate Pat Robertson, the whole conflict between "Islam and the West" is a contest to determine whether "the moon God of Mecca known as Allah is supreme, or whether the Judeo-Christian Jehovah, the God of the Bible, is supreme."[33]

Not all talk about God is, in fact, about the one true God. Some of it is about false gods, and much of it is about culture, territory, and identity and therefore deeply divisive and especially dangerous in an interconnected and interdependent world. It is time for

Reality Check: Combating Extremism

Almost every time I give a talk in the West about Islam and Christianity, I get asked whether Muslims and Christians worship the same God. And almost every time after I have answered the question, I get asked why both the question and the answer matter for combating extremism. Before the year 2001 these two issues hardly ever surfaced in discussions of Christianity and Islam. Except among a handful of experts, there was little interest in the problem of the "same God" (though I remember well talking about it as a young boy with my father). Muslim extremism was a nonissue. The change was brought about by the destructive reality of Muslim terrorism.

Today, many non-Muslims have come to see Islam as a threat and consider Muslim extremists as the tip of the sword brandished against them and their way of life. They wonder about the supposed violent propensities of the God to whom Muslims owe ultimate allegiance, about the attributes of the One who defines Muslim visions of the good life and shapes the fundamental values that motivate their actions and inspire their hopes. What seem like glaring differences in lifestyle, values, and practices (especially suicide bombings!) make many people doubt that Muslims worship the "same God" Christians and Jews do. Hence the persistent question about the same God and about extremism.

A Multipronged Approach

But what is the link between having the same (or a different) God and extremism, if there is any connection at all? Does the claim, which I make in this book, that Muslims and Christians have a common and similarly understood God matter for combating extremism?

Answers to this last question range all the way from "It doesn't matter at all" to "Ultimately, that's all that matters." Almost no one holds these two positions in a pure and consistent way. But, on the one side, many think that combating extremism with military or police force[1] or by promoting democratic institutions in majority Muslim countries is paramount;[2] religion is not only secondary, but also a mere reflection of other underlying forces and therefore unimportant. On the opposite side are those who think that force of arms or change of social institutions cannot even begin to solve the problem of Muslim extremism, because it is fundamentally rooted in the violent nature of the Muslim God.[3] These are the two extremes. Most analysts are somewhere in the middle, combining multiple approaches to combating extremism—the "force of arms," for instance, with the "force of ideas," and support for democratic institutions and judicial reform with cultural and interreligious dialogue.[4] I count myself among advocates of multipronged approaches, with an important exception.

When I lecture to my students about religion and extremism, I first explore the causes of extremism and then discuss possible ways of combating it. As to the causes, I have a mantra for them. When it comes to extremism (as when it comes to most things in life), *all monocausal explanations are suspect*. Translation: extremism does not have a single cause (say, perceived injustice suffered or dangerous religious convictions); it always has multiple causes—political, economic, cultural, religious, and more. And if the causes are many, the solution cannot be one. Multipronged approaches are necessary—from struggles for greater justice in international relations, to the recrafting of political institutions, to reforming judicial systems, to improving the quality of education and media, to fostering religious understanding and the purification of religious convictions.

Now the exception. I reject military approaches to combating extremism, though I support nonmilitary coercive measures, such as policing and economic sanctions. Far from being effective in combating extremism, the use of military force only exacerbates the problem. If I am correct—I am aware that I am making a controversial claim and that people much more knowledgeable than I disagree with me—that's an important pragmatic reason against military solutions. But in my judgment, moral reasons are even weightier than pragmatic ones. The war in Iraq, partly waged to combat extremism, was an unjust and therefore morally unacceptable war; to a lesser degree the same is arguably true of the war in Afghanistan.

There is a consistent Christian tradition, prevalent in the early church and then resurfacing during the Protestant Reformation, that condemns all use of military force as incompatible with the way of Christ. But even from a classical Christian perspective shaped by Augustine, which embraces the just-war idea, these wars or any other wars that may be waged to combat extremism must be condemned as unjust and incompatible with Christian convictions.[5] Some key criteria for just war cannot be met—above all, just cause for war (because combating extremism through military means as a rule involves preemptive use of force) and immunity for noncombatants (because terrorists hide among civilians), to name just two. At best, what could be defended within that tradition is targeted attacks against terrorist themselves or their direct supporters.

I mention my opposition to military approaches to combating extremism not because I hope to persuade those who disagree with me. This is not the place to develop an argument for my position. Instead, I mention it because for me it elevates the importance of alternative approaches, including addressing the problem through theological engagement with religious traditions. There is no reason why those who disagree with me on military approaches would not agree with me on the importance of theological approaches.

So the first part of the answer about the relevance of this book for combating extremism is that multipronged approaches are necessary, and engagement with religious convictions and practices, such as I undertake here, is one such prong, essential but insufficient in and of itself. Now, that tells you what you shouldn't expect from this book with respect to the problem of extremism—to provide you with a magic bullet (if a declared opponent of military solutions to the problem of extremism is permitted to use the metaphor). But what *can* you expect?

To start with, remember this is a book written by a Christian and addressed to Christians. It is a Christian take on Muslims' convictions, an account of how Christians should relate to Muslims, not a prescription for what Muslims should believe and how they should live. Can a book addressed to Christians have any bearing on *Muslim* extremism? It can. Note that highly negative views of Islam are widespread among Christians.[6] True, I know of no Christian who acts on these views by using terrorist means, but many do so by inflammatory rhetoric and advocating an all-out clash between Muslim and Christian civilizations. Extremism on one side often feeds extremism on the other side; negative views and negative actions often elicit corresponding and even augmented negative views and actions in return.[7] So combating highly negative—and, importantly, inaccurate and prejudiced—Christian views of Muslims is a significant contribution to combating Muslim extremism.

Although this is a book for Christians, an important but secondary audience is Muslims themselves. I am offering a Christian suggestion to Muslims about how Muslims and Christians together might think about the one God we understand and worship in partly different ways and about how to live in the one world we share in light of our convictions about God. The suggestion I offer is an invitation to Muslims to reflect on the matter and determine the extent to which their thoughts, faithful to the sources of their faith, resonate with what I propose. *To the extent that* Muslims are able to accept this invitation, important consequences follow for combating extremism.

The Common God and Combating Extremism

Here are ten ways in which major strands in the argument of the book contribute to combating extremism. All of them concern the environment in which extremism thrives rather than extremists themselves, for almost by definition extremists, zealous believers in the combat mode that they often are, are unreachable by reason. An environment that discourages extremism will contain:

1. *Discourse about truth*. Extremism thrives where reasoned debate about important issues of public concern is absent. And inversely, where extremism thrives, such reasoned debate tends to shut down. As the content of this book exemplifies, in their normative versions the Christian and Muslim faiths are not about irrational stances or blind passions. Believers in both faiths use reason and make truth claims. Some think this is a major problem for relations between these faiths; when their truths clash, religious people fight. Hence a prevalent propensity today to keep questions of truth out of discussions of religion. Yet this is wrongheaded. Religious truth claims, like any other truth claims, invite counterclaims and encourage public debate. Respectful debate about the truth claims of religious groups is one of the best antidotes against religiously motivated or legitimized violence.

2. *Acknowledgment of a common God*. For Muslims and Christians each to worship a different God would mean that one group is made up of idolaters while the other worships the true God, and that the two groups have a very different (though not necessarily *completely* incompatible) set of ultimate values. An extreme version of this position on the Christian side is a radical contrast between the "moon god" of

Muslims and Yahweh of Jews and Christians. If, on the other hand, my argument is right and Christians and Muslims have a common God, they will have a larger set of overlapping ultimate values, which will provide them with a common moral framework in which to debate their differences rather than feeling that they have to resort to violence (chapters 4 and 5).

3. *Belief that God is loving and just.* It is not just any set of values that Muslims and Christians agree on by having a common God. If they both agreed that God were a fierce and irrational deity whose whims must be obeyed, this would be detrimental to their relations and would in fact underwrite extremism. But if Christians and Muslims agree that God is both loving—beneficent toward all and merciful toward transgressors—and just, bridges between them can and ought to be built, and extremism loses religious legitimacy. Love and justice are divine and therefore ultimate values. All human practices must be measured against these values (chapters 5, 8, and 9)

4. *Adherence to the command to love neighbors.* If God commands believers to hate all infidels and love only coreligionists, extremism has a religious sanction. On the other hand, if God commands believers to love all neighbors—utterly irrespective of their creeds—then we have strong religious reasons to oppose extremism and work for caring and just relations among peoples of all religions. In a sense, if we embrace God's command to love neighbors, the more religious we are, the less extremist we will be (chapters 5 and 6).

5. *A healthy sense of the fear of God.* Most religious extremists fight for their causes in the name of God. The appeal to God transmutes their own causes into God's causes. It would seem that the allegiance to God in love and fear would play into the extremists' hands. And yet this is not so. "No god but God"—a fundamental conviction that Christians share with

Muslims—is an anti-extremist creed! First, if Muslims and Christians agree that they should love God above all things, then God will matter to them more than anything in the world, including their respective religious communities or political visions. Second, if they believe that the God to whom they owe ultimate allegiance is the God of love and justice who commands people to love their neighbors and do justice, they will reject all causes and forms of struggle incompatible with love and justice. The fear of the one and common God, the beginning of political wisdom, will thus help drive out the demon of extremism (chapter 13).

6. *A stand against injustice.* Real or perceived injustice is one of the main causes of extremism. Agreement that God is just and that, because we are commanded to love all, we should work toward justice for all—toward better understanding of what is just in concrete situations (say, the problem of Palestine) and toward implementing just solutions—will help curb extremism (chapters 6 and 12).

7. *A stand against prejudice.* Extremism thrives by feeding on prejudice and the demonization of others; it starves when the light of knowledge falls on others and their humanity becomes manifest (this holds true even when that humanity proves to be flawed). Prejudice and demonization are forms of falsehood, and falsehood in assessing others is always a form of injustice. Commitment to love and justice is a commitment to learn the truth about others—the pleasant and the unpleasant—and to understand their motivations and aspirations. Commitment to love and justice is also commitment to truth about oneself and to deeper understanding of one's own relation to others (chapter 11).

8. *A stand against compulsion in religion.* The command to love neighbors implies granting them freedom to choose their religion (or not to practice any religion). Real or perceived "compulsion in religion" in majority Muslim countries is a cause of much of Christian extremism. Complete freedom

of religion—to believe, to express one's beliefs publicly, to practice religion in private and public, to propagate religion, and to change religion—would go a long way in curbing Christian extremism (chapter 11).

9. *A stand against disrespect.* As the violence triggered by the film *Submission* and the Danish cartoons has shown, the ire of the extremists is often inflamed when others insult the sacred symbols of the Muslim faith. The command to love neighbors demands that we refrain from such disrespect. We don't need to agree with the views of Muslims; we just need to be civil rather than mean-spirited as we disagree (chapters 1 and 13).

10. *A stand against political exclusivism.* Extremism thrives where people do not have legitimate and effective ways of expressing their perspectives on common life and attending to their grievances. In an interconnected and interdependent world, commitment to the one God and to love for all people demands pluralistic political institutions in which each religious group's voice can be heard and in which the state is impartial toward all overarching perspectives on life (chapter 12).

The main thrust of all ten suggestions is this. The claim that Christians and Muslims, notwithstanding their important and ineradicable differences, have a common and similarly understood God (1) delegitimizes religious motivation to violence between them and (2) supplies motivation to care for others and to engage in a vigorous and sustained debate about what constitutes the common good in the one world we share.

ACKNOWLEDGMENTS

I have been thinking off and on since my boyhood about how Christians should respond to the God of the Muslims. I grew up in the north of Yugoslavia and did not know many Muslims at that time. But my father did, and some of them he knew quite well. He taught me that Christians and Muslims believe in the same God and set me on the course that resulted in this book. For this, and innumerable other blessings imparted, I dedicated this book to him, one of the very best human beings I have ever known.

After my father's initial lessons, it took me a while, though, to start actually crafting in a sustained way a proper Christian response to the God Muslims worship. The occasion was 9/11 and its aftermath. My reflections picked up momentum after the publication of the Muslim document "A Common Word Between Us and You" and the Christian "Yale Response," of which I was the primary drafter. In the public reaction to these documents—especially in the critical sort of reaction—the question of whether Muslims and Christians worship the same God soon emerged as the heart of the debate. To all who participated in one way or another in these discussions I am grateful for stimulating my own thinking. I must also mention here my friend Tim Collins, who alerted me to "The Common Word" even before it was officially published.

I delivered lectures on the topic at Evangelical-Theological Seminary in Osijek, Croatia (2008); Regent's Park College in Oxford, England (2008); the Reformed Theological Seminary, Orlando, Florida (Kistenmacher Lectures, 2008); Florida Southern College, Lakeland, Florida (Warren Willis Lecture, 2008); the First Baptist Church in Ann Arbor, Michigan (Morikawa Lectures, 2009); and the Pittsburgh Theological Seminary, Pittsburgh, Pennsylvania

(Henderson Lectures, 2010). I am grateful to the organizers as well as to the audiences for spirited discussions.

At the Yale Center for Faith and Culture, I organized two sessions of the series of consultations about "God and Human Flourishing" on whether Christians and Muslims believe in the same God. Bruce Chilton, John Hare, Aref Nayed, Jacob Neusner, Peter Ochs, Amy Plantinga Pauw, Christoph Schwöbel, Reza Shah-Kazemi, and Denys Turner were involved as paper writers and discussants. I have learned much from them, at points even more than I thought I needed to know. I am thankful to my friend Alonzo McDonald and his Agape Foundation for financially supporting these events (as well as for being an active participant in the discussions!).

Many friends have read and commented on the manuscript as it was being written. H. R. H. Prince Ghazi bin Muhammad bin Talal, Yasir Qadhi, Reza Shah-Kazemi, and Mona Siddiqui offered invaluable Muslim responses to portions of the text. I could not have done the book without them, even though I was not always able to follow their lead. Alon Goshen-Gottstein read the whole manuscript with a keen eye toward how it touches broader interfaith relations, especially in relation to Judaism, the original monotheistic faith, without which neither Christianity nor Islam would exist. Keith DeRose helped me in puzzling out the meaning of "the same" as applied to the one God Muslims and Christians worship. Ronald Rittgers, who taught with me a course on Martin Luther while he was at Yale, helped clarify my thinking about Luther's stance toward the God of Muhammad. Finally, I discussed many themes of the book with Awet Andemicael. She also helped with research and commented extensively and ably on the content as well as style of just about the whole manuscript.

I am particularly grateful to my past and present co-workers at the Yale Center for Faith and Culture—Neil Arner, Joseph Cumming, Terry Dumansky, Sven Ensminger, Elena Lloyd-Sidle, Ryan McAnnally-Linz, Amanda Ogden, Stephen Ogden, Libby Masback, Andrew Saperstein, and Melissa Yarrington. As we discussed the manuscript at our regular staff meetings, they were unsparing with their time and wise in their counsel. So also was Sean Larson, my former student at Yale. A very special thanks goes to two co-workers, Elena and Ryan. They worked as my primary research assistants, Elena covering Islam and Ryan everything else. Both were simply superb, and they saved me countless hours of work and much frustration. Jan O'Dell, my assistant, kept things moving at the office and shielded me from unnecessary intrusions.

I wrote this book in the course of two semester-long sabbaticals. I am grateful to Yale University and the dean of Yale Divinity School, Harold Attridge, for setting me free from teaching. But Yale paid for only one of these sabbaticals. A gift of Steve and Denise Adams paid for the other. Needless to say, without their generosity, for which I am deeply grateful, much of the content of this book would still be swirling somewhere in my head rather than being encoded in this book.

Finally, I am grateful to my editor and friend Roger Freet and his staff, who ably shepherded the whole project.

NOTES

Introduction: The One God and the Great Chasm

1. Muslims make up approximately 20 percent of the world's population; Christians, 33 percent. See "World Religions (2005)," Association of Religion Data Archives, http://www.thearda.com/QuickLists/Quick List_125.asp.

2. The *World Christian Database* estimates that between 2000 and 2005 Islam grew at an annual rate of 1.84 percent and Christianity at an annual rate of 1.38 percent. See Qassem Zein, "The List: The World's Fastest Growing Religions," *Foreign Policy,* May 14, 2007, http://www.foreign policy.com/articles/2007/05/13/the_list_the_worlds_fastest_growing _religions (accessed July 25, 2010). The *World Christian Encyclopedia* (Oxford: Oxford Univ. Press, 2001) projects that by 2050 Christianity will make up 34.3 percent of the world population and Islam 25 percent.

3. See Jose Casanova, *Public Religions in the Modern World* (Chicago: Univ. of Chicago Press, 1994); "Public Religions Revisited," in *Religion: Beyond a Concept,* ed. Hent de Vries (New York: Fordham Univ. Press, 2008), 101–19.

4. The U.S. Census Bureau and the United Nations both expect the world population to exceed nine billion people by 2050. See http://www.census .gov/ipc/www/idb/worldpop.php (accessed May 17, 2010); and Population Division of the Department of Economic and Social Affairs of the United Nations Secretariat, *World Population Prospects: The 2008 Revision,* http://esa.un.org/unpp (accessed May 17, 2010).

5. See Steven Solomon, *Water: The Epic Struggle for Wealth, Power, and Civilization* (New York: HarperCollins, 2010), 367–486.

6. See John Micklethwait and Adrian Wooldridge, *God Is Back: How the Global Revival of Faith Is Changing the World* (New York: Penguin, 2009), 298.

7. Text and video available at http://blog.christianitytoday.com/ctpolitics /2009/01/rick_warrens_in.html (accessed July 25, 2010).

8. Joe Schimmel, "Did Rick Warren Pray to Allah in the Name of a Muslim Prophet?" http://cupofjoe.goodfight.org/?p=88 (accessed July 25, 2010).

9. "Rick Warren's Invocation: Prayer That Equated Allah (Satan) with God," http://truedsicernment.com/2009/01/20/rick-warrens-invocation -prayer-that-equated-allah-satan-with-god/ (accessed July 25, 2010).

10. Lord Brian Griffiths, personal correspondence, November 18, 2008.

11. "U.S. Is 'Battling Satan' Says General," BBC News, October 17, 2003, http://news.bbc.co.uk/2/hi/americas/3199212.stm (accessed July 25, 2010).

12. Pat Robertson, "Why Evangelical Christians Support Israel," http://www. patrobertson.com/Speeches/IsraelLauder.asp (accessed July 26, 2010).

13. See The Encyclopedia of Islam (Leiden: Brill, 2002), s.v. "Allah," "Ilah." The association of the Allah of Islam with a "moon god" is hard to rec-oncile with the Qur'anic verse Fussilat, 41:37, which says, "Among His Signs are the Night and the Day, and the Sun and the Moon. Do not adore the sun and the moon, but adore Allah, Who created them, if it is Him you wish to serve."

14. See Jürgen Habermas, "A Reply," in An Awareness of What Is Missing: Faith and Reason in a Post-secular Age (Malden, MA: Polity, 2010), 72–83.

15. Even though Lincoln never joined a church and read little theology, the speech was theologically profound. Indeed, as Mark Noll argued recently (following in part Reinhold Niebuhr, one of the greatest Amer-ican theologians of the twentieth century): "The second inaugural rep-resented a moral theology superior to that which came from the nation's most distinguished theologians" ("'Both . . . Pray to the Same God': The Singularity of Lincoln's Faith in the Era of the Civil War," Journal of the Abraham Lincoln Association 18 [1997]: 19).

16. Frederick Douglass, Life and Times of Frederick Douglass (1882; Mineola, NY: Dover, 2003), 266.

17. Abraham Lincoln, "The Second Inaugural Address," in The Language of Liberty: The Political Speeches and Writings of Abraham Lincoln, ed. Joseph R. Fornieri (Washington, DC: Regnery, 2003), 696–98.

18. Lincoln alludes here to Matt. 7:1.

19. Abraham Lincoln, "Meditation on the Divine Will," in The Collected Works of Abraham Lincoln, ed. Roy P. Basler, 9 vols. (New Brunswick, NJ: Rutgers Univ. Press, 1953–55), 5:403.

20. On al-Ghazali, see Frank Griffel, Al-Ghazali's Philosophical Theology (Oxford: Oxford Univ. Press, 2009).

21. See Sayyid Qutb, Milestones (CreateSpace, 2005). On Qutb, see John Esposito, The Future of Islam (Oxford: Oxford Univ. Press, 2010), 67–68. On Qutb's "political thinking," see Miroslav Volf, A Public Faith: How

Followers of Christ Should Serve the Common Good (Grand Rapids: Baker, 2011), introduction.

Chapter 1: The Pope and the Prince: God, the Great Chasm, and the Building of Bridges

1. "Pope Says Peace Implies Respect for Religious Symbols," *Zenit,* February 20, 2006, http://www.zenit.org/article-15327?l=english (accessed July 25, 2010). Prior to the incident with the Danish caricatures, Benedict XVI had expressed concern that in Europe today freedom of expression seems to include the right to desecrate religious symbols. He insisted that "respect for that which another group holds sacred, especially for the sacred in the highest sense, for God," is fundamental to all cultures (Joseph Ratzinger, "The Spiritual Roots of Europe: Yesterday, Today, and Tomorrow," in Joseph Ratzinger and Marcello Pera, *Without Roots: The West, Relativism, Christianity, Islam,* trans. Michael F. Moore [New York: Basic, 2006], 78).

2. In Nouakchott, the capital of Mauritania, there was a peaceful prayer vigil during which the protesters read the Qur'an and said prayers all night (see Hamza Yusuf, "Refinement of the Hearts" [Audio CD, Sandala Productions]).

3. Ratzinger, "Spiritual Roots," 78.

4. In Ana Belen Soage, "The Muslim Reaction to Pope Benedict XVI's Regensburg Address," *Cross Currents* (January 2007): 138.

5. The pope mentioned the threat present "in the contempt for God and the cynicism that considers mockery of the sacred to be an exercise of freedom." The title of the pope's sermon is "His 'vengeance' is the cross: a love to the end. This is the God we need . . ." For the text of the sermon, see the following anthology of speeches and sermons made during the pope's trip to Bavaria in 2006: Sandro Magister, "Munich, Altötting, Regensburg: Diary of a Pilgrimage of Faith," *Chiesa Online,* September 14, 2006, http://chiesa.espresso.repubblica.it/articolo/83684?eng=y (accessed July 25, 2010).

6. See "Pope's Explanations Not Good Enough for Radical Islam," *AsiaNews,* September 18, 2006, http://www.asianews.it/index.php?l=en&art=7245 (accessed July 25, 2010).

7. See "Pope Benedict's Regensburg Address and the Muslim Reaction (Part II)," *Benedict Blog,* September 19, 2006, http://popebenedictxvinews.blogspot.com/2006/09/pope-benedicts-regensburg-address-and.html (accessed July 25, 2010).

8. For the official Vatican English translation of the pope's speech, see, Benedict XVI, "Faith, Reason and the University: Memories and Re-

flections," *The Holy See,* September 12, 2006, http://www.vatican.va /holy_father/benedict_xvi/speeches/2006/september/documents/hf _ben-xvi_spe_20060912_university-regensburg_en.html (accessed July 25, 2010).

9. Benedict XVI, "Faith, Reason and the University."

10. Wilhelm Baum, "Manuel II Palaiologos (1392–1425 A.D.)," *Online Encyclopedia of Roman Emperors,* http://www.roman-emperors.org/manuel2 .htm (accessed July 25, 2010).

11. Though European culture, especially its technology and trade, has marched triumphantly across the planet, "at the hour of its greatest success, Europe seems hollow," complained the pope in an earlier text (Ratzinger, "Spiritual Roots," 66). Its moral and cultural core has been eaten away by the acids of relativism. As a religion, Islam, on the other hand, sees itself as ascendant, he argued, maybe failing to note that encounter with modernity and globalization has exposed Islam to challenges similar to those facing Christianity. Muslims act out of persuasion that "they have something to say to the world" and that, indeed, they "are the essential religious force of the future" (Joseph Cardinal Ratzinger, *Salt of the Earth: Christianity and the Catholic Church at the End of the Millennium: An Interview with Peter Seewald,* trans. Adrian Walker [San Francisco: Ignatius, 1997], 246). Through immigration and high birth rates Islam is spreading in the Western world. Some forms of Islam are more violent than others, but all of them are, in Pope Benedict's judgment, essentially incompatible with the democratic traditions whose pillars are the inviolable dignity of human beings and the separation of political and religious spheres. The West is free and pluralistic; Islam is by "its inner nature" totalitarian and therefore also violent (Ratzinger, *Salt of the Earth;* see also Samir Khalil Samir, S.J., "When Civilizations Meet: How Joseph Ratzinger Sees Islam," *Chiesa Online,* April 5, 2006, http://chiesa.espresso.repubblica.it /articolo/53826?eng=y [accessed July 25, 2010]). Manuel II did put things brusquely, reflecting the historical context in which he was living, but, even writing six centuries ago and living under a Turkish siege, he articulated at least *something* of what Benedict XVI himself thinks. In response to the uproar in Muslim communities over his remarks, the pope expressed his regret "for the reactions in some countries to a few passages of my address at the University of Regensburg, which were considered offensive to the sensibility of Muslims." As a quotation from a medieval text, these words, he said, "do not in any way express my personal thought" (Benedict XVI, "Angelus (Castel Gandolfo)," *The Holy See,* September 17, 2006, http:// www.vatican.va/holy_father/benedict_xvi/angelus/2006/documents/hf _ben-xvi_ang_20060917_en.html [accessed July 25, 2010]).

12. In addition to describing the emperor's words as "surprisingly brusque," he also uses the word "forcefully" to describe the words of Manuel about "things evil and inhuman" in Islam (the German original is even stronger than "forcefully": *zuschlagen*). See paragraph 3 at http://www.vatican.va /holy_father/benedict_xvi/speeches/2006/september/documents/hf_ben xvi_spe_20060912_university-regensburg_en.html (accessed July 25, 2010).

13. Joseph Cardinal Ratzinger, *Truth and Tolerance: Christian Belief and World Religions,* trans. Henry Taylor (San Francisco: Ignatius, 2004), 54.

14. Ratzinger, *Salt of the Earth,* 244.

15. On this issue as it relates to freedom to witness and change one's religion, see chapters 11 and 12.

16. Wolfgang Krebs reads Benedict XVI to mean that in Islam the "God-as-will" account of God is an aberration, just as Benedict XVI claims that Duns Scotus's view is an aberration of the proper Christian view of God (see *Das Papstzitat von Regensburg: Benedikt XVI. im 'Kampf der Kulturen'* [Berlin: Rombos, 2007], 209). I read the pope to say that "God-as-will" is how mainstream Islam understands God.

17. Most of the Regensburg lecture was not about Islam, but about the perils of severing faith from reason (faith as obedience to arbitrary law or expression of mere feeling) and reason from faith (reason as scientific and instrumental rationality). And yet, the lecture as a whole very much concerned the Christian relationship to Islam. Its central thought was, in George Weigel's words, "that our idea of God (or lack of an idea of God) profoundly shapes the way we think about both what is good and what is wicked, and how we think about the appropriate methods for advancing the truth in a world in which there are profound disagreements about the truth of things" ("Pope on a Mission to Surprise," *Standpoint,* October 2008, http://www.standpointmag.co.uk/pope-on-a-mission-to -surprise-october [accessed July 26, 2010]).

18. "Open Letter to His Holiness Pope Benedict XVI," http://amman message.com/media/openLetter/english.pdf.

19. Aref Nayed argues that even scholars who stress divine transcendence most radically, like Ibn Hazm, do not sever God from reason: "God freely chooses, in His compassion towards His creatures, to self-consistently act reasonably so that we can use our reason to align ourselves with His guidance and directive" ("A Muslim's Commentary on Benedict XVI's 'Faith, Reason and the University: Memories and Reflections,'" Masud.co.uk, http://www.masud.co.uk/ISLAM/misc/commentary_on _benedict.php). For the important but complicated debate between Aref Nayed and Alessandro Martinetti about God-as-reason and God-as-will,

see Sandro Magister, "The Church and Islam: A Sprig of Dialogue Has Sprouted in Regensburg," trans. Matthew Sherry, *Chiesa Online,* October 30, 2006, http://chiesa.espresso.repubblica.it/articolo/93245?&eng=y.

20. John Paul II, *Insegnamenti* 8, no. 2 (1985): 497; quoted during a general audience on May 5, 1999, http://www.vatican.va/holy_father/john _paul_ii/audiences/1999/documents/hf_jp-ii_aud_05051999_en.html.

21. Thomas Aquinas, however, argued that baptized Christians who are stubborn heretics should be executed (*Summa Theologiae* [hereafter referred to as *ST*] II–II, Q.11, A.3), and "bodily compulsion" should be used to make apostates and heretics "fulfill what they have promised" (*ST* II–II, Q.10, A.8).

22. For popular criticism of Islam as violent, see Sam Harris, *The End of Faith: Religion, Terror, and the Future of Reason* (New York: Norton, 2004); Christopher Hitchens, *God Is Not Great: How Religion Poisons Everything* (Boston: Twelve Books, 2007).

23. William Chittick argues that at the most external level, Islam is a religion of law; it tells people what to do and what not to do. At the deepest level, however, Islam is a religion that "points the way to achieving nearness to God" (*Sufism* [Oxford: Oneworld, 2000], 7).

24. In his response to the "Common Word," Daniel Madigan, S.J., notes, rightly, the primacy of God's love for humanity in Christianity and the secondary status of human love for God and neighbor. "Does the Word become incarnate simply to remind us of a few important verses from Deuteronomy and Leviticus?" he asks rhetorically ("A Common Word Between Us and You: Some Initial Reflections," official website of A Common Word, http://www.acommonword.com/index .php?page=responses&item=51). To say, however, that love of God and neighbor is second in importance to God's own love is in no way to suggest that love of God and neighbor is not central.

25. Sunan al-Tirmidhi, *Kitab al-Da'awat, Bab al-Du'a fi Yawm 'Arafah,* Hadith no. 3934.

26. "A Common Word Between Us and You," in *A Common Word: Muslims and Christians on Loving God and Neighbor,* ed. Miroslav Volf, Ghazi bin Muhammad, and Melissa Yarrington (Grand Rapids, MI: Eerdmans, 2010), 36.

27. *Sahih Muslim, Kitab al-Iman,* 67–1, Hadith no. 45. See also the parallel saying: "None of you has faith until you love for your brother what you love for yourself" (*Sahih al-Bukhari, Kitab al-Iman,* Hadith no. 13).

28. "A Common Word," in Volf, Ghazi bin Muhammad, and Yarrington, eds., *Common Word,* 43–44.

29. See Mark Durie, "Notes of Christians," *Resources on "A Common Word Between Us and You,"* February 4, 2008, http://www.acommonword.blogspot .com/; "On the Yale Response," *Resources on "A Common Word Between Us and You,"* February 5, 2008, http://www.acommonword.blogspot.com/; Patrick Sookhdeo, *Global Jihad* (McLean, VA: Isaac, 2007).

30. "A Common Word," 49.

31. See Richard Rorty, "Religion as Conversation-Stopper," *Common Knowledge* 3 (1995): 1–6. Rorty later backed away from the position that religion should be totally excluded from the public square ("Religion in the Public Square: A Reconsideration," *Journal of Religious Ethics* 31 [2003]: 141–49).

32. On individuals and communities as moral agents, see Reinhold Niebuhr, *Moral Man and Immoral Society* (1932; Louisville, KY: Westminster John Knox, 2001).

33. Nicholas Wolterstorff suggests that not even God loves justice simply for the sake of the principle of justice (*Justice: Rights and Wrongs* [Princeton, NJ: Princeton Univ. Press, 2007], 82).

34. See Miroslav Volf, *Exclusion and Embrace* (Nashville: Abingdon, 1996), 224–25; "God, Justice, and Love," *Books & Culture* (January/February 2009): 26–28.

35. The first major interfaith event on these issues, involving many signatories of the "Common Word" and the "Yale Response," took place at Yale on July 24–31, 2008, and it was generally hailed as a major success. For partial proceedings, see *A Common Word at Yale,* "Loving God and Neighbor in Word and Deed: Implications for Christians and Muslims," Yale Center for Faith and Culture, http://www.yale.edu/faith/acw/acw -2008-conf.htm (accessed July 25, 2010).

36. You can read the "Yale Response"—with additional explanatory footnotes—in Volf, Ghazi bin Muhammad, and Yarrington, eds., *A Common Word,* 51–78.

37. John Piper, "A Common Word Between Us?," *Desiring God,* January 23, 2008, http://www.desiringgod.org/Blog/1032_a_common_word _between_us/ (accessed July 25, 2010).

38. Some Christians accuse Muslims of worshipping "another God," because Muslims deny the Trinity (see John Baker, "Should Christians 'Respect' Other Religions?," *True Discernment,* May 19, 2009, http://truediscern ment.com/2009/05/19/should-christians-respect-other-religions/ [accessed July 25, 2010]).

39. See Pope Paul VI, "Declaration on the Relation of the Church to Non-Christian Religions, *Nostra Aetate,*" *The Holy See,* October 28, 1965,

http://www.vatican.va/archive/hist_councils/ii_vatican_council/docu
ments/vat-ii_decl_19651028_nostra-aetate_en.html (accessed July 25,
2010).

40. "Text of Pope's Remarks to Muslim Leaders at Castel Gandolfo," *Catholic News Service,* September 25, 2006, http://www.catholicnews.com
/data/stories/cns/0605438.htm (accessed July 25, 2010).

41. "Meeting with Muslim Religious Leaders, Members of the Diplomatic
Corps and Rectors of Universities of Jordan: Address of His Holiness
Benedict XVI," *The Holy See,* May 9, 2009, http://www.vatican.va
/holy_father/benedict_xvi/speeches/2009/may/documents/hf_ben-xvi
_spe_20090509_capi-musulmani_en.html (accessed July 25, 2010).

42. "Meeting with Muslim Religious Leaders." Reference to the first encyclical of Benedict XVI is to *Deus est caritas,* no. 16.

43. For the text of Prince Ghazi's welcome speech to Pope Benedict XVI, see
http://acommonword.com/en/news-pope-benedict-xvi-visits-jordan/25
-news/312-welcome-speech-by-muslim-prince-ghazi.html (accessed July
25, 2010).

Chapter 2: A Catholic Cardinal and the One God of All

1. For an excerpt from his account of the siege and fall of Constantinople,
see http://www.deremilitari.org/resources/sources/constantinople3.htm
(accessed July 25, 2010).

2. As quoted in Nancy Bisaha, *Creating East and West: Renaissance Humanists and the Ottoman Turks* (Philadelphia: Univ. of Pennsylvania Press,
2004), 2.

3. Aeneas Silvius Piccolomini (Pius II), *Epistola ad Mahomatem II (Epistle
to Mohammed II),* ed. and trans. Albert R. Baca (New York: Peter Lang,
1990), 23.

4. Aeneas Sylvius Piccolomini, *Reject Aeneas, Accept Pius: Selected Letters
of Aeneas Sylvius Piccolomini (Pope Pius II),* trans. Thomas M. Izbicki,
Gerald Christianson, and Philip Krey (Washington, DC: Catholic Univ.
of America Press, 2006), 311. Ironically, Arabic manuscripts from Spain
and Sicily as well as Muslim commentaries had been at least as important as Greek versions from the Byzantine Empire in reintroducing
the philosophy of Aristotle to the Latin-speaking West (see Williston
Walker et al., *A History of the Christian Church,* 4th ed. [1918; New York:
Scribner, 1985], 132–34).

5. Piccolomini, *Reject Aeneas,* 313.

6. Bisaha, *Creating East and West,* 68.

7. Piccolomini, *Reject Aeneas,* 313.

8. Piccolomini, *Reject Aeneas,* 314.

9. Piccolomini, *Reject Aeneas,* 315.

10. On Pius II and the crusade, see Nancy Bisaha, "Pope Pius II and the Crusade," in *Crusading in the Fifteenth Century: Message and Impact,* ed. Norman Housley (Houndmills, UK: Palgrave Macmillan, 2004), 39–52.

11. Piccolomini, *Reject Aeneas,* 317.

12. Piccolomini, *Reject Aeneas,* 316.

13. Pius II, "The Commentaries of Pius II: Book 1," trans. Florence Alden Gragg, ed. Leona C. Gabel, *Smith College Studies in History* 22 (1936–37): 72.

14. Piccolomini, *Epistola,* 2.

15. Piccolomini, *Epistola,* 13.

16. Piccolomini, *Epistola,* 21.

17. Piccolomini, *Epistola,* 30–34.

18. Piccolomini, *Epistola,* 19, 184.

19. Piccolomini, *Epistola,* 113. Nicholas was more subtle on this matter. On the one hand, he stated: "There has always seemed to me to be as much difference between Muhammad's paradise and Christ's paradise as there is between sensible things and intellectual things—or between visible things, which are temporal, and invisible things, which are eternal." Yet he granted that it is possible to understand the sensual pleasures that abound in the Qur'an as symbols of intellectual pleasures ("Cribratio Alkorani," *Nicholas of Cusa's De pace fidei and Cribratio Alkorani,* trans. Jasper Hopkins [Minneapolis: Banning, 1994], 149–53).

20. As quoted in Bisaha, *Creating East and West,* 15.

21. Piccolomini, *Epistola,* 39–40.

22. Piccolomini, *Epistola,* 27.

23. Piccolomini, *Epistola,* 66–67.

24. Piccolomini, *Epistola,* 51.

25. As quoted in Mandell Creighton, *A History of the Papacy from the Great Schism to the Sack of Rome* (London: Longmans, 1903), 3:329.

26. Commenting on the stance of Nicholas of Cusa toward Muslims and the Ottoman Empire, Lamin Sanneh notes that he—along with John of Segovia—"faced the shock of the fall of Constantinople not by rushing forward into a crusade-for-our-time call to arms, but by cultivating the art of cultural understanding" ("The Fall of Constantinople and the Fall of the Twin Towers: The Muslim World and the West," VirtueOnline, http://www.virtueonline.org/portal/modules/news/article.php?storyid=8490).

27. See R. W. Southern, *Western Views of Islam in the Middle Ages* (Cambridge, MA: Harvard Univ. Press, 1962), 90–92.

28. Pope Nicholas V, who tried to organize a crusade against the Turks, had charged Nicholas of Cusa in 1455 with "a mission to the whole Germany and England to further it" (Henry Bett, *Nicholas of Cusa* [London: Methuen, 1932], 97). But Nicholas did not leave his diocese. What he did do a bit later, also at the request of the pope, was to write "a refutation of the errors of Islam." The refutation took the form of a "sifting" of the Qur'an, not a simple denunciation and refutation of its errors.

29. Nicholas of Cusa, "De pace fidei," in *Nicholas of Cusa's De pace fidei and Cribratio Alkorani,* 1.

30. Nicholas of Cusa, "De pace fidei," 68.

31. Nicholas of Cusa, "De pace fidei," 68.

32. For this thesis, see Florian Hamann, "Koran and Konziliarismus: Anmerkungen zum Verhältniss von Heymericus de Campo and Nikolaus von Kues," *Vivarium* (February 2005): 275–91.

33. Nicholas of Cusa, "De pace fidei," 5. Similarly, the Sufi Muslim poet Fakhruddin Iraqi (1213–89) wrote: "Love where you may, you will have loved Him; turn your face whatever way, it turns toward Him—even if you know it not" (*Divine Flashes,* trans. William C. Chittick and Peter Lamborn Wilson [New York: Paulist, 1982], 7:85).

34. See, for instance, Bonaventure, *The Soul's Journey into God* 3:4.

35. For Plato's argument that, in everything they desire, human beings desire the Good, see *Meno* 77–78 and *Gorgias* 466–68, in *Dialogues of Plato,* trans. B. Jowett (Oxford: Clarendon, 1875), 1:277–78; 2:336–40.

36. Nicholas of Cusa, "De pace fidei," 68.

37. Nicholas of Cusa, "De pace fidei," 6.

38. See Donald F. Duclow, "Life and Works," in *Introducing Nicholas of Cusa,* ed. Christopher M. Bellitto, Thomas M. Izbicki, and Gerald Christianson (New York: Paulist, 2004), 44.

39. It is for this reason that Nicholas could say, in his more polemical mode, both that the author of the Qur'an was "the god of this world . . . who blinds the minds of unbelievers, so that the light of the Gospel of the glory of Christ, who is the image of the invisible God, does not shine in them" and that "the beauty or truth or clarity" found in the Qur'an is "a ray of the most lucid Gospel" ("Cribratio Alkorani," 23, 41).

40. See Plato, *Gorgias* 509e5–6; cf. *Protagoras* 358b–d.

41. Nicholas of Cusa, "De pace fidei," 5. Nicholas speaks not just of Muhammad's errors, but also of his "perverse intent, because he did not intend to lead men to that goal-of-rest to which Christ showed the way, but rather sought his own glory under the guise of that goal." He immediately, however, insists that "*ignorance* was the cause of Muhammad's error and malevolence" ("Cribratio Alkorani," 9, emphasis added).

42. Nicholas of Cusa, "Cribratio Alkorani," 238.

43. In the *hadith,* Muhammad says: "The best that I have said—myself, and the prophets that came before me—is 'There is no god but God, He Alone, He hath no associate, His is the sovereignty and His is the praise and He hath power over all things'" (*Sunan al-Tirmidhi, Kitab al-Da'awat, Bab al-Du'a fi Yawm 'Arafah,* Hadith no. 3934).

44. Nicholas of Cusa, "De pace fidei," 10.

45. The great Jewish medieval thinker Maimonides held a similar view. According to David Novak, for Maimonides, "Christianity and Islam are true when they are variations of themes most completely presented in Judaism; and they are in error when they contradict Judaism" ("The Mind of Maimonides," *First Things,* February 1999, http://www.first things.com/article/2008/12/003-the-mind-of-maimonides-44 [accessed July 25, 2010]).

46. See Piccolomini, *Epistola,* 66.

47. Nicholas of Cusa, "Cribratio Alkorani," 88.

48. Nicholas of Cusa, "Cribratio Alkorani," 88.

49. Nicholas of Cusa, "Cribratio Alkorani," 88.

50. Nicholas of Cusa, "De docta ignorantia," *Nicholas of Cusa: Selected Spiritual Writings,* trans. H. Lawrence Bond (New York: Paulist, 1997), 57 (quoting Augustine).

51. See Augustine, *The Literal Meaning of Genesis* 4.3.6–4.6.13; Pseudo-Dionysius, *The Divine Names* 9.2, 13.3; Boethius *On the Trinity* 2–3.

52. Nicholas of Cusa, "De pace fidei," 15.

53. Nicholas of Cusa, "De pace fidei," 23. In his discussion of the Trinity in the *Summa Theologiae,* Thomas Aquinas insists that "the supreme unity and simplicity of God exclude every kind of plurality of absolute things" (*ST* I, Q.30, A.3).

54. Nicholas of Cusa, "Cribratio Alkorani," 107.

55. Nicholas of Cusa, "De docta ignorantia," 1:14.

56. See Augustine, *On the Trinity* bks. 5–8; Thomas Aquinas, *ST* I, Q.3, 11, 30, 31.

57. Nicholas of Cusa, "Cribratio Alkorani," 49.

58. Nicholas of Cusa, "Cribratio Alkorani," 111.

59. Nicholas of Cusa, "Cribratio Alkorani," 53.

60. Nicholas of Cusa, "Cribratio Alkorani," 52.

61. Nicholas of Cusa, "Cribratio Alkorani," 62.

62. Nicholas of Cusa, "Cribratio Alkorani," 64.

63. *Sunan al-Tirmidhi, Kitab al-Da'awat, Bab al-Du'a fi Yawm 'Arafah,* Hadith no. 3934.

64. Nicholas of Cusa, "De pace fidei," 26.

65. Nicholas of Cusa, "De pace fidei," 26.

66. Nicholas of Cusa, "Cribratio Alkorani," 86.

67. Nicholas of Cusa, "Cribratio Alkorani," 60.

68. Nicholas of Cusa, "De pace fidei," 26.

69. Nicholas of Cusa, "De pace fidei," 23.

70. Nicholas of Cusa, "Cribratio Alkorani," 108.

71. Nicholas of Cusa, "De pace fidei," 5.

72. Nicholas of Cusa, "De pace fidei," 5.

Chapter 3: A Protestant Reformer and the God of the Turks

1. Quoted in Max Kortepeter, "The Turkish Question in the Era of the Fifth Lateran Council (1512–1517)," in *Essays on Islamic Civilization: Presented to Niyazi Berkes,* ed. Donald P. Little (Leiden: Brill, 1976), 162.

2. Alan Palmer, *The Decline and Fall of the Ottoman Empire* (New York: Evans, 1992), 9.

3. John Bohnstedt, "The Infidel Scourge of God: The Turkish Menace as Seen by German Pamphleteers of the Reformation Era," *Transactions of the American Philosophical Society* 56, no. 9 (1968): 42.

4. Adam S. Francisco, *Martin Luther and Islam: A Study in Sixteenth-Century Polemics and Apologetics* (Leiden: Brill, 2007), 49.

5. "Luther's 1530 Preface to the Tract on the Religion and Customs of the Turks," in Sarah Henrich and James L. Boyce, "Martin Luther—Translations of Two Prefaces on Islam: Preface to the *Libellus de ritu et moribus Turcorum* (1530) and Preface to Bibliander's Edition of the Qur'an (1543)," *Word & World* 16 (Spring 1996): 260.

6. Philip K. Hitti, *The Arabs: A Short History* (Princeton, NJ: Princeton Univ. Press, 1943), 120.

7. David Nicholas, *The Evolution of the Medieval World: Society, Government and Thought in Europe, 312–1500* (London: Longman, 1992), 275; D. M. Dunlop, *Arab Civilization to A.D. 1500* (London: Longman, 1971), 20.

8. Nicholas, *Evolution of the Medieval World,* 112; Hitti, *Arabs,* 143, 146. Other contributions include the development of "Arabic" numerals, the invention of the concept of "zero," an astonishingly accurate estimation of the circumference of the earth, and the translation and preservation of important ancient Greek and Persian philosophical and scientific texts.

9. Marshall G. S. Hodgson, "The Role of Islam in World History," in *Rethinking World History: Essays on Europe, Islam, and World History,* ed. Edmund Burke III (Cambridge: Cambridge Univ. Press, 1993), 97.

10. Martin Luther, *The Large Catechism* (hereafter referred to as *LC*), 2:66,

in *The Book of Concord: The Confessions of the Evangelical Lutheran Church,* ed. Robert Kolb and Timothy J. Wengert (Minneapolis: Fortress, 2000).

11. Martin Luther, "The Smalcald Articles," 4:10, in Kolb and Wengert, eds., *Book of Concord.*

12. Martin Luther, "On the Jews and Their Lies," in *Luther's Works* (hereafter referred to as *LW*), ed. Jaroslav Pelikan and Helmut T. Lehmann, 55 vols. (Philadelphia: Fortress, 1955–86), 47:293.

13. Martin Luther, "Heerpredigt wider den Türken," in *D. Martin Luthers Werke Kritische Gesamtausgabe* (hereafter referred to as *WA* [*Weimarer Ausgabe*]; Weimar: Hermann Böhlau, 1883–), 30/2:173.

14. See Heiko Augustinus Oberman, *Luther: Man Between God and the Devil,* trans. Eileen Walliser-Schwarzbart (New Haven, CT: Yale Univ. Press, 2006), 5.

15. Nevertheless, throughout his life, Luther had considered the papacy the greatest threat to the church and the gospel.

16. Luther, *LC,* 2:67.

17. Luther, "On the War Against the Turk," *LW,* 46:180–81.

18. Cited in Henrich and Boyce, "Martin Luther," 259.

19. Henrich and Boyce, "Martin Luther," 259.

20. Luther, "Sermon for the Twenty-Sixth Sunday After Trinity," in *Sermons of Martin Luther,* electronic edition (Charlottesville, VA: InteLex Corporation, 1995), 5:383–84.

21. Martin Luther, *WA,* 51:150, 38–39.

22. Luther, *LC,* 2:64.

23. Luther, *LC,* 2:63.

24. Luther, *WA,* 53:150, 14; *LW,* 15:315.

25. Luther, *WA,* 53:328, 3–6.

26. Martin Luther, *WA,* 53:286, 8. In one sermon Luther notes that "the human body and soul are not so completely one as the Triune God" (cf. Luther, "Trinity Sunday, Second Sermon," in *Sermons of Martin Luther,* 8:29).

27. Luther, *LW,* 15:315. That last claim seems too strong, for why could we not say that whether God is the Trinity or not is simply a matter of adding or not adding one feature to God's being (the way you may or may not add an additional wing to a house)? But Luther knows—and many Muslim theologians agree with him and the whole Christian tradition on that issue—that God is not composite, so that you can add or subtract "features" from God. Still, even though God's being is not composite (so that, from the Christian perspective, God either is the Holy Trinity or is not God), our *knowledge* of God is composite; we can add

features to our knowledge of God. We can know and describe God partially—with characteristics or attributes of God missing, and yet refer in
our descriptions to the one true God (see also chapter 7).

28. See Luther, *WA*, 30/2, 207.

29. See Luther, "Heidelberg Disputation," *LW*, 31:57–58.

30. Luther, *WA*, 53:150, 21–23. In the *Large Catechism* Luther writes: "Here in
the Creed you have the entire essence, will, and work of God exquisitely
depicted in very brief but rich words. In them are comprehended all our
wisdom, which surpasses all human wisdom, understanding and reason.
Although the whole world has sought painstakingly to learn what God
might be and what he might think and do, yet it has never succeeded in
the least. But here you have everything in richest measure. For in all three
articles God himself has revealed and opened to us the most profound
depths of his fatherly heart and his pure, unutterable love" (*LC* 2:63–64).

31. Luther, *WA*, 53:152, 3; 53:151, 25–26.

32. Luther, *WA*, 51:150, 18–21.

33. Luther, *WA*, 53:152, 14–15.

34. Luther, "Heerpredigt wider den Türken," *WA*, 30/2:173, 4–5.

35. Luther, "Sermon for Trinity Sunday," in *Sermons of Martin Luther*, 8:13.

36. Luther, "Second Sermon for the Nineteenth Sunday After Trinity," in
Sermons of Martin Luther, 5:223.

37. Luther, "Second Sermon," 5:223.

38. Luther, *LC*, 2:66.

39. Luther, "Sermon for the Nineteenth Sunday After Trinity," 5:223.

40. Erasmus, *Consultatio de bello Turcis inferendo*, in *Documents on the Later
Crusades, 1274–1580*, trans. and ed. Norman Housley (London: Macmillan, 1996), 178.

Chapter 4: How Do We Decide?

1. Another clear confirmation from the Qur'an that Muslims worship
the same God as Jews and Christians is the verse that reads: "To those
against whom war is made, permission is given (to fight), because they
are wronged—and verily, God is Most Powerful for their aid—(They
are) those who have been expelled from their homes in defiance of
right—(for no cause) except that they say, 'Our Lord is God.' Had not
God checked one set of people by means of another there would surely
have been pulled down monasteries, churches, synagogues, and mosques,
in which the name of God is commemorated in abundant measure" (Al
Hajj, 22:39–40). The Qur'an here affirms that the "name of God" is
invoked in synagogues and churches no less than in mosques.

2. Baradan Kuppusamy, "Can Christians Say 'Allah'? In Malaysia, Muslims Say No," *Time,* January 8, 2010, http://www.time.com/time/world/article/0,8599,1952497,00.html (accessed July 25, 2010).

3. Quoted in Michelle Vu, "Is Calling the Christian God 'Allah' Wrong?," *Christian Post,* August 23, 2007, http://www.christianpost.com/article/20070823/is-calling-the-christian-god-allah-wrong/index.html (accessed July 25, 2010).

4. Mark Durie, *Revelation? Do We Worship the Same God?* (Upper Mt. Gravatt, QLD: CityHarvest, 2006), 1.

5. For Muslims, Arabic is a sacred language, because it is the language of their revelation; Christians do not have an equivalent. The Bible is fundamentally translatable, whereas, though translated, the Qur'an is not translatable (on the significance of "translatability" and "intranslatability," see Lamin Sanneh, *Translating the Message: The Missionary Impact on Culture,* 2nd ed. [Maryknoll, NY: Orbis Books, 2008]). The Qur'an is the Word of God, strictly speaking, only in Arabic, whereas a translation is an interpretation and also loses its sacred quality. For Muslim speakers of Arabic, "Allah" is the word for the true God in what they deem a sacred language; it has special meaning and even special power. For Christian speakers of Arabic it is a word for the true God in an ordinary language with no special power. But this difference is not reason enough to preclude the use of "Allah" for God by Arabic-speaking Christians.

6. Andrew Saperstein, Rick Love, and Joseph Cumming, "Answers to Frequently Asked Questions Regarding the Yale Response to 'A Common Word Between Us and You,'" in Miroslav Volf, Ghazi bin Muhammad, and Melissa Yarrington, eds., *A Common Word: Muslims and Christians on Loving God and Neighbor* (Grand Rapids, MI: Eerdmans, 2010), 182.

7. On tattoos of crosses as identification marks of Copts, see Otto F. R. Meinardus, *Two Thousand Years of Coptic Christianity* (Cairo: American Univ. in Cairo Press, 1999), 265–66.

8. See Christian Fraser, "Egypt's Coptic Christians Battle for ID Cards," BBC News, December 26, 2009, http://news.bbc.co.uk/2/hi/middle_east/8424599.stm (accessed July 25, 2010).

9. Gottlob Frege uses this example in trying to illustrate the difference between "sense" and "reference." Since the "evening star" and the "morning star" both denote the same heavenly body, the planet Venus, the referent is the same. But the sense of the "evening star" is different from the sense of the "morning star," because the first expression tells you that you will see the star in the west at twilight and the second that you will see it in the east at dawn ("On Sense and Reference," in *Translations*

from the Philosophical Writings of Gottlob Frege, ed. Peter Geach and Max Black [Oxford: Blackwell, 1970], 56–78).

10. One could complicate the matter even more, as Thomas Hobbes did, and inquire whether a ship made entirely out of the replaced planks would be the same ship as the original one. See Roderick M. Chisholm, *Person and Object: A Metaphysical Study* (London: Routledge, 2002), 89–92.

11. Keith DeRose, personal communication, January 2, 2010.

12. I take the apostle Paul to say that an idol is nothing (see 1 Cor. 10:19). Some Christians disagree. From the contrast between the "table of the Lord" and the "table of demons" (1 Cor. 10:21) they conclude that, in worshipping idols, people in fact worship demons. Tertullian, an early Christian apologist and the father of Latin Christianity, thought so. Arguing against idol making and not just idol worshipping, Tertullian asks rhetorically, "For how have we *renounced* the devil and his angels, if we *make* them?" (*On Idolatry,* in *The Ante-Nicene Fathers,* vol. 3, ed. Alexander Roberts and James Donaldson [Grand Rapids, MI: Eerdmans, 1978], 64).

13. Ludwig Feuerbach, *The Essence of Christianity,* trans. George Eliot (Amherst, NY: Prometheus, 1989).

14. See Moshe Halbertal and Avishai Margalit, *Idolatry,* trans. Naomi Goldblum (Cambridge, MA: Harvard Univ. Press, 1992), 140.

15. For the argument that in everything they desire, human beings desire the Good, see Plato, *Meno* 77–78 and *Gorgias* 466–68, in *Dialogues of Plato,* trans. B. Jowett (Oxford: Clarendon, 1875), 1:277–78; 2:336–40.

16. Among Muslims who agree with this position, there is debate as to whether the term "Gospel" refers to the four Gospels or to the words of Jesus recorded in the Gospels.

17. For a defense of this position from a Muslim perspective, see Reza Shah-Kazemi, "Do Muslims and Christians Believe in the Same God?" (unpublished paper presented at the Yale Center for Faith and Culture consultation on "The Same God?," September 23–24, 2009), 6–7. On the basis of Al Ma'idah, 5:46–48, Shah-Kazemi argues that the relationship of succeeding prophets to previous ones is that of "confirmation." See also his text "Light Upon Light? The Qur'an and the Gospel of John" (forthcoming).

18. Asad's principal sources for his translation and explanation are al-Tabari, al-Razi, al-Zamakhshari, and al-Qurtubi as well as the contemporary commentator Rashid Rida.

19. Muhammad Asad, *The Message of the Qur'an* (Bristol, UK: Book Foundation, 2003), 79. For Muslims, the original message revealed to Moses and Jesus is salvific for those who genuinely follow it. This is conveyed in Al Ma'idah, 5:65–66: "If the followers of the Bible would but attain to

[true] faith and God-consciousness, We should indeed efface their [previous] bad deeds, and indeed bring them into gardens of bliss; and if they would but truly observe the Torah and the Gospel and all [the revelation] that has been bestowed from on high upon them by their Sustainer, they would indeed partake of all the blessings of heaven and earth." On the second verse here Asad comments: "The expression 'partake of all the blessings of heaven and earth' . . . is an allusion to the blessing which accompanies the realization of a spiritual truth, as well as to the social happiness that is bound to follow an observance of the moral principles laid down in the genuine teachings of the Bible. It should be borne in mind that the phrase 'if they would but truly observe the Torah and the Gospel,' etc., implies an observance of those scriptures in their genuine spirit" (182).

20. Peter Geach argues that "a sufficiently erroneous thought of a God will simply fail to relate to the true and living God at all" ("On Worshipping the Right God," in *God and the Soul* [London: Routledge & Kegan Paul, 1969], 111).

21. Calvinists, claiming to follow the Reformed theology of John Calvin (1509–64), argued that God predestines some human beings to salvation and some to damnation and held that human beings cannot reject God's grace. Arminians adopted and developed the views of Jacobus Arminius (1560–1609). They believed that God wills for human beings to have the power to reject God's grace, so that even though God knows who will reject it and therefore be damned, God does not will their damnation. See Jaroslav Pelikan, *Reformation of Church and Dogma (1300–1700)*, vol. 4 of *The Christian Tradition* (Chicago: Univ. of Chicago Press, 1984), 232–39.

22. Durie, *Revelation*, 85.

23. John Piper uses this text to argue for basically the same approach as Durie's. Jesus is the picture of God. To determine whether Christians and Muslims worship the same God, you look at the picture of God in the Qur'an and then you look at Jesus. If the match is perfect, then God is the same (see the video presentation "A Common Word Between Us?," http://www.desiringgod.org/Blog/1032_a_common_word_between _us/ [accessed July 25, 2010]).

24. Jews often did not share the Christian belief that they worship the same God as Christians. Unlike Muslims, whom Jews considered pure monotheists, in the Middle Ages Christians were perceived as apparent idolaters because of their belief in the Trinity, worship of Jesus Christ, and use of images in worship (see Halbertal and Margalit, *Idolatry*, 210). Maimonides, for instance, maintained that, unlike Muslims, Christians

are idolaters (Maimonides, *The Guide for the Perplexed,* 2nd ed., trans. M. Friedlander [1904; New York: Dover, 1956], 1:50).

25. Halbertal and Margalit, *Idolatry,* 147.

Chapter 5: A Common God and the Matter of Beliefs

1. *Nostra Aetate,* http://www.vatican.va/archive/hist_councils/ii_vatican _council/documents/vat-ii_decl_19651028_nostra-aetate_en.html (accessed July 25, 2010).

2. Herbert E. J. Cowdrey, *Pope Gregory VII: 1073–1085* (Oxford: Clarendon, 1998), 493–94.

3. Gregory VII, "Letter to Anzir, King of Mauretania," *The Christian Faith in the Doctrinal Documents of the Catholic Church,* ed. Jacques Dupuis (New York: Alba House, 2001), 418–19.

4. In his discussion of the question of whether Jews and Christians worship the same God, Alon Goshen-Gottstein notes that theological differences in understandings of God within Judaism are "no less significant than the differences between Judaism and Christianity" ("God Between Christians and Jews—Is It the Same God?," unpublished manuscript, 9).

5. Jan Assmann argues compellingly that the difference between God and the world is fundamental to monotheism (*Die Mosaische Unterscheidung, Oder der Preis des Monotheismus* [Munich: Carl Hanser, 2003], 57, 62).

6. This argument is very different from the following one: "Since there is only one God, two persons who claim to be monotheists must be worshipping the same God." In response, Peter Geach rightly and dryly notes: "One may shoot at an animal that is not there to be shot at" ("On Worshipping the Right God," in *God and the Soul* [London: Routledge & Kegan Paul, 1969], 108). "To worship" is an intentional verb, and just as one can shoot at an imaginary target, one can direct one's worship at an *imagined* God who is very different than the one true God.

7. Karl Barth, *Dogmatics in Outline,* trans. G. T. Thompson (New York: Harper & Row, 1959), 48–49.

8. Consider idolatry, which is the opposite of the worship of the true God; it is the worship of that which is not God. Idolatry is not merely an isolated sin, that is, one among many sins. It is not even the biggest sin of them all. Instead, idolatry is the "the head of unrighteousness," to use Tertullian's phrase. "In idolatry," he writes, "all crimes are detected and in all crimes idolatry" (*On Idolatry,* in *The Ante-Nicene Fathers,* vol. 3, ed. Alexander Roberts and James Donaldson [Grand Rapids, MI: Eerd-

mans, 1978], 61). When human beings worship a wrong god, they align their thoughts, desires, energies, and actions—their whole being—with a wrong set of fundamental values. Idolatry is the obverse of the proper worship of the true God.

9. See Miroslav Volf, Ghazi bin Muhammad, and Melissa Yarrington, eds., *A Common Word: Muslims and Christians on Loving God and Neighbor* (Grand Rapids, MI: Eerdmans, 2010).

10. The implication is that God, just by being alone God, also alone deserves total human devotion. "The words 'He Alone,' remind Muslims that their hearts must be devoted to God Alone" (Volf, Ghazi bin Muhammad, and Yarrington, eds., *A Common Word,* 31–32).

11. See Nicholas of Cusa, "De pace fidei," in *Nicholas of Cusa's De pace fidei and Cribratio Alkorani,* trans. Jasper Hopkins (Minneapolis: Banning, 1994), 65.

12. *Sahih Muslim, Kitab al-Iman,* Hadith no. 45.

13. All Ten Commandments except one can be found in Al Isra', 17:20–39.

14. For a brief commentary on this verse, see Reza Shah-Kazemi, *My Mercy Encompasses All* (Berkeley, CA: Counterpoint, 2007), 32.

15. See Mark Durie, *Revelation? Do We Worship the Same God?* (Upper Mt. Gravatt, QLD: CityHarvest, 2006), 87. Durie cites a booklet by P. Newton and M. Raffiqul-Haqq, *Allah: Is He God?,* which has a more extended discussion.

16. For example, *Sahih al-Bukhari,* Hadith no. 8806.

17. See, for example, the story recorded in Shaykh Shihab al-Din Abu Hafs 'Umar Suhrawardi, *Rasa'il javamardan,* 114–15, which Leonard Lewisohn cites ("'Ali ibn Abi Talib's Ethics of Mercy in the Mirror of the Persian Sufi Tradition," in *The Sacred Foundations of Justice in Islam,* ed. M. Ali Lakhani, Reza Shah-Kazemi, and Leonard Lewisohn [Bloomington, IN: World Wisdom, 2006], 125).

Chapter 6: A Common God and the Matter of Practices

1. For a recent attempt, see Michael Wenrich, "Glauben Juden, Christen und Muslime an denselben Gott? Systematisch-theologische Annäherungen an eine unzugängliche Frage," *Evangelische Theologie* 67 (April 2007): 246–63.

2. Reza Aslan, *How to Win a Cosmic War: God, Globalization, and the End of the War on Terror* (New York: Random House, 2009), 4.

3. See Martha Crenshaw, "Explaining Suicide Terrorism: A Review Essay," *Security Studies* 16 (2007): 154.

4. Muslim religious leadership almost uniformly condemns terrorism. *The*

Amman Message, endorsed by most leading Muslims, may serve as an example. In it we read: "On religious and moral grounds, we denounce the contemporary concept of terrorism that is associated with wrongful practices, whatever their source and form may be. Such acts are represented by aggression against human life in an oppressive form that transgresses the rulings of God, frightening those who are secure, violating peaceful civilians, finishing off the wounded, and killing prisoners; and they employ unethical means, such as destroying buildings and ransacking cities: *Do not kill the soul that God has made sacrosanct, save for justice* (6:151)" (http:// ammanmessage.com/index.php?option=com_content&task=view&id= 16&Itemid=30&limit=1&limitstart=2 [accessed July 25, 2010]).

5. True, some influential Muslim clerics disagree, like Sheik Qaradawi, one of the most prominent television personalities of the Muslim world and a member of the Muslim Brotherhood: "He who carries out a martyrdom operation . . . sells himself to Allah in order to buy Paradise in exchange" (MEMRI Special Dispatch Series, no. 542, July 24, 2003, quoted in Matthias Küntzel, "Suicide Terrorism and Islam," *American Foreign Policy Interests* 30 [2008], http://www.matthiaskuentzel.de/con tents/suicide-terrorism-and-islam [accessed July 25, 2010]). Still, he and others like him are a minority.

6. Matthias Küntzel writes, "For a Muslim deliberately to be sent to certain death has been considered sacrilege within Islam. Even the founders of the Islamist movement—Hassan al-Banna, Abu Mawdudi and Sayyid Qutb—never recommended that form of jihad. That is why in Soviet-occupied Afghanistan between 1979 and 1989 not a single suicide attack took place. The systematic employment of Muslims as guided human bombs with the aim of killing as many people as possible was not seen in the first 1360 years of Islam, but was invented only 25 years ago" ("Suicide Terrorism and Islam").

7. Alon Goshen-Gottstein, "God Between Christians and Jews—Is It the Same God?" (unpublished manuscript), 18.

8. See Karl Marx, "Economic and Philosophical Manuscripts," in *Early Writings,* trans. Rodney Livingstone and Gregor Benton (New York: Penguin, 1992), 356–57.

9. See Jacques Maritain, *The Range of Reason,* http://maritain.nd.edu/jmc /etext/range08.htm#p103 (accessed July 25, 2010).

10. Augustine, *Homilies on the Gospel According to St. John, and His First Epistle,* vol. 29, Library of Fathers of the Holy Catholic Church (Oxford: Parker, 1948), homily 7, n. 2, p. 1180; n. 5, p. 1183.

11. Luther, *Large Catechism (LC),* 1:1–2.

12. Chronicle of Fulcher of Chartres, http://www.historyguide.org/ancient /fulcher.html (accessed July 25, 2010).

13. *De Expugatione Terrae Sanctae per Saladinum* [The Capture of the Holy Land by Saladin], ed. Joseph Stevenson, Rolls Series (London: Longmans, 1875), trans. James Brundage, *The Crusades: A Documentary History* (Milwaukee, WI: Marquette Univ. Press, 1962), 159–63; http://www.fordham .edu/halsall/source/1187saladin.html (accessed July 25, 2010).

14. See A. R. Azzam, *Saladin* (Harlow, UK: Pearson, 2009), 190–91.

15. See Margaret Jubb, *The Legend of Saladin in Western Literature and Historiography* (Lewiston, NY: Mellen, 2000).

16. Gotthold Ephraim Lessing, *Nathan the Wise,* trans. Ronald Schechter (Boston: Bedford/St. Martin's, 2004), 34.

Chapter 7: The One God and the Holy Trinity

1. The "Verse of the Sword" reads: "But when the forbidden months are past, then fight and slay the Pagans wherever ye find them, and seize them, beleaguer them, and lie in wait for them in every stratagem (of war); but if they repent, and establish regular prayers and practice regular charity, then open the way for them: for God is Oft-Forgiving, Most Merciful."

2. For the use of the biblical injunction to kill whole peoples as a justification for violence in the Spanish conquest of the Americas, see Juan Ginés de Sepúlveda, *Tratado sobre las justas causes de la guerra contra los indios* (México D. F.: Fondo de Cultura Económica, 1986), 79. For an opposing view, see Bartolomé de Las Casas, *The Devastation of the Indies: A Brief Account,* trans. Herma Briffault (Baltimore, MD: Johns Hopkins Univ. Press, 1992). For appeals to the biblical narrative of the extermination of Canaanites in British debates about the colonization of North America, see Alfred A. Cave, "Canaanites in a Promised Land: The American Indian and the Providential Theory of Empire," *American Indian Quarterly* 12, no. 4 (1988): 277–97.

3. Rowan Williams, "A Common Word for the Common Good," http://acommonword.com/lib/downloads/Common-Good-Canterbury-FINAL-as-sent–14–7–08–1.pdf (accessed July 25, 2010).

4. See Habib Ali al-Jifri, "Loving God and Loving Neighbor," in Miroslav Volf, Ghazi bin Muhammad, and Melissa Yarrington, eds., *A Common Word: Muslims and Christians on Loving God and Neighbor* (Grand Rapids, MI: Eerdmans, 2010), 83.

5. Interestingly enough, Orthodox churches do not accept the Athanasian Creed, though this has nothing to do with the substance of its position

on the essential unity of God and the distinctness of the Persons, my sole interest in this section. Instead, it is related to inter-Christian debates about the precise nature of the relation between the first and the second Persons of the Trinity. See Jaroslav Pelikan, *The Spirit of Eastern Christendom (600–1700)*, vol. 2 of *The Christian Tradition* (Chicago: Univ. of Chicago Press, 1974), 183–98; J. N. D. Kelly, *The Athanasian Creed* (New York: Harper & Row, 1964), 44–48.

6. Aref Ali Nayed, "The Same God?" (unpublished paper for the consultation on "The Same God?," Yale Center for Faith and Culture, September 23–24, 2009), 8.

7. Maimonides, *The Guide for the Perplexed*, trans. M. Friedlander (1904; New York: Dover, 1956), 1:50. On Maimonides, see Harry Wolfson, "Maimonides on the Unity and Incorporeality of God," *Jewish Quarterly Review* 56 (1965): 124–34; David Novak, "The Mind of Maimonides," *First Things* (February 1999): 27–33. For an alternate interpretation of Maimonides that is more generous toward Christians, see Alon Goshen-Gottstein, "God Between Christians and Jews—Is It the Same God?" (unpublished manuscript).

8. Gregory of Nyssa, *Commentary on the Song of Songs*, trans. Casimir McCambley (Brookline, MA: Hellenic College Press, 1987), 145. See the discussion and literature in Kathryn Tanner, *Christ the Key* (Cambridge: Cambridge Univ. Press, 2010), 212–14.

9. Some contemporary Christians, even theologians, take the Qur'an's denial of the divine sonship of Christ at face value and conclude that therefore Muslims and Christians have a radically different God—one God has a Son and the other cannot have a son (e.g., Ergun Caner, president of Liberty Baptist Theological Seminary, whose remarks are reported in Mark Oppenheimer, "A Dispute on Using the Koran as a Path to Jesus," http://www.nytimes.com/2010/03/13/us/13beliefs.html?hp [accessed July 25, 2010]). However, a careful comparison of the Qur'an with the patristic Christian trinitarian debates makes clear that the great Christian theologians do *not* affirm what the Qur'an denies.

10. Rowan Williams, "Christians and Muslims Before the One God: An Address Given at al-Azhar al-Shari, Cairo, on 11 September 2004," *Islam and Christian-Muslim Relations* 16 (2005): 188–89.

11. Williams, "Christians and Muslims," 188.

12. Among contemporary theologians who write in classical theological mode, Karl Barth is one significant exception. He does claim that God was Christ and not merely that Christ was God (*Church Dogmatics*, trans. G. W. Bromiley [1936; London: Clark, 2004], 2:1, 381; 2:2, 249). But in Barth, this claim is tied up, I believe, with his peculiar and im-

plausible doctrine of election. It may be significant that the "Christian atheist" theologian Thomas J. J. Altizer makes the same claim: God was Jesus, and Jesus's death was the "self-annihilation" of God (*The Gospel of Christian Atheism* [Philadelphia: Westminster, 1966], 44).

13. To note that Christians reject the claim that "God was Christ" is not to suggest that there are no differences between Christianity and Islam when it comes to the person of Christ. To the contrary, the most important differences between these two faiths lie precisely there, in the Christian affirmation of the divinity of Christ and the Muslim rejection of it. The point I am making is more modest: there is agreement between Muslims and Christians that it is not appropriate to say "God was Christ" and that therefore there is significantly more agreement on the nature of God than may be superficially apparent.

14. Fakhr al-Din al-Razi, *Al-Tafsir al-kabir* (Beirut: Dar Ehia al-Tourath al-Arabi, 2000), 4.271, as quoted in Reza Shah-Kazemi, "Do Muslims and Christians Believe in the Same God?" (unpublished paper presented at the Yale Center for Faith and Culture consultation on "The Same God?," September 23–24, 2009), 10.

15. Nicholas of Cusa, "De pace fidei," in *Nicholas of Cusa's De pace fidei and Cribratio Alkorani,* trans. Jasper Hopkins (Minneapolis: Banning, 1994), 26.

16. Seyyed Hossein Nasr, "We and You: Let Us Meet in God's Love," a lecture delivered at the "Common Word" meeting with Pope Benedict XVI, November 6, 2008, 2.

17. For arguments that Christians described in the Qur'an are a deviant sect, see Jane McAuliffe, *Qur'anic Christians* (Cambridge: Cambridge Univ. Press, 1991).

18. Augustine, *The Trinity,* trans. Edmund Hill (Brooklyn: New City Press, 1991), 1.8 (70).

19. Augustine, *The Trinity* 6.9 (211).

20. As quoted in Shah-Kazemi, "Do Muslims and Christians Believe in the Same God?," 6.

21. I have tried to show here that the Christian teaching about the incarnation of the Word in Jesus Christ does not require a division in the divine essence. However, this leaves untouched other objections Muslims might have to Christian claims about Christ. The Qur'an, for instance, says, "Christ, the son of Mary, was no more than a Messenger; many were the Messengers that passed away before him. His mother was a woman of truth. They had both to eat their (daily) food. See how God doth make his signs clear to them; yet see in what ways they are deluded away from the truth!" (Al Ma'idah, 5:75). According to this verse, Christ is no more than a prophet. True, he is a unique prophet, for of no other

prophet is it said that he is God's "word" and "a spirit from Him" (Al Nisa', 4:171). In chapter 2 we saw that Nicholas of Cusa used this verse from the Qur'an to argue that, properly understood, it requires Muslims to accept the divinity of Christ. Nevertheless, normative Islam does not accept this argument and considers Jesus only a prophet. For Christians, on the other hand, Christ is emphatically more than a prophet; he is the incarnation of God. It remains to be seen whether this gap in convictions can be bridged here. But whether or not it is bridged, the way Christians understand the incarnation does not require them to divide the single divine essence.

22. Two of the greatest twentieth-century theologians did so. See Barth, *Church Dogmatics* 1:1, 355–59; Karl Rahner, *The Trinity,* trans. Joseph Donceel (New York: Crossroad, 1970), 103–15.

23. Augustine, *The Trinity* 7.7 (224–25).

24. See Augustine, *The Trinity* 15.39 (426). The Fourth Lateran Council (1215) underscored the same idea: "A likeness is not able to be noted between Creator and creature unless a greater unlikeness is to be noted between them" (DS 806). The major twentieth-century Catholic theologian Hans Urs von Balthasar is fond of speaking of "likeness, but always greater unlikeness" (see, for instance, *Theologik* [Einsiedeln: Johannes, 1985–87], 2:77).

25. On God's inconceivability, see the classic text by Pseudo-Dionysius, *The Divine Names,* in *Pseudo-Dionysius: The Complete Works,* ed. and trans. Colm Luibhéid and Paul Rorem (Mahwah, NJ: Paulist, 1987), 47–131.

26. For example, the Jewish philosopher Maimonides emphasizes the inadequacy of human knowledge of God (*The Guide for the Perplexed,* 1:50–60). In the Christian tradition, Thomas Aquinas holds this position (*Summa Theologiae* I, Q.3, Prol.), as do Pseudo-Dionysius and others. The Ash'arite school of Islamic theology holds that the divine essence is indescribable, and many Sufis emphasize this theme (see Muhammad al-Niffari, *The Mawaqif and Mukhatabat,* ed., Arthur J. Arberry [Cambridge: Cambridge Univ. Press, 1935], 158).

27. Denys Turner, "The 'Same' God: Is there an 'Apophatic' Solution, or, Who's to Know?'" (unpublished paper for the consultation on "The Same God?," Yale Center for Faith and Culture, September 23–24, 2009), 16–17.

28. Turner, "The 'Same' God," 17.

29. Turner argues that "a plurality of gods is ruled out by God's oneness, because counting is ruled out in every way" ("The 'Same' God," 17). If that were the case, however, would it not follow that you would be just as

right in saying that there are thirty-nine gods as you would be in saying that there is only one god? In either case, according to Turner, you would be making a category mistake rather than a numerical error. But that doesn't seem quite right. The affirmation that God is one excludes the possibility of there being others in any way like God, and in that sense *is* a form of numbering, though of a different kind from the ordinary numbering of created entities.

30. *Dabru Emet,* a document published in 2000 by a team of Jewish scholars in response to the ongoing reexamination of the attitude toward Judaism in Christian churches, is a recent and notable exception, and it articulates well a shift in the attitude of many Jews. In its opening proposition, it states unequivocally: "Jews and Christians worship the same God." It adds that "Christian worship is not a viable religious choice for Jews," and yet it claims that "through Christianity, hundreds of millions of people have entered into relationship with the God of Israel" (http://www.jcrelations.net/en/?item=1014 [accessed July 25, 2010]). See also Alon Goshen-Gottstein, "God Between Christians and Jews," 15–16.

31. Marcion (ca. 110–160) taught that the God of the Jewish scriptures was not the same as the Heavenly Father of Jesus. He considered the Jewish God, whom he recognized as the creator of the physical world, to be inept and vengeful, whereas Jesus's God was loving and saved humans from their suffering. See Alister McGrath, *Heresy: A History of Defending the Truth* (New York: HarperCollins, 2009), 127–32. Catharism was a religious movement that flourished especially in southern France in the eleventh to thirteenth centuries. Like Marcionites, Cathars believed in the existence of two gods, including an evil god connected with matter and associated with the god of the Old Testament. See Malcolm Barber, *The Cathars: Dualistic Heretics in Languedoc in the High Middle Ages* (Essex: Pearson Education, 2000).

32. Not much is known about Sabellius, who sparked a controversy in Rome in the early third century with his teachings, which blurred the distinction between the Father and the Son. See Jaroslav Pelikan, *The Christian Tradition,* vol. 1, *The Emergence of the Catholic Tradition* (Chicago: Univ. of Chicago Press, 1975), 176–80.

33. Arius (ca. 256–336) was a Christian from Alexandria, Egypt, whose views about the Son's relation to the Father launched a fierce controversy in the first half of the fourth century. The First Council of Nicea (325) and the First Council of Constantinople (381) dealt extensively with the settlement of the Arian crisis. The result was the Nicene Creed. See

Richard Hanson, *The Search for the Christian Doctrine of God* (1988; London: Clark, 2005).

34. Athanasius of Alexandria (293–373) was the chief opponent of Arius's doctrines. His views were highly influential in the formulation of the Nicene doctrine of the Trinity. See Khaled Anatolios, *Athanasius* (London: Routledge, 2004).

35. See J. N. D. Kelly, *Early Christian Doctrines,* 5th ed. (San Francisco: HarperSanFrancisco, 2000), 83–137, 223–79.

36. See Søren Kierkegaard, *Philosophical Fragments,* trans. Howard V. Hong and Edna H. Hong (Princeton, NJ: Princeton Univ. Press, 1985), 14–18.

37. See Barth, *Church Dogmatics* 1:1, 295–333.

38. Williams, "A Common Word for the Common Good."

Chapter 8: God's Mercy

1. So the title of Mark Juergensmeyer's book, *Terror in the Mind of God: The Global Rise of Religious Violence* (Berkeley: Univ. of California Press, 2000).

2. For an exploration of such people from variety of religious traditions, see Juergensmeyer, *Terror in the Mind of God.*

3. See Miroslav Volf, Ghazi bin Muhammad, and Melissa Yarrington, eds., *A Common Word: Muslims and Christians on Loving God and Neighbor* (Grand Rapids, MI: Eerdmans, 2010). See also http://www.acommon word.com.

4. See Naveed S. Sheikh, *Body Count: A Quantitative Review of Political Violence Across World Civilizations* (Amman, Jordan: Royal Islamic Strategic Studies Centre, 2009).

5. *Sahih al Bukhari, Kitab al-Adab,* bk. 18, Hadith no. 5999. I recognize, of course, that God is categorically different from creatures. Nevertheless, when we humans try to understand something of God's nature, we find ourselves compelled to turn to created realities as a basis for metaphor, since created realities are what we know, and we generally learn by relating the unknown to the already known.

6. See Volf, Ghazi bin Muhammad, and Yarrington, eds., *A Common Word,* 51–75.

7. See Joseph Norment Bell, *Love Theory in Later Hanbalite Islam* (Albany: State Univ. of New York Press, 1979).

8. See Marshall G. H. Hodgson, *The Venture of Islam: Conscience and History in a World Civilization,* vol. 2, *The Expansion of Islam in the Middle Periods* (Chicago: Univ. of Chicago Press, 1974), 125.

9. Plato, *Symposium* 200, in *The Dialogues of Plato,* trans. B. Jowett (Oxford: Clarendon, 1875), 2:50–52.

10. See Reza Shah-Kazemi, "God, 'The Loving,'" in Volf, Ghazi bin Muhammad, and Yarrington, eds., *Common Word,* 102–4. On the whole issue, see also Reza Shah-Kazemi, *My Mercy Encompasses All: The Koran's Teachings on Compassion, Peace and Love* (Emeryville, CA: Shoemaker & Hoard, 2007).

11. There are ninety-nine names of God mentioned in the Qur'an, which refers to them as the Most Beautiful Names (*al-asma al-husna*): "And to God belong the Most Beautiful Names—so invoke Him by them . . ." (Al A'raf, 7:180); and also "He is God, the Creator, the Maker, the Shaper. To Him belong the Most Beautiful Names. All that is in the heavens and the earth glorify Him, and He is the Mighty, the Wise" (Al Hash, 59:22–24). The Beautiful Names have been a major source for Muslim theological reflection.

12. Al-Ghazali, *The Ninety-Nine Beautiful Names of God,* trans. David B. Burrell and Nazir Daher (Cambridge: Islamic Texts Society, 1992), 119.

13. Abu Hamid al-Ghazali, *The Alchemy of Happiness,* trans. Claud Field (Gloucester, UK: Dodo, 2008), 46; cf. al-Ghazali, *Ninety-Nine Beautiful Names,* 54.

14. Muhammad ibn Jarir al-Tabari, in *An Anthology of Qur'anic Commentaries,* vol. 1, *On the Nature of the Divine,* ed. Feras Hamza and Sajjad Rizvi, with Farhana Mayer (Oxford: Oxford Univ. Press, 2008), 306.

15. See Nicholas Wolterstorff, *Justice: Rights and Wrongs* (Princeton, NJ: Princeton Univ. Press, 2007), 109–34.

16. Seyyed Hossein Nasr, "We and You: Let Us Meet in God's Love" (unpublished lecture delivered at the "Common Word" meeting with Pope Benedict XVI, November 6, 2008), 2.

17. Quoted in Shah-Kazemi, "God, 'The Loving,'" 106.

18. See Wolterstorff, *Justice,* 180–206.

19. *Salih al-Bukhari, Kitab al-Iman,* Hadith no. 13, and *Salih Muslim, Kitab al-Iman,* 67–1, Hadith no. 45.

20. "Common Word," in Volf, Ghazi bin Muhammad, and Yarrington, eds., *Common Word,* 44.

21. Al-Ghazali, *Ninety-Nine Beautiful Names,* 53.

22. Al-Ghazali, *Ninety-Nine Beautiful Names,* 30.

23. Al-Ghazali, *Ninety-Nine Beautiful Names,* 73.

24. Al-Ghazali, *Ninety-Nine Beautiful Names,* 73.

25. Al-Ghazali, *Ninety-Nine Beautiful Names,* 74.

26. Søren Kierkegaard, *Works of Love,* ed. and trans. Howard V. Hong and

Edna H. Hong (Princeton, NJ: Princeton Univ. Press, 1995), 280–99; *Eighteen Upbuilding Discourses,* ed. and trans. Howard V. Hong and Edna H. Hong (Princeton, NJ: Princeton Univ. Press, 1990), 55–78.

27. In the song "Grace," Bono, lead singer of the rock band U2, writes that "Grace finds goodness in everything."

Chapter 9: Eternal and Unconditional Love

1. At that time I did not realize that most people, including children, are strong "essentialists"—believers that it is an inner essence that makes a thing into something, not an outward appearance (see Paul Bloom, *How Pleasure Works: The New Science of Why We Like What We Like* [New York: Norton, 2010], 211–70).

2. Augustine, *Homilies on the Gospel According to St. John, and His First Epistle,* vol. 29, Library of Fathers of the Holy Catholic Church (Oxford: J. H. Parker, 1848), homily 7, nn. 4–5, p. 1182.

3. Karl Barth, probably the greatest twentieth-century theologian, issues a warning: "If we say with 1 John 4 that God is love, the obverse that love is God is forbidden until it is mediated and clarified from God's being and therefore from God's act what the love is which can and must be legitimately identified with God" (*Church Dogmatics,* trans. G. W. Bromiley [1936; London: Clark, 2004], 2:1, 276).

4. See Ludwig Feuerbach, *The Essence of Christianity,* trans. George Eliot (Amherst, NY: Prometheus, 1989).

5. Reza Shah-Kazemi, "God, 'The Loving,'" in Miroslav Volf, Ghazi bin Muhammad, and Melissa Yarrington, eds., *A Common Word: Muslims and Christians on Loving God and Neighbor* (Grand Rapids, MI: Eerdmans, 2010), 107.

6. Shah-Kazemi, "God, 'The Loving,'" 94.

7. Shah-Kazemi, "God, 'The Loving,'" 94.

8. Shah-Kazemi, "God, 'The Loving,'" 94.

9. See William Chittick, *The Sufi Path of Knowledge: Ibn al-'Arabi's Metaphysics of Imagination* (Albany: State Univ. of New York Press, 1989), 130.

10. For a recent affirmation by a preeminent Sufi thinker that God's love is eternal and that it underlies all other loves, indeed, for an affirmation that God is love, see Seyyed Hossein Nasr, *The Garden of Truth: The Vision and Promise of Sufism, Islam's Mystical Tradition* (San Francisco: HarperOne, 2007), 61.

11. Wahhabism is the name, applied mostly by others, to the conservative movement that traces its intellectual roots to Ibn Abd al-Wahhab. It is marked by an interpretation of Ibn Taymiyya's teachings on God's unity

that is so strident that it ends up condemning a wide range of fairly mainstream Muslim practices as *shirk*, the ultimate sin of associating other beings with God. For two different perspectives on Wahhabism, see Natana J. DeLong-Bas, *Wahhabi Islam: From Revival and Reform to Global Jihad* (Oxford: Oxford Univ. Press, 2004); and Hamid Algar, *Wahhabism: A Critical Essay* (Oneonta, NY: Islamic Publications International, 2002).

12. Ibn Taymiyya's argument against the view—advocated by Mu'tazilites— that God's wise design in creating the world was to benefit human beings goes as follows: "If it be supposed that the existence or nonexistence of an act of kindness were indifferent to the agent, then he would not know such an act on his part to be good. Rather, such an act would be considered absurd in the minds of rational thinkers" (quoted in Joseph Norment Bell, *Love Theory in Later Hanbalite Islam* [Albany: State Univ. of New York Press, 1979], 69–70).

13. Bell summarizes Ibn Taymiyya's stance: "God's love for himself is necessarily the greatest of all loves, and his love for certain men and their acts is subordinate to this first love" (*Love Theory,* 72).

14. Ibn 'Arabi, a great Sufi master and a representative of a direction in Islam to which Ibn Taymiyya was not sympathetic, even though Ibn Taymmiya also considered himself to be a Sufi, thought similarly. He argued that God creates because God loves. What is it that God loves? God loves God's own self and God loves to be known by creatures. "If there were not for this [divine] love, the world would never have appeared," writes Ibn 'Arabi (*The Ringstone of Wisdom,* trans. Caner Dagli [Chicago: Kazi, 2004], 261–62). On Ibn 'Arabi's understanding of God's love, see William C. Chittick, *Ibn 'Arabi: Heir to the Prophets* (Oxford: Oneworld, 2007), 35–51.

15. Mosab Hassan Yousef draws this contrast in a lengthy interview for BBC occasioned by the publication of his book *Son of Hamas: A Gripping Account of Terror, Betrayal, Political Intrigue, and Unthinkable Choices* (Carol Stream, IL: Saltriver, 2010). See http://www.bbc.co.uk/world service/news/2010/03/100303_mosab_newaudio.shtml (accessed July 25, 2010).

16. Thomas Aquinas, *Summa Contra Gentiles,* trans. Anton C. Pegis (Notre Dame, IN: Univ. of Notre Dame Press, 1975), 1:80:6.

17. Augustine, *The Trinity,* trans. Edmund Hill (Brooklyn: New City, 1991).

18. Abu Hamid al-Ghazali, *The Revival of Religious Sciences,* vol. 6, bk. 36. This passage was translated from the Arabic by Reza Shah-Kazemi.

19. See chapter 2 for Nicholas of Cusa's reflections on the intimate connection between the trinitarian nature of God and what he calls "divine

fecundity," or God's creativity. For a more recent argument, see Hans Urs von Balthasar, *Theo-Drama*, vol. 2, trans. Graham Harrison (San Francisco: Ignatius, 1990), 266; Junius Johnson, "Christ and Analogy: The Metaphysics of Hans Urs von Balthasar" (Ph.D. diss., Yale University, 2010).

20. The grand alternative of "divine self-love" versus "divine love of the other" reaches as deep down as you can get to the foundations of reality. However, it is not a divide that places Muslims (more precisely those Muslims who affirm that God loves God's own self) on one side and all Christians on the other. Some very prominent Christians, a small minority, would be on the "Muslim" side of that divide, like the early Karl Barth and Karl Rahner, two of the greatest twentieth-century Christian theologians. They affirmed God's eternal love, but denied that there is love among divine "Persons" (see Barth, *Church Dogmatics* 2:2, 280, where Barth writes of God as the object of God's own love; and Karl Rahner, *The Trinity*, trans. Joseph Donceel [New York: Herder & Herder, 1970], 106).

21. For the idea that God's favors are showered on all—just and unjust, deserving and undeserving—in the Qur'an, see Al Isra', 17:20: "Of the bounties of thy Lord we bestow freely on all—these as well as those: the bounties of thy Lord are not closed (to anyone)."

22. This distinction has a long history in Christian thought, going back at least to Augustine, who advises "love for the persons and a hatred for their vices" (*St. Augustine: Letters 211–270*, trans. Roland Teske [Hyde Park, NY: New City, 2005], 211.11). This phrase is the source of the common saying, "Love the sinner, hate the sin."

23. William Shakespeare, *Measure for Measure*, 2.2, in *The Riverside Shakespeare*, ed. G. Blakemore Evans (Boston: Houghton Mifflin, 1974), 560.

24. In the Qur'an we find a very similar idea: "On the Day when every soul will be confronted with all the good it has done, and all the evil it has done, it will wish there were a great distance between it and its evil. But God cautions you (to remember) Himself. And God is full of kindness to those that serve Him" (Al 'Imran, 3:30). The distance between the soul and its evil presupposes a distinction between the doer and the deed.

25. Martin Luther, "Heidelberg Disputation," *Luther's Works*, ed. Jaroslav Pelikan and Helmut T. Lehmann, 55 vols. (Philadelphia: Fortress, 1955–86), 31:57.

26. Shah-Kazemi, "God, 'The Loving,'" 90–91.

27. Martin Luther, *D. Martin Luthers Werke Kritische Gesamtausgabe* (Weimar: Hermann Böhlau, 1883–), 51:150, 38–39.

28. For a discussion of Jesus as the "Mercy of God," see Scott Dolff, "Mercy, Human and Divine" (Ph.D. diss., Yale University, 2009), 34–119.

29. With some notable exceptions, especially in recent centuries, most Christians have thought that the self-giving character of God's love is not incompatible with the reality of eternal punishment of those who refuse to be redeemed by God's love. That punishment itself has been seen as a mode of God's love (see, for example, Eleonore Stump, "Dante's Hell, Aquinas's Moral Theory, and the Love of God," *Canadian Journal of Philosophy* 16 [1986]: 181–98)—a difficult thought that underscores the fundamental importance for Christians of the conviction that God is love.

30. Aeneas Silvius Piccolomini (Pius II), *Epistola ad Mahomatem II (Epistle to Mohammed II),* ed. and trans. Algert R. Baca (New York: Peter Lang, 1990), 2.

31. Luther, "Heidelberg Disputation," 31:306.

32. This story is from Abu al-Qasim al-Qushayri, *Risala,* and is retold by Sheykh Hamza Yusuf, *Poor Man's Book of Assistance,* audio recording (Hayward, CA: Alhambra Productions).

33. The "Verse of the Sword" has played an inglorious role in the "external relations" of Muslims (relations to all non-Muslims). The verse reads: "But when the forbidden months are past, then fight and slay the Pagans wherever ye find them, and seize them, beleaguer them, and lie in wait for them in every stratagem (of war); but if they repent, and establish regular prayers and practice regular charity, then open the way for them: for God is Oft-Forgiving, Most Merciful" (Al Tawbah, 9:5). According to 'Abdul Hamid A. Abu Sulayman, this verse, along with Al Tawbah, 9:123, played a central role in classical jurisprudence "in determining the Islamic position pertaining to the relations among nations." This was possible because some jurists "took an extreme position in interpreting this verse. They claimed that this verse abrogated all preceding verses pertaining to patience (*sabr*), persuasion (*hasna*), tolerance (*ta ikrah*), and the right to self-determination (*lasta 'alayhim bi musaytir*)" (*Towards an Islamic Theory of International Relations: New Directions for Methodology and Thought* [Herndon, VA: International Institute of Islamic Thought, 1993], 119, 44).

34. On the issue of just war in Islam, see John Kelsay, *Arguing the Just War in Islam* (Cambridge, MA: Harvard Univ. Press, 2007).

35. See John Mark Mattox, *Saint Augustine and the Theory of Just War* (New York: Continuum, 2006).

36. For a contemporary restatement of an argument that the pursuit of just war is motivated by love, see Oliver O'Donovan, *The Just War Revisited* (Cambridge: Cambridge Univ. Press, 2003).

37. See David Clough and Brian Stiltner, *Faith and Force: A Christian Debate About War* (Washington, DC: Georgetown Univ. Press, 2007), 6.

38. Recall that according to the Qur'an God's mercy encompasses all things; "mercy" is God's way of relating to all creatures. Now, consider the following three verses from the Qur'an:

> Nor can Goodness and Evil be equal. Repel (evil) with what is better: then will he between whom and thee was hatred become as if he were thy friend and intimate. (Fussilat, 41:34)

> We [God] ordained therein [in the Torah] for them: "Life for life, eye for eye, nose for nose, ear for ear, tooth for tooth, and wounds equal for equal." But if anyone remits the retaliation by the way of charity, it is an act of atonement for himself. (Al Ma'idah, 5:45)

> It may be that God will grant love (and friendship) between you and those whom you (now) hold as enemies. For God has power (over all things); and God is Oft-Forgiving, Most Merciful. God forbids you not, with regard those who fight you not for (your) faith nor drive you out of your homes, from dealing kindly and justly with them: For God loves those who are just. (Al Mumtahinah, 60:7–8)

Might Muslims be able to affirm that the command to love the neighbor includes the command to love the enemy? If God's mercy is ultimate in God's relation to humans, if evil ought to be overcome by good, and if the Most Merciful One does not forbid kindness to enemies, but considers it a more noble way, does it not follow that we *should* be benevolent and beneficent toward our enemies, that we *should* love them? With humans, as with God, mercy would then encompass justice.

39. "Common Word," in Volf, Ghazi bin Muhammad, and Yarrington, eds., *Common Word*, 47–48.

40. "Loving God and Neighbor Together," in Volf, Ghazi bin Muhammad, and Yarrington, eds., *Common Word*, 55.

41. I take the story from Paul L. Heck, *Common Ground: Islam, Christianity, and Religious Pluralism* (Washington, DC: Georgetown Univ. Press, 2009), 108.

42. *Takfiris* are what the American media often call "jihadists," that is, a small minority of Salafi Muslims who consider themselves fit to accuse other Muslims of having fallen away from the faith and of no longer being Muslims. In addition, they reject political authority (even Islamic political authority that does not conform to their interpretation of Islam),

they reject the traditional rules for jihad, and they believe in suicide as a legitimate method of jihad (against all traditional scholarship and jurisprudence). See Vincenzo Oliveti, *Terror's Source: The Ideology of Wahhabi-Salafism and Its Consequences* (Birmingham, UK: Amadeus, 2002), 43–48.

Chapter 10: The Same God, the Same Religion?

1. G. W. F. Hegel, *Introduction to the Philosophy of History,* trans. Leo Rauch (Indianapolis, IN: Hackett, 1988), 53.
2. So Jean-Jacques Rousseau, *The Social Contract or Principles of Political Right,* trans. G. D. H. Cole, http://www.constitution.org/jjr/socon.htm (accessed July 26, 2010), 4.8.
3. Alexander Wolff, "Prisoners of War," *Sports Illustrated,* http://sports illustrated.cnn.com/events/1996/olympics/storyolympic/yuhoops2.html (accessed July 26, 2010).
4. On this most recently, see Paul L. Heck, *Common Ground: Islam, Christianity, and Religious Pluralism* (Washington, DC: Georgetown Univ. Press, 2009), 213–14.
5. See Timothy Fitzgerald, *The Ideology of Religious Studies* (Oxford: Oxford Univ. Press, 2000), 3–118.
6. Gotthold Ephraim Lessing, *Nathan the Wise,* trans. Ronald Schechter (Boston: Bedford/St. Martin's, 2004), 70.
7. Lessing, *Nathan the Wise,* 72.
8. Lessing, *Nathan the Wise,* 73.
9. Nicholas of Cusa advocated a version of this view. Though he argued that all religions are variants of the same faith, he did not consider them all equally true, but believed that the Christian faith is the true religion, all others being more or less true variants of it (see chapter 2). For a similar position formulated more recently from a Muslim perspective, see Reza Shah-Kazemi, *The Other in the Light of the One* (Cambridge, UK: Islamic Texts Society, 2006).
10. For Jewish reflection on the matter, see Alon Goshen-Gottstein, "God Between Christians and Jews—Is It the Same God?" (unpublished manuscript), 8–9.
11. See James Dunn, ed., *Jews and Christians: The Parting of the Ways, A.D. 70–135* (Grand Rapids, MI: Eerdmans, 1999).
12. Denys Turner, "The 'Same' God: Is There an 'Apophatic' Solution, or, Who's to Know?" (unpublished paper for the consultation on "The Same God?," Yale Center for Faith and Culture, September 23–24, 2009), 6.

13. Samuel P. Huntington, "The Clash of Civilizations?," *Foreign Affairs* 72 (1993): 27.

14. See, among others, Ingolf U. Dalferth, "'I Determine What God Is!': Theology in the Age of 'Cafeteria Religion,'" *Theology Today* 57 (April 2000): 5–23, http://findarticles.com/p/articles/mi_qa3664/is_200004 /ai_n8879113/ (accessed March 26, 2010).

15. Janet I. Tu, "'I Am Both Muslim and Christian,'" *Seattle Times*, June 17, 2007.

16. Patrick Oppmann, "Episcopal Minister Defrocked After Becoming a Muslim," April 2, 2009, http://www.cnn.com/2009/US/04/02/muslim .minister.defrocked/ (accessed July 26, 2010).

17. Combining Christianity and Islam is not just a Western phenomenon. In Lagos, the second most populous city in Nigeria, a country rocked by violence between Muslims and Christians, Shamsuddin Saka is a minister of a congregation that has on its lectern both the Qur'an and the Bible. He was born a Muslim, and after returning from a pilgrimage to Mecca, he decided to start a new ministry. He preaches what he calls "Chrislam," a combination of Islam and Christianity. Abraham's children should be under the same religious roof, he reasons. See "Chrislam," *Religion & Ethics Newsweekly*, February, 13, 2009, http://www.pbs .org/wnet/religionandethics/episodes/february–13–2009/chrislam /2236/ (accessed March 26, 2010).

18. Joseph Cumming, "Muslim Followers of Jesus?," *Christianity Today*, December 2009, http://www.christianitytoday.com/globalconversation /december2009/index.html (accessed March 27, 2010).

19. On the significance of the phenomenon of translation, see Lamin Sanneh, *Translating the Message: The Missionary Impact on Culture*, 2nd ed. (Maryknoll, NY: Orbis Books, 2008).

20. See Miroslav Volf, *A Public Faith: How Followers of Christ Should Serve the Common Good* (Grand Rapids, MI: Baker, 2011); "Christliche Identität und Differenz: Zur Eigenart der christlichen Präsenz in den modernen Gesellchaften," *Zeitschrift für Theologie und Kirche* 3 (1995): 357–75.

21. See David Martin, *On Secularization: Towards a Revised General Theory* (Surrey, U.K.: Ashgate, 2005), 142–44.

22. See the many popular books on Jesus or God as one's "friend," e.g., Jill Savage, *Real Moms . . . Real Jesus: Meet the Friend Who Understands* (Chicago: Moody, 2009); Henry T. Blackaby, *Created to Be God's Friend: How God Shapes Those He Loves* (Nashville: Nelson, 1999); John D. Sloan, *Our Faithful Friend: Embracing God's Intimacy* (Grand Rapids, MI: Zondervan, 1994).

23. Martin Luther, *D. Martin Luthers Werke Kritische Gesamtausgabe* (Weimar: Hermann Böhlau, 1883–), 30/2:207.

24. The text of Al Fatihah reads: "In the name of God, Most Gracious, Most Merciful. Praise to God, the Cherisher and Sustainer of the world; Most Gracious, Most Merciful; Master of the Day of Judgment. Thee do we worship, and Thine aid we seek. Show us the straight way. The way of those on whom Thou has bestowed Thy Grace, those whose (portion) is not wrath and who go not astray."

25. What I say here has only partial bearing on what in Serbian was called *dvovjerstvo,* a person's "being of two faiths" in the sense of outwardly practicing Islam while remaining at heart a Christian. During the Ottoman rule in the Balkans, Christians would sometimes convert to Islam out of sheer necessity—say, to escape Turkish taxes that they could not pay—while secretly retaining their Christian faith. In these cases, conversion was forced and the embrace of Islam disingenuous, whereas I have in mind cases of hybrid religiosity in which both faiths—or elements of both faiths—are embraced voluntarily.

Chapter 11: Prejudices, Proselytism, and Partnership

1. See Nick Cumming-Bruce and Steven Erlanger, "Swiss Ban Building of Minarets on Mosques," *New York Times,* November 29, 2009, http://www.nytimes.com/2009/11/30/world/europe/30swiss.html?_r=1&scp=1&sq=switzerland%20minaret&st=cse (accessed July 26, 2010).

2. See the U.S. Department of State's *2009 Report on International Religious Freedom* for countries such as Saudi Arabia and Algeria, http://www.state.gov/g/drl/rls/irf/2009/index.htm (accessed July 26, 2010).

3. See Ralph Blumenthal and Sharaf Mowjood, "Muslim Prayers and Renewal Near Ground Zero," *New York Times,* December 8, 2009, http://www.nytimes.com/2009/12/09/nyregion/09mosque.html?_r=1&fta=y (accessed July 26, 2010). The website of the Cordoba Initiative, the group that plans to build Cordoba House, is www.cordobainitiative.org.

4. Olivier Roy notes that "there has almost never been an example in Muslim history to parallel today's terrorist acts." He suggests that "the real genesis of Al Qaeda violence has more to do with a Western tradition of individual and pessimistic revolt for an elusive ideal world than with the Koranic conception of martyrdom" (*Globalized Islam: The Search for a New Ummah* [New York: Columbia Univ. Press, 2004], 42–43).

5. See Miroslav Volf, *Exclusion and Embrace: A Theological Exploration of Identity, Otherness, and Reconciliation* (Nashville: Abingdon, 1996), 250–53.

6. On the relation between truthfulness and justice, see Miroslav Volf, *The End of Memory: Remembering Rightly in a Violent World* (Grand Rapids, MI: Eerdmans, 2006), 54–56.

7. The declaration on religious freedom of the Second Vatican Council was the first official document in which freedom of religion was clearly embraced by the Catholic Church; see http://www.vatican.va/archive /hist_councils/ii_vatican_council/documents/vat-ii_decl_19651207 _dignitatis-humanae_en.html (accessed July 26, 2010). It was considered highly innovative at the time (1960s) and was debated strenuously. See chapter 12.

8. H. R. H. Prince Ghazi bin Muhammad, "On 'A Common Word Between Us and You,'" in *A Common Word: Muslims and Christians on Loving God and Neighbor,* ed. Miroslav Volf, Ghazi bin Muhammad, and Melissa Yarrington (Grand Rapids, MI: Eerdmans, 2010), 6.

9. During some periods the Christian cross-cultural missionary impulse has been subdued, as in the case of Protestants from their inception in 1517 to about 1794, when William Carey started the modern Protestant missionary movement; see William Carey, *An Enquiry into the Obligations of Christians to Use Means for the Conversion of the Heathens* (Whitefish, MT: Kessinger, 2004).

10. David Rennie, "Bible Belt Missionaries Set Out on a 'War for Souls' in Iraq," *Daily Telegraph,* December 27, 2003, http://www.telegraph.co.uk /news/worldnews/northamerica/usa/1450359/Bible-Belt-missionaries -set-out-on-a-war-for-souls-in-Iraq.html (accessed July 26, 2010).

11. So Jonathan Bonk, executive director of the Overseas Ministries Study Center, who writes: "The most eloquent and doggedly persistent voices raised against the opium trade in China, for example—foisted on a relatively defenseless country by Western business and political interests in order to support the East India Company's operations and armies in India—were missionary. Businessmen and missionaries in the Treaty Ports were often at odds, since missionaries tended to get in the way of 'good' business by drawing attention to ethical lapses at virtually every level. Missionaries were in the forefront, for example, in exposing Leopold's gigantically lucrative 'business' in his Congo (he actually owned the Congo), bringing back to this country photos of the mounds of hands and feet chopped off of hapless victims who failed to meet Leopold's quotas for rubber and ivory" (personal communication, March 29, 2010).

12. For example, Samuel Huntington slips back and forth between the terms "Christianity" and "the West" without noting a distinction between them ("The Clash of Civilizations?" *Foreign Affairs* 72 [1993]: 209).

13. Quoted in Bernard Lewis, *The Crisis of Islam: Holy War and Unholy Terror* (New York: Modern Library, 2003), xv.

14. See Umej Bhatia, "The Sea Speaks Arabic," *History Today* 55, no. 5 (2005): 12–14.

15. See, for example, Christine Schirrmacher, "Islamic 'Mission' (Da'wah)," http://www.worldevangelicals.org/resources/pdf/Islamic_Mission __Da%27wah_.pdf (accessed July 26, 2010).

16. Seyyed Hossein Nasr, "We and You: Let Us Meet in God's Love" (unpublished lecture delivered at the "Common Word" meeting with Pope Benedict XVI, November 6, 2008), 14.

17. The whole verse, important to many more progressive Muslims, reads: "To thee we sent the Scripture in truth, confirming the scripture that came before it, and guarding it in safety: so judge between them by what God hath revealed, and follow not their vain desires, diverging from the truth that hath come to thee. To each among you have we prescribed a Law and an Open Way. If God had so willed, he would have made you a single people, but (His plan is) to test you in what He hath given you; to strive as in a race in all virtues. The goal of you all is to God; it is He that will show you the truth of the matters in which ye dispute."

18. This is reported as a response to the question of Ali to Muhammad, who sent him to fight Khaibar, "Allah's Messenger, on what issue should I fight with the people?" (*Sahih Muslim,* 31:5917, http://www.usc.edu/schools /college/crcc/engagement/resources/texts/muslim/hadith/muslim/031 .smt.html#031.5917 [accessed July 26, 2010]). See also *Sahih al-Bukhari* (1) 2:24: Allah's Apostle said: "I have been ordered (by Allah) to fight against the people until they testify that none has the right to be worshipped but Allah and that Muhammad is Allah's Apostle, and offer the prayers perfectly and give the obligatory charity, so if they perform all that, then they save their lives and property from me except for Islamic laws and then their reckoning (accounts) will be done by Allah" (http://www.usc.edu/schools /college/crcc/engagement/resources/texts/muslim/hadith/bukhari/002 .sbt.html#001.002.024 [accessed July 26, 2010]).

19. For a critique of this position by some of the most influential Muslim leaders and scholars today, see "Open Letter to His Holiness Pope Benedict XVI," 1, http://ammanmessage.com/media/openLetter/english.pdf (accessed April 2, 2010).

20. Ayatollah Shaykh Muhammad Husayn Fadlallah, *Afaq al-Hiwar al-Islami al-Masihi* (Beirut: Dar al-Malak, 1998), 110. This passage was translated from the Arabic by Joseph Cumming.

21. For further reflection on the nature of Christian witness, see Miroslav

Volf, *A Public Faith: How Followers of Christ Should Serve the Common Good* (Grand Rapids: Baker, 2011), chapter 6.

22. Not all worldly benefits are extrinsic to the good news. Clearly Jesus commissioned his disciples to proclaim and to heal. Muslims and Christians agree that faith is good for this life and not just for the afterlife.

23. Eboo Patel, *Acts of Faith: The Story of an American Muslim, the Struggle for the Soul of a Generation* (Boston: Beacon, 2008).

24. See David Johnston, *Earth, Empire and Sacred Text: Muslims and Christians as Trustees of Creation* (London: Equinox, 2010).

25. Ruth Turner, personal communication, May 19, 2010.

26. See Tim O'Keefe, *Epicureanism* (Berkeley: Univ. of California Press, 2009).

27. Christian Smith and Melinda Lundquist Denton, *Soul Searching: The Religious and Spiritual Lives of American Teenagers* (Oxford: Oxford Univ. Press, 2005), 165.

28. See Philip Rieff, *The Triumph of the Therapeutic: Uses of Faith After Freud* (New York: Harper & Row, 1966), 232–61.

29. See Andrew Delbanco, *The Real American Dream: A Meditation on Hope* (Cambridge, MA: Harvard Univ. Press, 1999), 96–118.

30. This observation fits with one of the central conclusions of the Grant Study—a study of well-adjusted Harvard sophomores begun in 1937, which, after more than seventy years of following its subjects, remains one of "the longest running, and probably most exhaustive, longitudinal studies of mental and physical well-being in history." In an interview in 2008, its longtime director, George Vaillant, was asked, "What have you learned from Grant Study men?" His response was, "The only thing that really matters in life are your relationships with other people" (Joshua Wolf Shenk, "What Makes Us Happy?," *Atlantic* [June 2009]: 36). Applied to the question of satisfaction, this suggests that deep and meaningful relationships give meaning to pleasure; pleasure without them is hollow.

31. See Sigmund Freud, *Civilization and Its Discontents,* trans. James Strachey (New York: Norton, 1961); see also Philip Rieff, *Freud: The Mind of the Moralist,* 2nd ed. (Garden City, NY: Doubleday, 1961), 217; Jan Assmann, *Die Mosaische Unterscheidung, Oder der Preis des Monotheismus* (Munich: Carl Hanser, 2003), 119–43.

32. Seyyed Hossein Nasr has called for a similar alliance of Christians and Muslims with a broader goal of struggling against secularism: "We live in a secularist world in which religions are each other's best friends. In any case, today our enemy, which in fact is common between us, is the materialistic, hedonistic, nihilistic and God-negating worldview that is so widespread, the worldview that negates the spiritual nature of humanity, denies the sacred and the transcendent, and seeks to shatter our hopes for

a blessed life everlasting. We have much to offer to each other in the central battle between truth and falsehood. But the offer can only be accepted if we first recognize each other as friends and not as enemies" ("We and You," 13). I don't disagree. To me, however, combating the prevalence of the managed pursuit of pleasure in our culture (which many secularist humanists oppose as well, Karl Marx being the most influential example) seems culturally more urgent. And it could be that a secularist, devoted to love of neighbor, may end up closer to God without knowing it than a religious person obsessed with love of self.

33. Abu Hamid al-Ghazali, *The Alchemy of Happiness,* trans. Claud Field (Gloucester, UK: Dodo, 2008), xii.

34. Al-Ghazali, *The Alchemy of Happiness,* xii.

35. As, for example, in Augustine's *Confessions,* esp. bks. 1–3, 11–12.

Chapter 12: Two Faiths, Common God, Single Government

1. See http://www.youtube.com/v/qtVTcvIyWdA (accessed April 29, 2010).

2. See Jan Assmann, *Moses the Egyptian: The Memory of Egypt in Western Monotheism* (Cambridge, MA: Harvard Univ. Press, 1997); *Die Mosaische Unterscheidung, Oder der Preis des Monotheismus* (Munich: Carl Hanser, 2003).

3. On this, see, for instance, Aziz al-Azmeh, "Monotheistic Monarchy," *Journal for the Study of Religions and Ideologies* 10 (Spring 2005): 133–49. Similarly, Regina M. Schwartz, *The Curse of Cain: The Violent Legacy of Monotheism* (Chicago: Univ. of Chicago Press, 1997).

4. See Jean-Jacques Rousseau, *The Social Contract or Principles of Political Right,* trans. G. D. H. Cole, http://www.constitution.org/jjr/socon.htm (accessed July 26, 2010), 4.8. For a contrary argument that polytheism, for all its defects, is more peaceable than monotheism, see David Hume, *The Natural History of Religion,* ed. H. E. Root (Stanford, CA: Stanford Univ. Press, 1956), 48–51.

5. See S. Gurumurthy, "Semitic Monotheism: The Root of Intolerance in India" (Madras: Center for Policy Studies), http://www.bjp.org/content /view/2655/ (accessed May 4, 2007).

6. See Jürgen Moltmann, *The Trinity and the Kingdom: The Doctrine of God,* trans. Margaret Kohl (Minneapolis: Fortress, 1993), 192–202.

7. So Kathryn Tanner, *Christ the Key* (Cambridge: Cambridge Univ. Press, 2010), 208–9.

8. See Hans Zirker, "Monotheismus und Intoleranz," *Mit den Anderen Leben,* ed. Konrad Hilpert and Jürgen Werbick (Düsseldorff: Patmos, 1995), 95–96.

9. See Joseph Ratzinger (Benedict XVI), *Introduction to Christianity*, trans. J. R. Foster (1969; San Francisco: Ignatius, 2004), 136.

10. See *The Encyclopedia of Islam and the Muslim World*, s.v. "Minorities" (New York: Macmillan Reference, 2004).

11. On closer inspection, the line demarcating the polar opposites of religious exclusivism and religious pluralism is not as sharp as it is often made out to be. Pluralists cannot avoid all exclusivism; some religions, like those involving human sacrifice, for instance, are always out. And exclusivists virtually never insist that others are totally different, totally false; instead, they affirm that other faiths have overlapping elements and shared truth with theirs.

12. See Jon Shields, *The Democratic Virtues of the Christian Right* (Princeton, NJ: Princeton Univ. Press, 2009).

13. Peter Berger, "The Desecularization of the World: A Global Overview," in *The Desecularization of the World: Resurgent Religion and World Politics*, ed. Peter Berger (Grand Rapids, MI: Eerdmans, 1999), 8.

14. Assmann, *Die Mosaische Unterscheidung*, 66.

15. Matt. 7:12; *Sahih Muslim, Kitab al-Iman*, Hadith no. 45.

16. Assmann, *Die Mosaische Unterscheidung*, 67–68.

17. See Daniel Boyarin, *A Radical Jew: Paul and the Politics of Identity* (Berkeley: Univ. of California Press, 1994). On Boyarin's thesis, see Miroslav Volf and Judith Gundry-Volf, "Paul and the Politics of Identity," review of *A Radical Jew* by Daniel Boyarin, *Books & Culture* (July/August 1997): 16–18.

18. Nicholas Wolterstorff, *The Mighty and the Almighty* (unpublished manuscript), 11, 4.

19. Wolterstorff, *Mighty and the Almighty*, 4.

20. For a similar use of the Golden Rule to underwrite pluralism as a political project, see Abdullahi Ahmed An-Na'im, *Islam and the Secular State* (Cambridge, MA: Harvard Univ. Press, 2008), 95.

21. Wolterstorff, *Mighty and the Almighty*, 10.

22. *St. Augustine: Letters 156–210*, trans. Roland Teske (Hyde Park, NY: New City, 2004), 185.2.11.

23. An-Na'im, *Islam and the Secular State*, 3.

24. Declaration on Religious Freedom, *Dignitatis humanae*, http://www.vatican.va/archive/hist_councils/ii_vatican_council/documents/vat-ii_decl_19651207_dignitatis-humanae_en.html (accessed July 26, 2010).

25. "Once a Muslim, Always a Muslim in Malaysia," *Asia Sentinel*, May 30, 2007, http://www.asiasentinel.com/index.php?Itemid=34&id=515&option=com_content&task=view (accessed July 26, 2010).

26. "Malaysian Court Refuses to Recognize Woman's Conversion to Christianity," *New York Times*, May 30, 2007, http://www.nytimes.com/2007

/05/30/world/asia/30cnd-malaysia.html?_r=1&scp=3&sq=lina%20joy&
st=cse (accessed July 26, 2010).

27. "Egypt's Religious Advisor Says Muslims Can Choose Own Religion,"
ABC News, http://www.abc.net.au/news/stories/2007/07/24/1987362
.htm?section=justin (accessed May 8, 2010). According to some reports
("Top Cleric Denies 'Freedom to Choose Religion' Comment," GulfNews.
com, July 24, 2007, http://archive.gulfnews.com/articles/07/07/25/10141696
.html [accessed July 26, 2010]), he is said to have reversed his position later
on, stating, "Islam prohibits a Muslim from changing his religion and . . .
apostasy is a crime, which must be punished."

28. See John Micklethwait and Adrian Wooldridge, *God Is Back: How the
Global Revival of Faith Is Changing the World* (New York: Penguin, 2009),
293. Most disturbing of all are the actual horrifying executions, such as
the beheading of a Somali Christian named Mansuur Muhammed by the
Islamist Shabab militia in 2008 (see "Somalia: Christian Aid Worker Be-
headed for Converting from Islam," Compass Direct News, October 27,
2008, http://english.freecopts.net/english/index.php?option=com_conte
nt&task=view&id=975&Itemid=9 [accessed July 26, 2010]). Condemned
for spying for the enemies of the mujahdeen and for being a *murtadd*
(an apostate), his head was cut off with a knife amid cries of "God is
great." Horrendous brutalities against apostates widen the chasm between Muslims and Christians to the point that extremists among the
latter think of Islam as a profoundly evil and demonic religion (for example, "Graham Disinvited from Prayer Event over Islam Comments,"
CNN, April 23, 2010, http://www.cnn.com/2010/US/04/23/graham
.islam.controversy/index.html?iref=allsearch [accessed July 26, 2010];
Chuck Baldwin, "Our Politically Correct Theologian-in-Chief," Covenant News, December 13, 2002, http://www.chuckbaldwinlive.com
/c2002/cbarchive_20021213.html [accessed July 26, 2010]). Most Christians understand, however, that evildoers often don the cloak of religion
in hopes of somehow sanctifying their base goals. They also know that
in a failed state like Somalia, in which the government does not exert
full sovereignty and militias rule over significant swaths of territory, life
is brutish and short for many, not just for the "apostates."

29. The Declaration on Religious Freedom of the Second Vatican Council notes this explicitly: "Revelation does not indeed affirm in so many
words the right of man to immunity from external coercion in matters
religious." The argument of the declaration is based on a biblical and
theological understanding of the dignity of person, not on an explicit biblical text. The revelation, the declaration states, "does, however, disclose
the dignity of the human person in its full dimensions. It gives evidence

of the respect which Christ showed toward the freedom with which man is to fulfill his duty of belief in the word of God and it gives us lessons in the spirit which disciples of such a Master ought to adopt and continually follow" ("Declaration on Religious Freedom," *Dignitatis humanae,* no. 9, http://www.vatican.va/archive/hist_councils/ii_vatican_council/docu ments/vat-ii_decl_19651207_dignitatis-humanae_en.html [accessed July 26, 2010]).

30. "Apostasy," *Catholic Encyclopedia,* http://www.newadvent.org/cathen /01624b.htm (accessed May 8, 2010).

31. The question of reciprocity was at the center of the debates about free-dom of religion during the Second Vatican Council, at which a declara-tion on religious freedom, one of the most innovative documents of that council, was issued. Initially, many bishops as well as theologians insisted on the asymmetrical relationship between the Catholic Church and other religious communities, whether Christian churches or other religions. Be-cause it is the "true religion," the Catholic Church felt that it could claim for itself what it was, under the same circumstances, unwilling to grant to others. Within the ranks of the Church, the strongest and most effective resistance to this position came from the then newly established Secretar-iat for Promoting Christian Unity, under the leadership of Cardinal Bea. Non-Catholics, the argument went, react negatively to the Church when it fails to act according to the principle of reciprocity (see Pietro Pavan, "Einleitung und Kommentar [Declaratio de libertate religiosa]," *Lexikon fur Theologie und Kirche* [Freiburg: Herder, 1967], 13, 704–5).

32. Gregory VII, "Letter to Anzir (Nacir), King of Mauretania," *The Chris-tian Faith in the Doctrinal Documents of the Catholic Church,* ed. Jacques Dupuis (New York: Alba House, 2001), 418–19.

33. The pope slightly distorted the original meaning of Ephesians 2, which refers to Christ on the cross, rather than to God, as "our peace."

34. See Sayyid Qutb, *Milestones* (Lahore: Kazi, 2007), 87–90. On Qutb's political theology, see Miroslav Volf, *A Public Faith: How Followers of Christ Should Serve the Common Good* (Grand Rapids, MI: Baker, 2011), introduction.

35. See Paul Heck, *Common Ground: Islam, Christianity, and Religious Pluralism* (Washington, DC: Georgetown Univ. Press, 2009), 166–68. Olivier Roy writes in a similar vein more generally about revivals in Islam: "The contemporary religious revival in Islam is targeting society more than the state and calling to the individual's spiritual needs" (*Glo-balized Islam: The Search for a New Ummah* [New York: Columbia Univ. Press, 2004], 3).

36. Abdullahi Ahmed An-Na'im argues for a similar position: "First, the

modern territorial state should neither seek to enforce Shariʿa as positive law and public policy nor claim to interpret its doctrine and general principles for Muslim citizens. Second, Shariʿa principles can and should be a source of public policy and legislation, subject to the fundamental constitutional and human rights of all citizens, men and women, Muslims and non-Muslims, equally and without discrimination" (*Islam and the Secular State,* 28–29).

37. So Mark Lilla, *The Stillborn God: Religion, Politics, and the Modern West* (New York: Knopf, 2007), 40.

38. See Volf, *A Public Faith,* chapter 6; Nicholas Wolterstorff, "The Role of Religion in Decision and Discussion of Political Issues," in Robert Audi and Nicholas Wolterstorff, *Religion in the Public Square: The Place of Religious Convictions in Political Debate* (Lanham, MD: Rowman & Littlefield, 1997), 67–120.

Chapter 13: The Fear of God and the Common Good

1. For a brief reflection on "secularization through religion," see Olivier Roy, *Globalized Islam: The Search for a New Ummah* (New York: Columbia Univ. Press, 2004), 40–41.

2. See Emily Gunzburger Makas, "Representing Competing Entities in Postwar Mostar" (presentation at the Woodrow Wilson International Center for Scholars, November 16, 2005. http://www.wilsoncenter.org/topics/pubs/MR318Makas.doc).

3. See Ivan Sarcevic, "Totalitarizam, teologija I simboli. Sakralizirana politika I nacionalizirana vjera: primjer Bosne i Hercegovine," *Nova Prisutnost* 8 (1/2010): 87–97.

4. "Sarajevo: Archbishop's Praise for Progress Towards Reconciliation," http://www.archbishopofcanterbury.org/1120 (accessed April 6, 2010).

5. For an alternate account, see William Cavanaugh, *The Myth of Religious Violence* (Oxford: Oxford Univ. Press, 2009), 123–80.

6. Peter Berger, "The Desecularization of the World: A Global Overview," in *The Desecularization of the World: Resurgent Religion and World Politics,* ed. Peter Berger (Grand Rapids, MI: Eerdmans, 1999), 1–18.

7. For a similar idea, see Plato, *Crito* 51, in *The Dialogues of Plato,* trans. B. Jowett (Oxford: Clarendon, 1875), 1:392–93.

8. See Roy, *Globalized Islam,* 17–21.

9. John Locke, *A Letter Concerning Toleration* (Indianapolis, IN: Hackett, 1983).

10. John Rawls, *Political Liberalism* (New York: Columbia Univ. Press, 1993).

11. Mark Lilla, *The Stillborn God: Religion, Politics, and the Modern West* (New York: Knopf, 2007), 309.

12. See Jose Casanova, *Public Religions in the Modern World* (Chicago: Univ. of Chicago Press, 1994); "Public Religions Revisited," in *Religion: Beyond a Concept,* ed. Hent de Vries (New York: Fordham Univ. Press, 2008), 101–19.

13. See Nicholas Wolterstorff, "The Role of Religion in Decision and Discussion of Political Issues," in Robert Audi and Nicholas Wolterstorff, *Religion in the Public Square: The Place of Religious Convictions in Political Debate* (Lanham, MD: Rowman & Littlefield, 1997), 87–91.

14. Plato, *Lysis* 214, in *The Dialogues of Plato,* trans. B. Jowett (Oxford: Clarendon, 1875), 1:58.

15. Plato, *Lysis.* Socrates goes on to undermine this position as well with a somewhat dubious argument expressed in the following rhetorical question: "Can like do any good or harm to like which he could not do to himself, or suffer anything from his like which he would not suffer from himself? And if neither can be of any use to the other, how can they be loved by one another?" (214 [1:59]).

16. Plato, *Lysis* 215 (1:60).

17. Plato, *Lysis* 216 (1:61).

18. Sigmund Freud, *Civilization and Its Discontents,* trans. James Strachey (New York: Norton, 1961), 61.

19. Plato, *Lysis* 215 (1:60).

20. Plato, *Euthyphro* 7, in *Dialogues of Plato,* 1:321.

21. Plato, *Euthyphro* 8 (1:323).

22. The occasion for the dialogue was Euthyphro's suit against his father. Euthyphro's father had bound and put in a ditch a field laborer who had killed a domestic servant in a fit of drunken passion, and the laborer died while the father was waiting for the diviner from Athens to tell him what should be done with the laborer. Euthyphro was persuaded that he knew that his father was a murderer. Socrates thought the persuasion was facile.

23. One need not have a common God to have a meaningful moral argument. Michael Walzer starts his book *Thick and Thin* on "moral argument at home and abroad" by recalling the image from the 1989 Velvet Revolution in then Czechoslovakia: "It is a picture of people marching in the streets of Prague: they carry signs, some of which say, simply, 'Truth' and others 'Justice.' When I saw the picture, I knew immediately what the signs meant—and so did everyone else who saw the same picture. Not only that: I also recognized and acknowledged the values that the marchers were defending—and so did (almost) everyone else. . . . The marchers shared a culture with which I was largely unfamiliar; they

were responding to an experience I had never had. And yet, I could have walked comfortably in their midst. I could carry the same signs" (*Thick and Thin: Moral Argument at Home and Abroad* [Notre Dame, IN: Notre Dame Univ. Press, 1994], 1).

Walzer's point is simple and profound: whether people are atheists or theists, whether they are Buddhists, Christians, or Hindus, whether they are from China, Senegal, or the United States, they will all know what those signs mean and likely identify with the rough contours of the social vision expressed in them. They may disagree in detail about what "justice" means and which people or what acts are to be deemed as just, and yet they also share a big-picture sense of what is just. They are, for instance, likely to agree that "grinding the face of the poor" is unjust (Isa. 3:15) and yet will debate strenuously whether in a given case or under a given economic system the face of the poor is in fact being ground. Muslims' and Christians' commonalities go even deeper than the moral minimum identified by Walzer—if Muslims and Christians have a common God and overlapping understandings of God's character and God's commands.

24. Westergaard came into an already tense environment at Yale. His visit to the campus coincided with the visit of Jytte Klausen, the author of the Yale University Press book *The Cartoons That Shook the World* (2009). Yale University made a controversial but, in my judgment, correct decision not to reprint the cartoons in that book, and that decision triggered an intense debate on campus and in the media in the United States (see Esther Zuckerman and Paul Needham, "Yale Press Panned for Nixing Cartoons of Muhammad," *Yale Daily News,* August 16, 2009, http://www.yaledailynews.com/news/art-news/2009/08/16/yale-press-panned-for-nixing-cartoons-of-muhammad/ [accessed July 26, 2010]).

25. Let me be clear, I am not suggesting that those who owe no allegiance to the God who loves and commands love of neighbor are unable to care. Many such people do care, and some of them care much more and more effectively than those who "fear God." I am suggesting that for Muslims and Christians, allegiance to the God who loves and commands love will provide a motivation to care for one another's well-being.

26. In this debate about rights and care for others, I suspect that most Christians, especially those living outside the United States, feel an affinity for philosopher Robert Scruton's position. He insists that freedom of speech "does not mean the freedom to produce images, however offensive, or to make insulting gestures." In a text titled "Respect, and a Real Debate," he distinguishes between criticism in the context of a debate about the content of a faith and the deeds of its followers (which should be encouraged)

and desecration of the symbols of a faith (which should be censured). His reasons for rejecting desecration? "A faith is not a system of intellectual beliefs; it is a way of life. And the symbols of that way of life are like family portraits, which stay on the wall and the desk, defining the place where we are, the place that is ours, the home that is sacred and not to be defiled. Those who spit on them are not regarded kindly." A condition for fruitful public debate about faith and its impact on social life is to refrain from spitting on the symbols of faith. "We must respect the icons of the Muslim faith," Scruton writes, "even if we think them ridiculous, indeed especially if we think them ridiculous. The cartoons that have precipitated the current crisis were worse than a mistake: they were an act of sacrilege, like trampling on the crucifix or spitting on the Torah. This is not a contribution to free speech but an obstacle to it" ("Respect, and a Real Debate," in *Muslims and Europe: A Cartoon Confrontation,* February 6, 2006, http://www.open democracy.net/faith-terrorism/muslim_cartoons_3244.jsp#one [accessed July 26, 2010]). With reasons such as these, many Christians around the world, including Pope Benedict XVI, objected to the publication of the Danish cartoons (see chapter 1). Part of the Christian condemnation of the cartoons stemmed from the fear that ridiculing sacred symbols of Islam might make acceptable the mocking of icons of Christianity. Many remembered Jens Jørgen Thorsen's depiction of Jesus on the cross with an erection (1973, in Denmark), the images of the crucifixion of pigs (1994, in Germany), and innumerable examples pouring scorn on the Virgin Mary in Europe and the United States—acts of sacrilege perpetrated against Christian symbols "as though this were some daring challenge to oppressive hierarchies and a bid for liberation" (Scruton, "Respect"). Christians worldwide therefore tend to resist unbridled freedom of speech. More generally, many Christians believe that a culture that celebrates mere transgression of boundaries as liberation and affirms the right to offend others is incongruous with love of God and love of neighbor. The cartoons were an expression of that same culture, just directed against Islam rather than Christianity. Many Christians protested vehemently.

27. See "To the Civilized World by the Professors of Germany," *Current History* 1 (January 1915): 25.

28. Karl Barth, "Biblical Questions, Insights, and Vistas," in *The Word of God and the Word of Man,* trans. Douglas Horton (New York: Harper, 1956), 69.

29. Barth, "Biblical Questions," 73.

30. Barth, "Biblical Questions," 74.

31. "Sacred canopy" describes the way in which people can use religious

symbols to sanctify social institutions by associating them with the order of the whole cosmos. See Peter Berger, *The Sacred Canopy: Elements of a Sociological Theory of Religion* (1969; New York: Anchor, 1990).

32. Reza Aslan, *How to Win a Cosmic War: God, Globalization, and the End of the War on Terror* (New York: Random House, 2009), 4.

33. Pat Robertson, "Why Evangelical Christians Support Israel," http:// www.patrobertson.com/Speeches/IsraelLauder.asp (accessed July 26, 2010).

Epilogue: Reality Check: Combating Extremism

1. Max Singer, "The Potential Dangers of a 'Real' *Jihad*," in *Radical Islam and International Security: Challenges and Responses,* ed. Hillel Frisch and Efraim Inbar (London: Routledge, 2008), 171–79; Laurent Murawiec, "Deterring Those Who Are Already Dead?," in Frisch and Inbar, eds., *Radical Islam and International Security,* 180–87.

2. Neil J. Kressel, *Bad Faith: The Danger of Religious Extremism* (Amherst, NY: Prometheus, 2007).

3. So, for instance, from an atheistic perspective, Wafa Sultan, *A God Who Hates: The Courageous Woman Who Inflamed the Muslim World Speaks Out Against the Evils of Islam* (New York: St. Martin's, 2009); and from a Christian perspective, Mosab Hassan Yousef, *Son of Hamas: A Gripping Account of Terror, Betrayal, Political Intrigue, and Unthinkable Choices* (Carol Stream, IL: Saltriver, 2010).

4. For instance, Tony Blair has argued, "It is as much the force of ideas as the force of arms that will secure our future" ("We Must Make Faith a Weapon," *Australian*, June 9, 2010, http://www.theaustralian.com.au/news /opinion/we-must-make-faith-a-weapon/story-e6frg6zo–1225877207290 [accessed July 26, 2010]).

5. For a defense from a Christian perspective of the war in Iraq, see Jean Bethke Elshtain, *Just War Against Terror: The Burden of American Power in a Violent World* (New York: Basic, 2003). For a critique, see Albert L. Weeks, *The Choice of War: The Iraq War and the Just War Tradition* (Santa Barbara, CA: ABC-CLIO, 2010).

6. For example, the Pew Forum on Religion and Public Life found in 2007 that, in the United States, 57 percent of white evangelical Christians hold "unfavorable" views of Muslims. That figure is substantially higher than the national figure of 35 percent. See "Public Expresses Mixed Views of Islam, Mormonism," http://pewforum.org/Public-Expresses-Mixed -Views-of-Islam-Mormonism.aspx (accessed July 26, 2010).

INDEX

Page numbers in **boldface** *indicate chapter and verse from the Bible and Qur'an.*